CENTRAL PENNSYLVANIA MARRIAGES
1700-1896

Compiled by

Charles A. Fisher

GENEALOGICAL PUBLISHING CO. INC.

Originally published: Selingsgrove, Pennsylvania, 1946
Reprinted by Genealgoical Publishing Co., Inc.
Baltimore, Maryland, 1974

Reprinted in paperback by Genealogical Publishing Company
Baltimore, Maryland, 2020

Paperback ISBN 9780806380155

CENTRAL PENNSYLVANIA MARRIAGES
(1700-1896)

Compiled by

DR. CHARLES ADAM FISHER, F.I.A.G.,
Historian and Genealogist,
Selinsgrove, Pennsylvania.

1946

CONTENTS
(Alphabetically Arranged)

NOTE.

Users of this compilation should remember that this is not a complete record of all marriages that took place in central Pennsylvania, but only such as the compiler was able to locate in public and private records. Many of these have never before been published.

	MAN	COUNTY	WOMAN
2/22/1858	Adams, Bernard	Northumberland	Anna Arnold (Henry)
9/12-1855	" George C.	"	Susan Klase (Valentine)
5/10/1792	Ainsworth, Samuel	Dauphin	Mary McEwen (Richard)
5/18/1846	Alleman, Samuel	"	Anna E. Holman, Harrisburg, Pa.
9/28/1871	" Horace	Snyder	Matilda Pierce, Gettysburg, Pa.
1788	Alexander, Hugh, Jr.	Perry	Jemima Patterson
1806	" Hugh	Mifflin	Elizabeth Brown (Alex)
1799	" James	Juniata	Jane Sanders
12/28/1809	" Samuel	Mifflin	Margaret Alexander (James)
12/28/1837	Alricks, Hamilton	Dauphin	Caroline Bull (Rev. Levi)
7/21/1796	" . James	"	Martha Hamilton (John)
2/—/1712	Anderson, Rev. James	Lancaster	Suit Garland (Sylvester)
12/27/1737	" " "	"	Rachael Wilson
8/22/1809	Angst, Daniel	Berks	Mary Zweier (Joseph)
3/6/1817	" John	"	Susanna Katterman
Pentacostal			
Tuesday, 1744	Anspach, John	Berks	Ann Elizabeth Fisher (Sebastian)
1/25/1820	Arnold, Peter	Snyder	Margaret Fisher (John)
10/6/1825	Apple, Daniel	"	Susan Orwig, Mifflinburg, Pa.
4/27/1824	Awl, Jacob M.	Dauphin	Fanny Horning
3/9/1843	" Dr. Robert	Northumberland	Elizabeth Bower
11/21/1849	" Dr. Robert	"	Rebecca Purcell(Peter)
4/27/1795	" Samuel	"	Mary Maclay
10/18/1860	Ayers, Alfred	"	Caroline Adams (James)
5/6/1817	" William	Dauphin	Mary E. Bucher (Jacob)
1826	Backus, Dr. S.S.	Snyder	Sarah Dietrick, Northampton County
3/10/1814	Bailey, Joel	Dauphin	Elizabeth Seidel, Berks County
1/14/1790	Banks, Andrew	Juniata	Elizabeth Lintner (Christian)
4/10/1827	" . David	"	Jane McAllister (William)
2/15/1883	Barber, Dr. I. Grier	Union	Kate Wittenmeyer
1838	Barker, Robert R.	"	Jane Forster (John), Center County
1833	Barner, Henry	Perry	Elizabeth Smith (Jacob)
2/10/1840	" Jacob	"	Elizabeth Wagner
2/21/1858	" Samuel	"	Amelia Gaugler (Jacob)
1/17/1856	Barthololomew, Jacob b	Northumberland	Charlotte Lyons (George)
8/19/1862	Bastion, Mathias D.	"	Lydia Poyer (Abitha)
5/18/1815	Beatty, George	Dauphin	Elizabeth White (William, 1st wife
11/22/1820	" "	"	Sarah Shrom (Caspor, 2nd wife
9/21/1830	" "	"	Catherine Shrom 3rd wife
6/9/1859	Beaver, Gabriel	Snyder	Harriet Steininger
4/15/1827	" George	Perry	Catherine Long (Jonathan)
12/3/1874	" Isaac (widower)	"	Kate Smith
1820	" Simon	Snyder	Elizabeth Oldt (John)
1/23/1838	" Thomas	"	Elizabeth Wilkins (Robert), Dauphin Co.
12/19/1861	" William H.	Snyder	Mary Ann Ulrich
1848	Beck, J. Jacob	Northumberland	Elizabeth Shadel (David)
10/15/1833	Bell, Joseph C.	"	Rebecca Campbell (John)
1819	" William	Dauphin	Elizabeth Hutman (Mathias)
10/8/1815	Bergstresser, Peter	Snyder	Elizabeth Ulrich (J.George Jr.)
3/14/1850	" Reuben	"	Araminta Wagenseller
11/9/1856	Bornheisel, Peter	Dauphin	Hannah Webner (Charlie)
1706	Bortram, Rev. William	"	Jane Gillespie, wid. of Aug. McClain
2/2/1854	Best, John	Northumberland	Caroline Hilgert
5/30/1830	Bickel, Andrew	Center	Nancy Moyer, of Virginia
6/—/1837	" Tobias	"	Elizabeth McAdams, Hamilton Co.,Ohio
175-	Blank, J. George	Lehigh	Elizabeth Steinmetz (Valentine)
5/14/1860	Blasser, Abraham D.	Northumberland	" Lenker (Adam)
8/25/1857	" Jacob D.	"	Harriet Leader (Marks)

Date	Name	County	Spouse
1/4/1838	Hlust, Dr. Joseph	Dauphin	Mary Benninger
1835	Hly, John	Union	Lydia Rhoads
5/17/1811	Boas, Frederick	Dauphin	Elizabeth Krause (David)
1828	Boas, William D.	Dauphin	Martha Ingram
5/3/1827	Bombaugh, Aaron	Dauphin	Maria Lloyd (Joseph)
3/18/1802	" Abraham	"	Catherine Reehm
3/26/1812	Barber, Thomas	Union	Elizabeth Clingan
1/18/1844	" Robert		Margaret B. Young
11/11/1847	" William		Mary Foster
1829	Bibighans, Dr. John	Snyder	Julia Swineford
1816	Bird, Sylvanus	Northumberland	Lena Tietsworth (Robert)
4/12/1859	Bloom, John	"	Matilda Shipman (Abraham)
8/23/1842	Bohner, Peter	"	Catherine Rebuck (Peter)
6/19/1864	Bohner, "	"	Susan Shaffer (Peter)
7/31/1713	Boone, George	Berks	Deborah Howell
1726	" Benjamin	"	Ann Farmer
3/26/1748	" William	"	Sarah Lincoln
1778	" "	"	Susan Parks, Reading, Pa.
1/9/1877	Bordner, Dr. H. H.	Snyder	Olivia J. Gross (John)
11/15/1848	Bower, Thompson	Lycoming	Catherine Gosh (Christian)
1794	Bowman, John F.	Dauphin	———— Jerse (Isaac)
8/25/1846	Boyer, Charles	Snyder	Sarah Missimer (Aaron)
1852	" Daniel S.	"	Leah Snyder, Berrysburg, Pa.
1743	" J. Henry		Magdalene Kirchner
11/26/1801	" J. Philip		Catherine Keeley
1728	Bright (Brecht), Michael	Berks	Margaret Simone
6/18/1819	Brown, Samuel T.	Northumberland	Nancy Woods
3/21/1854	" William C.	Perry	Margaret Mitchell (William)
6/3/1852	Bruner, Capt. Charles	Northumberland	Louisa Weiser
1/1/1852	Bryson, Capt. James	"	Margaret Montgomery (William)
2/3/1820	" William B.	"	Rebecca Caldwell
3/27/1792	Bucher, J. Jacob	Dauphin	Susan M. Hortter (J. Valentine)
1/17/1820	" John C.	"	Ellen Isett (Jacob)
11/20/1861	" Hon. Joseph C.	Union	Mary E. Walls (John)
12/8/1831	" Francis	Northumberland	Mary Ann Masser
12/15/1858	" John W.		Hester Beard (James)
5/17/1831	Buchler, William	Dauphin	Henrietta Snyder, Franklin County
3/23/1830	Burchfield, Lewis	Juniata	Jane McKennen (Patrick)
1747or1748	Burd, James		Sarah Shippen (Edward)
4/6/1824	Burke, Michael	Dauphin	Mary Ann Finley
6/13/1823	Burns, James	Mifflin	Cartes Steely (Lazarus)
12/13/1815	Buyers, William F.	Northumberland	Martha Hunter (Alexander)
1817	Calder, William	Dauphin	Mary Kirkwood
1/5/1820	Cameron, William		Elinor McLaughlin (Hugh)
10/18/1852	Cameron, William B.	Dauphin	Elizabeth Bastedo (Gilbert)
11/22/1854	Campbell, Andrew W.	Mifflin	Mary J. Wilson (George)
12/17/1810	" David		Elizabeth Wilson
12/5/1844	" "		Eunice Smith
1/9/1857	" Goodman		Ada J. Elston
6/6/1817	" Isaac		Sophia Garrison
10/30/1862	" Isaac W.		Sarah J. Humbert
9/18/1858	" John G.		Emma Sharp
1813	" Joseph	Mifflin	Elizabeth Oliver (Joseph)
1/9/1840	" Obed	Northumberland	Elizabeth Teats (John)
5/20/1850	" Peter G.		Susan Barlinger
11/3/1818	" Robert		Ann Moore, 1st wife
4/1/1827	" "		Sarah Broes, 2nd wife
8/2/1832	Carpenter, David	Lycoming	Mary Ware
2/11/1836	" "	"	" Mitchelltree
5/4/1847	" Jesse B.	"	Phoebe Carpenter
3/4/1806	" John	"	Mary Campbell (John)

-2-

Date	Name	County	Spouse
12/22/1846	Carpenter, John J.	Lycoming	Mary Marshall
6/—/1840	Casey, Joseph C.		Mary Ann Knettle, Carlisle, Pa.
11/6/18)8	Cattrell, William	Dauphin	Letitia Wilson
10/28/1865	Caveny, Samuel B.	Juniata	Mary M. Cassell
1/12/1863	Cawley, J. Harrison	Northumberland	Elizabeth Koch (Jonas)
10/17/1850	Chamberlin, Lemuel	Northumberland	Mary Hoffman (John C.)
6/4/1864	Chester, Theodore	"	Louise Wolf (Abraham)
8/13/1824	Clark, James	"	Jane Sweeney
9/13/1838	" "		Sarah Crawford
3/24/1812	" Mark		Ann Stockman (Nathaniel)
8/5/1819	" Walter		Esther Hill
1802	" William	Dauphin	Sarah Patterson
9/—/1824	" ", Jr.		Hannah Brewster
3/27/1856	Clemens, Peter	Northumberland	Caroline Brouse (Samuel), Snyder Co.
11/2/1856	Clement, David	"	Sarah Wolverton
3/23/1860	" Henry	"	Catherine Geist (John)
1834	" Ira T.	"	Sarah Hartz, Shamokin, Pa.
5/18/1854	" Gen. John Kay	"	Mary S. Zeigler (Isaac)
5/27/1819	Clingan, Flavel	Union	Mary Ann Scott
10/7/1817	" George	Union	Elizabeth Scott
1/5/1813	" Thomas	"	Margaret Lewis
3/25/1856	" "	"	Mary E. Sedam
2/?/1868	" Pascal L.	"	Maria L. Zuber
1/3/1870	" Scott	"	Clarissa Clingan
6/12/1856	" William	"	Mary E. Dean
5/10/1864	" "		Elizabeth Finney
5/18/1833	Clinger, Henry Daniel	Berks	Susan Wagner (Abraham)
11/13/1845	Close, Henry L.	Mifflin	Francina Ramsey (William)
1/11/1810	Cochran, William		Rachael Gross (Christian)
3/3/1804	" John		Mary Hart
1/25/1836	Coldren, Elijah	Snyder	Susan Fisher (J. George)
11/15/1845	Cooper, James	Northumberland	Jane Sunderland
2/—/1857	Cotnor, Davis M.	Mifflin	Mary Childs, Perry County
1/25/1824	Cover, John	Dauphin	Polly Fetter, Allentown, Pa.
9/23/1830	Cox, Daniel W.	Union	Hannah Weidensaul
1802	Crain, Richard M.	Dauphin	Elizabeth Whitehill (Robert)
5/10/1853	Crawford, Dr. David M.	Juniata	Ellen Jackman (James)
7/4/1831	Cressinger, Rev. John B.	Northumberland	Mary Baumgardner
1873	Cronimiller, J. P.	Union	Louisa Shindle, Snyder County
7/3/1839	Culbertson, Dr. James	Mifflin	Mary Steel (Robert)
2/26/1846	Cummings, Alexander	Northumberland	Mary E. Mogan (Robert)
11/6/1817	" James	"	Fanny Billmeyer (Andrew)
3/14/1850	Davenport, George	N. Y. State	Mary Arnold
10/27/1862	Davies, Newton H.	Dauphin	Anna Van Horn (William)
8/2/1840	Davis, John	Mifflin	Jane McCallister (Gershom)
10/20/1863	Denning, Henry C.	Dauphin	Kate Whitman
9/7/1867	Deppen, Joseph	Northumberland	Eva Hoffman, (Jacob)
6/21/1848	Dewart, William L.	"	Rosetta Van Horn (Espy)
11/—/1829	Dickerman, Dr. Clark		Eliza Knapp, 1st wife
10/14/1833	" "		Sarah Chandler, 2nd wife
3/10/1869	" Charles H.	Northumberland	Joy Ivy Carter (William)
1825	Dieffenbach, Jacob	Columbia	Mary Hughes (Garrett), Snyder County
10/14/1864	Dill, Andrew H.	Union	Catherine Slifer (Eli)
4/10/1866	Dissinger, David C.	Northumberland	Fannie Clement (Ira T.)
9/26/1839	Diven, James L.	Perry	Elizabeth Junkin (John), 1st wife
11/20/1849	" "	"	Mary Irwin (Robert), 2nd wife
7/30/1844	Dock, George		Clara Rehrer (Thomas)
1818	" William		Margaret Gilliard
12/17/1857	Dodge, Joseph R.	Northumberland	Mary Ann Hine (Jacob)
11/14/1811	Doty, Dr. Ezra	Juniata	Rebecca (Lewis) North, wid. of Daniel
1/4/1793	Dougal, Dr. Charles E.	Northumberland	Annie Oakes (Samuel)

10/14/1793	Dougal, James	Union	June Starett
7/3/1818	" Dr. James S.	Northumberland	Sarah Pollock (William)
1/2/1849	" William P.	Union	Sarah Ann Clingan
6/10/1833	Dougherty, Philip	Dauphin	Mary W. Clark (John)
1/21/1799	Douty, John	Northumberland	Mary Mertz, (Peter)
6/5/1798	DOWNEY, JOHN	DAUPHIN	Alice Brady (James)
1832	Dreisbach, Martin, 3rd	Union	Elizabeth Kleckner
7/28/1864	" Hiram	Northumberland	Rebecca Houghton (James)
1/5/1865	Dressler, Jacob B.	"	Susan Hays
12/25/1857	" John	"	Leah Bordner (Jonathan)
12/25/1853	Duey, Samuel	Dauphin	Susan Zarker (Benjamin)
1815	Dull, Casper	Mifflin	Jane Junkin (James)
6/25/1884	Duncan, John F.	Union	Clara L. Gardner
1/23/1851	Earley, Aaron D.	Dauphin	Amanda Mark (Rev. George)
1800	Eckman, Charles	Northumberland	Margaret DeWitt
7/—/1826	" Jacob	"	Emma Gulick
11/23/1852	" Peter	"	Angeline Shipe
8/7/1851	Edwards, Oliver	Dauphin	Rachael Chandler (Jonathan)
9/12/1810	Egolf, Joseph	"	Barbara Loose
4/10/1725	" Michael	(Germany)	Mary Voutsh (Martin)
1/14/1757	" "	"	Elizabeth —————
3/23/1835	" "	Cumberland	Mary McManus (Carmack)
1803	" Valentine	"	Elizabeth Martin (David)
1/5/1808	Ehrenfeld, August C.	Mifflin	Charlotte Stitzer
1/19/1860	Eicholtz, Jacob E.	Lancaster	Harriet Erisman
3/2/1854	Elder, James	Dauphin	Rebecca Whitehill (John)
1740	Elder Rev. John	"	Mary Baker (Joshua)
3/23/1799	" Thomas	"	Catherine Cox (Col. Cornelius)
5/30/1813	" "	"	Elizabeth Jones (Robert)
3/17/1814	Elliott, William P.	Mifflin	Emily Smith
1/9/1857	Elston, Abraham		Marinda Campbell (Robert)
1/23/1855	Emerick, Michael	Northumberland	Hannah Tressler (Jacob)
3/9/1837	Enslow, Samuel	Perry	Eliza McNeal (James)
5/20/1836	Ent, Samuel	Northumberland	Lucy Clayton (William)
6/2/1845	Eppley, Daniel	Dauphin	Louisa Geiger (Bernhart)
11/9/1835	ERLENMEYER, REV. CHAS G.	Snyder	Catherine Steel, New Buffalo, Pa.
9/23/1838	ESTERLINE, SAMUEL	Center	Catherine Stover
3/5/1818	Etter, George	Dauphin	Nancy Shelly (Abraham)
3/24/1850	Ettinger, William	Center	Sophia M. Kurts
8/13/1844	Evans, S. Owen	Juniata	Amelia Kremer (Hon. George)
3/9/1812	Ewing, Rev. James		Prudence Manifold
4/—/1819	Ewing " "		Justina Grove (Jacob), York County
1851	" " "		Elizabeth Jennings
1840	EYSTER, DR. JOSEPH	Snyder	Elizabeth Houts
4/19/1796	Fahnstock, Obed	Dauphin	Anna Maria Gessell
1/19/1806	Fairchild, Solomon	Lycoming	Elizabeth Lutsey
12/23/1852	" "	Northumberland	Emily Lines
3/29/1834	Farley, Abraham	Union	Rebecca Wolf (Michael)
6/4/1868	" Jacob	"	Mary E. Brown
5/—/1857	" Michael	"	Hannah Hoy (John)
12/18/1856	Fasold, Daniel	Northumberland	Elizabeth Bartol (Jacob)
	" Valentine		Christiana Xander
11/1/1715	Feg, Leonard (Son of John) N.Y. State		Anna Catherine Sheetz
12/7/1823	Fegley, Solomon	Northumberland	Maria Eva Klase
9/3/1839	Fetter, Herman	Northampton	Christiana Christman
1729	Fetterolf, Peter		Anna Maria Rothermel (John)

-4-

12/30/1865	Findley, Gov. William		Mary Irwin (Archibald)
10/30/1865	Finney, James		Anna Mary Clingan
6/7/1835	Fisher, Charles	Snyder	Phoebe Bergstresser (Peter)
11/24/1864	" Calvin	"	Matilda Miller
12/15/1885	" Benjamin F.	(Lehigh,Iowa)	Ann Parker
11/24/1844	" David	Northumberland	Abigail Shipman
4/—/1838	" Daniel	Snyder	Amelia Laudenslager (Valentine, Jr.)
3/13/1845	" Christian, Jr.	"	Lydia Hendershot
2/6/1883	" Franklin L.	Dauphin	Ella Lock
11/28/1832	" George	Snyder	Rebecca Gemberling, 1st wife
6/13/1850	" "	"	Susan Snyder, 2nd wife
1845	" Henry	"	Catherine Hildebitle
1797	" John	"	Catherine Hosterman (Peter)
9/19/1830	" "	"	Lydia Witmer (John)
10/14/1868	" Jeremiah	(Indiana)	Lydia Gruber
1/16/1802	" J. George	Snyder	Mary Magdalene Rhoads (Francis W.)
1816	" J. Jacob	"	Philipina Schrantz, 1st wife
1820	" " "	"	Rebecca Speece, 2nd wife
5/16/1813	" J. Michael	"	Catherine Elizabeth Morr (Philip)
10/4/1888	" J. Nelson	(Tenn.)	Mary Murphrey
12/—/1847	" Joseph	Union	Mary McCullough
1/4/1750	" Peter	(N.Y.State)	Anna Dorothea Ball
10/12/1805	" "	"	Christina Lawyer
12/25/1827	" William	Northumberland	Eleanor Blue
12/5/1853	" William A.	"	Christiana Varts
10/7/1886	" William I.	(Lehigh, Iowa)	Ella Mitchell
6/5/1845	Fleming, Robert J.	Dauphin	Sarah A. Poor (Charles)
6/--/1808	Follmer, Daniel	Northumberland	Margaret Rood (James)
10/15/1829	" "	"	Sarah Lantz
10/5/1854	" Henry E.	"	Ellen Buckman (William)
9/25/1798	Forster, John	Dauphin	Mary Elder (John), 1st wife
7/9/1833	" "	"	Margaret Law (Benjamin), 2nd wife
5/4/1848	Fortner, John		Mary A. Campbell (Isaac)
3/12/1845	Fox, Edwin		Sophia " "
11/29/1804	" John, Jr.	Dauphin	Sarah Shonberger
2/4/1808	" Thomas	"	Barbara Baum
11/25/1827	Francis, Samuel	Berks	Catherine Koch
5/14/1843	" William	"	Juliana Steinmetz (Michael)
1805	Frantz, John	"	Mary Fricker (Anthony)
1821	Fretz, Matthias	Dauphin	Eliza Penrose (Joseph)
4/6/1734	Galbraith, James	Philadelphia	Elizabeth Bertram
1/1/1863	" William B.	Northumberland	Mary A. House (George)
1/1/1900	Garman, G. Calvin	(Elkhart, Ind.)	Carrie Green
1842	" , George B.	Snyder	Leah Fisher
12/13/1896	" Jonathan F.	(Michigan)	Anna Wingart
8/12/1834	Gass, Joseph	Northumberland	Maria Roker
6/8/1813	Gast, Christian	Center	Elizabeth Meyer (Philip)
2/15/1857	Geuger, Anthony E	Northumberland	Mary E. Klopp
10/28/1847	Gause, Lewis H.	Dauphin	Sarah Moore (Levi)
2/12/1843	Geary, Gen. John W.	"	Mary Ann Logan (James)
6/28/1854	Gearhart, E. McClay	Northumberland	Rosanna Gossler (Samuel)
4/6/1837	Goddes, J. Michael		Fanny Savage, Orange Co. N. Y.
3/2/1797	" , Robert	Lebanon	Jane Sawyer (John)
3/23/1810	" "	"	Mrs. Martha McClure
1/20/1846	Geiger, Hiram R.	Mifflin	Elizabeth Blattenborger
-1807	" , John	Dauphin	Mary Schoch (John)
2/15/1819	" , Joseph	"	Sarah Rupley
12/12/1824	Geist, John	"	Susan Frederick
7/14/1839	Gemberling, Samuel G.	Union	Matilda Kline

10/15/1854	Gemberling, Reuben		Sarah Ritter
10/14/1855	" William H.	Snyder	Amanda Forry (John)
3/19/1840	" Jonathan	"	Sarah Bickhart
12/26/1854	" Sephares	"	Rose Ann Picard
1793	" Philip	"	Eva Glass (George)
9/30/1866	" William B.	"	Caroline Fisher
2/25/1864	Getter, Jacob B.	Northumberland	Thursa Rhodes (William)
1846	Gift, Isaac	Snyder	Eveline Overmire
1795	" Jeremiah	"	Catherine Kline (Christopher)
1826	" John	"	Elizabeth Kern (John)
1840	" Michael	"	Anna Kleckner (John)
7/4/1861	Gold, Edwin T.	Northumberland	Sarah Cooner
12/1/1799	Good, Adam	Snyder	Mary Magdalene Ulrich (George)
2/7/1833	" John	"	Hannah Wagner
7/20/1828	Goodman, Peter	Montour	Sarah Van de Mark
3/17/1807	" Philip	"	Jane Campbell (John)
7/27/1847	Goodwill, Robert	Northumberland	Catherine Wake (Philip)
3/5/1840	Gorgas, William R.	Dauphin	Elizabeth Rummel
6/31/1797	Goy, J. Frederick	Snyder	Catherine Zeller
10/30/1845	Graham, George W.	Union	Eliza Budd, Peekskill, N. Y.
9/23/1852	Grant, William T.	Northumberland	Rachael Yoxtheimer (Henry)
1847	Gray, P. W.	"	Margaret Frantz (John), Snyder Co.
1804	Green, Innis	Dauphin	Rebecca Murray (Col. John)
11/18/1858	Greenawalt, Jeremiah K.	"	Anna L. Wolfersberger (George)
12/12/1791	Greenough, Ebenezer	Northumberland	Abigail Israel
9/21/1852	" William I.	"	Mary C. Baldy (Peter)
4/10/1834	Gudykunst, Charles	Union	Margaret Stitzel
6/30/1794	Gundy, Christian	"	Mary Magdalene Follmer
4/7/1795	Gundrum, George	Berks	Catherine E. Weise (Adam)
3/15/1866	Gutelius, George C.	Snyder	Amelia Beaver
2/20/1858	Haag, Beneville K.	Northumberland	Sarah Schuck (Philip)
12/8/1864	" George W.	"	Susan Leinbach
12/6/1835	Haas, John S.	"	Margaret Deppen
10/23/1855	" Dr. Joseph	"	Mary F. Peal (Dr. John)
11/28/1858	Hackenberg, Albert	"	Maria Brouse (Samuel), Snyder Co.
12/18/1849	Hage, Hother	Dauphin	Mary Kendig (Henry)
9/30/1857	Haile, Lawrence	Northumberland	Catherine Maringer (Peter)
4/8/1799	Haines, Lawrence	Snyder	Anna Maria Motz (G. Peter)
1/6/1807	Hamilton, Hugh		Rosanna Boyd (Capt. Adam)
	Hanna, John A.	Dauphin	Mary Harris
10/—/1819	Harris, James, Jr.	Union	Sarah Bell
5/12/1791	" Robert	Dauphin	Elizabeth Ewing (Rev. John)
9/28/1726	Hartlein, J. Jacob	Berks	Julia Dressler
10/13/1842	Hartman, Harrison	Northumberland	Elizabeth Haag (John)
1/11/1835	Hassinger, Joseph	Snyder	Sophia Klose (Solomon)
12/12/1861	Hauck, Andrew	Union	Elizabeth Fisher (Daniel)
1729	Hayes, Patrick	Dauphin	Jean ————
8/25/1824	Hayes, John	Mifflin	Jane Alexander (John)
9/12/1834	" Samuel W.		Margaret Moore (Archibald)
1/19/1847	Hays, James	Union	Jane Clingan (Flavel)
3/5/1861	" William W.		Mary Dry (Dr. Stephen)
7/3/1864	Hayward, Richard W. Jr.	Dauphin	Susan Funston, Philadelphia, Pa.
10/23/1860	Heim, Daniel	Northumberland	Mary Hornberger (George)
12/29/1831	Hench, Nicholas	Perry	Catherine Hamilton (George)
1852	Henderson, Dr. John	Mifflin	Margaret Isenberg
3/20/1787	" James		Margaret Wiggins (John)
9/28/1854	Herman, George	Snyder	Hannah Fisher
2/15/1830	Herr, Daniel	Dauphin	Sarah Gilbert (Boise)
5/12/1803	Hiester, Gabriel, Jr.	Berks	Mary Otto (Dr. John)

—6—

11/26/1835	Hilbish, John A.	Snyder	Amelia Fisher (J. Michael)
12/25/1848	Hill, George		Martha Beiler (Beuhler)(Samuel)
2/3/1790	Hill, Samuel	Dauphin	Nancy Beaty (James)
12/—/1755	Hills, John	(England)	Sarah Lewis
1794	" Stephen		Margaret Ashby
11/10/1864	Himmelreich, George W	Union	Elizabeth Slear
4/16/1857	Hoch, A. S.	Northumberland	Amelia Saltsman (William),Snyder Co.
1822	Holman, Samuel	Dauphin	Sarah Hertz (Daniel)
12/30/1866	Hoover, Henry	Northumberland	Mary Bindley
11/3/1804	Hoover, Philip		Mary Conrad (Philip)
5/25/1854	Hopewell, John U.	Northumberland	Sarah C. Young
1/7/1805	Houston, James	Lycoming	Anna Wright
2/2/1836	Howard, Laird	Union	Jane Barber (Thomas)
12/26/1854	Hower, Charles	Snyder	Amanda Nicholas
1841	Hoyer, B. F.	Dauphin	Margaret A. Kershner (Elias)
1850	" George	"	Justina Hippey (William)
10/15/1844	Huber, Levi	Schuylkill	Margaret Stackpole (Thomas)
10/13/1607	Hummel, David	Dauphin	Susan Kunkle (Christian)
3/3/1833	" "	"	Barbara Shearer
3/25/1806	" Frederick		Barbara Metzger (Jacob)
1751	" J. Jacob	Berks	Eva Maria De Turck
3/18/1813	" Valentine	Dauphin	Elizabeth Walborn (Christian)
1749	" Geo. Philip	Berks	Barbara Seb
1766	" J. Martin	"	Anna Catherine ————
1759	" John	"	Juliana ————
ca. 1764	" Andrew	"	Elizabeth Catherine ————
ca. 1779	" J. Jacob	"	Elizabeth Heffner
ca. 1792	" J. Frederick	Snyder	Elizabeth Becker (Michael)
ca. 1803	" John	Union	Catherine Weary
ca. 1803	" Capt.J.Jacob	Snyder	Nancy Bower
ca. 1814	" Jacob F.	"	Margaret Kline (Barnhart)
ca. 1815	" Samuel		Catherine Slough
8/19/1896	Huse, Eugene W.	(Nebraska)	Della Fisher (Benjamin)
1/1/1843	Ingram, Samuel D.	Dauphin	Malvina Geiger (John)
2/15/1851	Irwin, Jarid C.	Northumberland	Anna S. Kiehl (George)
1838	" Dr. John	Perry	Jane Bell
11/24/1840	" Philip	Dauphin	Ann Etter (George)
2/6/1868	" Robert H.	Union	Mary Ann Fisher (Daniel)
12/21/1861	Jackson, Elisha B.		Lavina Barstow, 1st wife
12/5/1864	" " "		Emma Foulton, 2nd wife
3/18/1824	" Evan O.		Elizabeth Campbell (John)
10/22/1850	" William W.	Perry	Catherine Adams (Levi), Dauphin Co.
9/10/1844	James, Charles R.	Union	Mary Evans
6/15/1847	Johnston, Alexander	Perry	Letitia Russell (Alexander)
5/—1835	" George	"	Margaret " "
3/16/1790	" James	"	Margaret Anderson (William)
1845	Jones, Uriah J.	Dauphin	" L. Trough
10/29/1811	Jordan, Benjamin		Mary Crouch (Edward)
6/23/1849	Jordon, Samuel D.	Northumberland	Elizabeth Tharp (James)
1811	Jury, Abraham	Dauphin	Mary Weise (Adam)
4/26/1846	Kantz, John	Snyder	Hannah Walborn (Jacob)
2/16/1841	Kapp, Amos E.	Northumberland	Margaret Withington
3/28/1852	Kauffman, John R.	"	Boann Shaffer (John)
12/14/1848	Kearny, Patrick	"	Catherine McAndrew (William)
4/8/1862	Keiser, Absalom B.	"	Mary Ann Goss (Joseph)
6/5/1856	Kuhres, Nathaniel E.	"	Catherine Hoffman (Henry D.)
1798	Kelker, John	Dauphin	Sabina Shantz (Henry)
11/11/1855	" Henry A.	"	Ellan Roberts (Col. James)

4/14/1825	Keller, Rev. Emanuel	Dauphin	Sabina Seltzer
2/10/1831	Kelly, David H.	Union	Mary Boker (Jacob)
6/15/1820	Kendig, Martin	Dauphin	Rebecca McFarland
1842	Keyner, William H.	"	Cassandra Loudrs (George)
1829	Kern, Daniel S.	Snyder	Sarah J. Parker
11/27/1854	Keefer, John B.	Northumberland	Catherine Boyer, Berks County
9/21/1847	Kelker, Immanuel M.	Dauphin	Mary Ann Beatty (George)
4/15/1866	Kerstetter, Simon P.	Northumberland	Elizabeth Bingaman
10/24/1815	" Solomon	Snyder	Barbara Zellers
9/1/1812	King, Peter	(Ohio)	Mary Magdalene Witmer (Peter, Jr.)
11/25/1831	Kinney, Frederick	Snyder	Lucy Gemberling (George)
11/7/1809	Kinter, John, Jr.	Dauphin	Elizabeth Miller
5/11/1841	Kinsloe, Robert M.	Mifflin	Sibella Ball (John)
5/18/1847	Kistler, David	Perry	Susan Rice (George), 1st wife
1/16/1864	"	"	Maria Anderson (William), 2nd wife
11/8/1849	Klase, John	Northumberland	Mary Evert (Solomon)
11/26/1854	" Solomon J.	"	Jane Withington
6/8/1829	Kleckner, David	Union	Esther Wingert (John)
1/—/1860	Kline, William F.	Northumberland	Margaret Wolverton
2/9/1856	Knauff, John	"	Susan Clinger (Henry)
9/12/1847	Kniss, Peter	"	Lucy A. Batdorf (John)
10/20/1827	Knouse, Charles	Snyder	Matilda Fetter
11/12/1752	Kratzer, Frederick	"	Anna M. Dorstlinger (Frederick)
4/3/1803	" Daniel	Snyder	Anna M. Spangler
9/—/1826	Krause, David	Dauphin	Catherine Orr, Philadelphia, Pa.
5/27/1811	Kremer, Hon. George	Snyder	Catherine Evans (Frederick)
1/6/1853	" Jacob	Union	Julia Allen (Isaac)
2/18/1851	" " B.	Montour	Anna C. Henderson
6/8/1843	Krick, John M.	Northumberland	Margaret Burns (Torrence)
10/5/1851	Kulp, Darlington	Berks	Elizabeth Gilbert (George)
10/20/1857	Kunkle, Daniel	Dauphin	Elizabeth Rutherford (Dr. William)
6/12/1861	Kutzner, William R.	Northumberland	Anna M. Douty (John B.)
11/15/1836	Laird, Samuel H.	Union	Elizabeth Clingan (Thomas)
9/14/1852	Lamberton, Robert A.	"	Anna Buehler (William)
6/22/1836	Landis, Samuel	Dauphin	Margaret Kinter (Isaac)
4/4/1864	Lawrence, Samuel M.	"	Hannah Groen (John)
3/19/1812	Lawson, Joseph	Union	Anna Clingan
10/19/1843	" William	"	Hannah Sanderson
1/15/1845	" John	"	Elizabeth Finney
4/27/1852	" James	"	Jane Clingan
10/25/1836	Lechner, Dr. Henry A.	Snyder	Mary Fisher (John)
4/1/1800	Loiby, John J.	Berks	Christiana Neifert (Jacob)
2/15/1844	" David	Union	Elizabeth Moyer (Jacob)
2/7/1855	" Isaac U.	Berks	" Mangel (Thomas)
6/6/1809	Leighow, John	Northumberland	Sarah Weimar (Peter)
1815	" Henry	"	Ellen Clark
5/29/1838	" William H.	"	Lourissa Vastine
10/2/1700	Leinbach, John, Sr.		Ann Elizabeth Kleiss
6/2/1737	" Frederick		Elizabeth Frey
11/2/1739	" J. Henry		Joanna Herman
8/12/1735	" John, Jr.		Catherine Riehm
3/17/1801	Leebrick, George	Dauphin	Mary Mohr, Union County
2/17/183—	" J. Philip		Hannah Mary Parke
7/23/1853	Leitzel, George B.	Northumberland	Christiana Schmeltzer (Daniel) 1st wife
1/—/1864	" " "	"	Catherine " " 2nd wife
6/13/1819	Leisenring, Jacob E.	"	Mary Bucher (Henry)
4/17/1877	Leiser, Andrew A.	Union	Susan Brickenstein
5/—/1849	" Dr. William	"	M—— L. Albright
12/17/1863	Lepley, James	"	Mary Fox (Daniel)

—8—

1/8/1800	Lingle, Paul	Center	Mary Spohn
5/24/1814	" Thomas		Susan Hinkle
12/1/1829	Long, Arthur B.	Mifflin	Anna E. Shaw (William)
11/6/1859	Longenecker, John S.		Margaret Peak (Nicholas)
6/3/1835	Loomis, Arthur W.	Dauphin	Maria Brubaker, 1st wife
4/2/1844	" " "		Mary Murray (Francis)
6/9/1805	Ludwig, Jacob	Berks	Maria Redcay (Elias)
12/27/1876	Leinbach, Cyrus	Northumberland	Kate Yoder (Moses)
10/2/1858	" John B.	"	Rebecca Dunkle
6/25/1786	Lesher, J. George		Anna Flickinger
3/22/1853	" Robert A.	Snyder	Sarah Vandling
6/3/1819	Lincoln, John	Union	Hannah Von Buskirk (Richard)
8/18/1852	" Richard V.B.	"	Anna M. Pellman (Samuel)
12/26/1867	Linn, James M.	"	Mary E. Billmeyer (Philip)
1/16/1838	Loomis, Dr. Justin R.	"	Sarah A. Freeman, Richfield Spg.,N.Y.
1/17/1854	" " " "	"	Mary Gilbert, 2nd wife
8/20/1873	" " " "	"	Augusta Tucker, 3rd wife
4/16/1769	Maclay, William	Northumberland	Margaret Harris (John)
1858	Melick, Dr. Solomon	Snyder	Mary Ann Rousk
1/24/1871	Marr, Addison G.	Union	Magdalene Sheriff, Mifflin County
6/16/1885	" Frank S.		Elizabeth D. Buckingham
12/17/1839	" David R.	Northumberland	Hettie Davis, 1st wife
1/22/1850	" " "	"	Harriet Matchin (Joseph), 2nd wife
6/17/1852	Markle, Martin		Helena Eith (Casper)
12/2/1862	Markley, George H.	Dauphin	Emma Snyder (Charles)
3/4/1823	Marshall, Andrew	Lycoming	Elizabeth Carpenter (John)
2/20/1866	Martin, Charles F.	Northumberland	Susan Rinehart (Charles)
1831	" Hugh	Dauphin	Hannah Maurer
9/19/1848	Martz, David	Northumberland	Barbara Miller
10/25/1860	" Frank	"	Margaret Fisher (John)
9/2/1865	" George O.	"	Emma L. Kooner
6/5/1859	" John	"	Elizabeth Weary (Peter)
1/39/1854	" John W.	"	Mary Ann Witmer (Peter)
9/19/1848	" Nathaniel F.	"	Elizabeth Samuels (George)
4/6/1841	" Solomon	"	Hannah Reed (John)
5/24/1756	" John	Berks	Rosina Hase (Melchoir)
12/5/1802	Masser, Henry	Northumberland	Mary Barbara Baldy (Paul)
5/--/1829	Mathers, James	Juniata	Jane Hutchinson (Rev. John)
3/25/1845	Maurer, Daniel C.	Lancaster	Sarah Rauch (Christian)
3/6/1833	Maus, Dr. Samuel G.	Montour	Anna Goodman (Philip)
10/11/1853	McAuley, John M.	Mifflin	Susan Stroup (John)
9/23/1802	McCleery, John	Northumberland	Mary Lytle
6/6/1866	" " "	"	Mary Helen Marr
10/2/1828	" Dr. William	"	Mary Pollock (William)
6/29/1867	McCormick, Col. Henry	Dauphin	Anna Criswell (John V.)
1830	" James	"	Eliza Buehler
5/26/1859	" " "	"	Mary Alricks (Herman)
12/21/1841	McDowell, John, Jr.	Mifflin	Mary Brisbin (James)
1/9/1847	McIlhenny, Samuel	Dauphin	Catherine Culp (Louis)
6/2/1866	McIntire, Charles J. F.	Juniata	Margaret Peale (William)
1826	McKee, Hugh	Mifflin	" Hannawalt (George)
1797	McWilliams, Robert	Northumberland	Jane Curry (Robert)
10/13/1853	" William W.	"	Catherine Caldwell (Alexander)
5/31/1791	Means, Robert	Mifflin	Hannah McKee
1807	Meiser, Frederick	Snyder	Magdalene Rine (Henry)
10/28/1851	Melick, Justus A.	Northumberland	Emeline Patchin
1/1/1856	Menges, John	"	Diana Frankenfield (John)
1/1/1861	" Peter R.	"	Mary D. Bieber (Daniel)
10/16/1826	Merrill, James	Union	Sarah Hepburn
11/3/1853	Mettler, Enoch		Mary Ann Robinson

Date	Name	County	Spouse
1/18/1872	Meyer, Hon. Henry	Center	Martha J. Taylor (Thomas)
1828	" Samuel	"	Esther Reynolds, 1st wife
7/7/1836	" "	"	Susan J. Russell
1/16/1836	Middlesworth, K.	Snyder	Elizabeth Bubb (Peter)
3/8/1810	Mifflin, Warner		Sarah Newlin (Thomas), 1st wife
10/18/1825	" "		Elizabeth Laws (Samuel), 2nd wife
9/26/1861	Miller, David R.	Dauphin	Christiana Gervick (Henry)
9/20/1856	Miller, Enoch	Union	Sarah Catherman (Frederick)
12/23/1820	" George	Northumberland	Mary M. Startzel (George)
3/22/1825	" John	Lancaster	Elizabeth Erb
1831	" Moses W.	Union	Mary Bertolet, Berks County
5/23/1853	Milliken, David B.	Perry	Elizabeth McCoy (Neal), 1st wife
4/11/1856	" "	"	Margaret Okeson (Daniel), 2nd wife
5/12/1838	Minaker, Joshua	Lycoming	Harriet Missimer (Aaron)
3/13/1845	Missimer, John	"	Lena Fisher
2/17/1848	" Philip M.	"	Harriet Reigle
6/3/1867	" Dr. Wm. H.	"	Rachael Nice
10/20/1803	Mitchell, David	Cumberland	Margaret Cochran (Samuel)
10/24/1837	" George V.	Mifflin	Elizabeth Taylor
5/5/1808	" Joseph	Dauphin	" Zearing (Henry)
3/15/1849	" William	"	Anglicia Ehrman (Christian)
1/19/1846	Mohler, John	Mifflin	Sarah Stroup (John)
11/16/1837	Montgomery, Dr. Daniel	Northumberland	Margaret Curry (William)
6/25/1857	" Hugh R.	"	Sarah Moll (Daniel)
1795	" James	"	Sarah Sheddan (James)
11/15/1825	" " Jr.	"	Jane Harrison, Union County
12/4/1857	" Robert G.	"	Susan Nesbit (Fleming)
ca. 1792	Moore, Archibald	Mifflin	Rebecca Junkin (William)
1845	Morrows, Dr. Thomas G.	Perry	Sarah Thompson
6/4/1833	Motz, George	Snyder	Elizabeth Freed
2/6/1840	" John	"	Sarah Moyer (Christopher)
12/11/1827	" John Jr.	Center	Elizabeth Fisher (Christian)
2/1/1842	Moyer, George C.	Snyder	Elixabeth Fisher (Michael)
3/27/1860	" Henry	"	Mary Dagle
1794	" John	"	Anna Margaret Miller (Frederick)
3/21/1825	" William	"	Margaret Fisher (Christian)
12/18/1860	" "	"	Sarah Hilbish (John A.) Perry Co.
3/31/1812	Mowrey, Charles	Mifflin	Mary Richmond (George)
7/8/1794	Muench, Rev. Chas. E.		Margaret Beiser
12/3/1855	" Jacob E.	Northumberland	Lavina Scholl
1799	Murdock, Robert A.		Mary Fisher (William)
6/22/1767	Murray, Lindley	Dauphin	Hannah Dobson
12/18/1853	Neagley, John	Dauphin	Elizabeth Murray (John)
2/18/1851	Neff, Dr. Peter D.	Center	Sarah Motz
1/15/1835	Newcomer, Jonas	Lycoming	Sophia Carpenter (John)
3/15/1827	Nicely, Joseph	Northumberland	Rebecca Fox
1810	Nissley, Martin	Dauphin	Ann Bomberger
1/5/1865	North, Calvin B.	Snyder	Anna Richter (Peter)
8/25/1840	Oakes, John H.	Union	Sarah Oakes (William)
3/14/1822	" Samuel	" ?	" Montgomery
2/13/1864	O'Conner, Dr. Martin	Dauphin	Susan Haldeman (Jacob M.)
10/15/1833	Ogden, Isaac B.	Montour	Priscilla Goodman (Philip)
1794	Orth, Christian H.	Dauphin	Rebecca Rahm (Conrad)
1795	Overmeyer, David	Union	Barbara Hochlander
1831	" "	Snyder	Catherine Bruce
5/14/1814	" B. Frank	(Ohio)	Magdalene Hendricks (Peter)
ca.1715	" J. George	(Germany	Anna Bane
1753	" Capt. J. George	Lancaster	Eva Rosenbaum
1760	" " " "	"	Barbara Focht (Jonas)

1808	Overmeyer, J. George	(Ohio)	Cath. Eve. Hoffman, Perry Co.,Ohio
5/16/1816	"　　　George L.	"	Mary Bowman (Geo) " " "
10/9/1823	"　　　Hugh	"	Eleanor Yost " " "
3/17/1768	"　　　J. Jacob	Germany	Eva Catherine Kemperlin
ca. 1798	"　　　Jacob	Union	Mary Gwynn (Hugh)
1828	"　　　Jacob	(Ohio)	Gordig Weaver, Perry County Ohio
8/5/1821	"　　　"	Snyder	Catherine Anderson
1830	"　　　"	Union	Mary Margaret Hummel, Snyder County
ca. 1790	"　　　J. George, Jr.	"	Maria Resrick
9/22/1793	"　　　J. Michael	"	Catherine Long (George)
4/29/1823	"　　　Michael	(Ohio)	Esther Hamer (Jacob), Perry Co.,Ohio
5/5/1833	"　　　John	"	Sarah Hendricks (Jacob), Sandusky Co.
1832	"　　　Louis	"	Rhoda Hammitt, Perry Co., Ohio
1783	"　　　Peter	"	Maria Eva Haney (Christopher)
ca. 1818	"　　　"	(Ohio)	Mary Hodge, Perry Co., Ohio
9/23/1824	"　　　"	?	Rosanna Bush
6/24/1838	"　　　"	(Ohio)	Elizabeth Hill, Sandusky Co., Ohio
1824	"　　Philip	Snyder	Margaret Swineford
4/6/1741	"　　J. Philip	(Germany)	Mary Graeber
ca.1792	"　　Philip	Union	Rosanna Bishop (Jacob?)
4/7/1825	Orwig, John	"	Maria Bright
4/18/1837	Ott, Jacob	Snyder	Catherine Good (Adam)
8/13/1805	"　J. Nicholas	Dauphin	Margaret Kissecker
8/2/1860	Otto, Washington	Northumberland	Harriet Bower
1/1/1752	Packer, James	Center	Rose Mendenhall, Chester County
5/22/1861	"　　John B.	Northumberland	Mary Cameron, Union County
9/28/1847	Painter, Ebenezer G.	Dauphin	Elizabeth Ewing (Rev. James)
5/28/1767	Pancoast, Adam	"	Abigail Boone (William)
3/26/1814	Pancoast, Hezekiah	"	Rachael " (Samuel)
3/2/1824	Pardoe, Thomas	Northumberland	Sarah House
1/2/1849	"　William	"	Lucy Troxel
4/26/1831	Parker, Andrew	Juniata	Ann Elizabeth Doty
5/9/1843	Parks, John	Snyder	Lydia Gemberling (Philip)
10/6/1836	Patterson, John	Juniata	Ellen Van Dyck (William)
1/24/1815	Pawling, Samuel	Snyder	Elizabeth Woodling (John)
1/18/1853	"　　Samuel B.	"	Leah Hoffman (John), 1st wife
5/15/1866	"　　" "	"	Hester Long (Benjamin), 2nd wife
10/12/1828	Pearson, John J.	Dauphin	Ellen Hayes (Samuel), 1st wife
7/13/1842	"　　" " "	"	Mary Briggs
9/19/1786	Pellman, Dr. Conrad	Berks	Mary Kline
2/6/1825	"　　Samuel	Union	Mary Wolf (Abraham), Berks Co.
12/5/1865	"　　Oliver K.	Union	Sallie Swengle
1859	Pennayl, David R.	Northumberland	Caroline Fry (Joseph)
6/28/1860	"　　William	"	Harriet C. Hull (Isaac)
1/24/1828	Pepperman, John	Lycoming	Priscilla Carpenter (John)
1797	Persing, John	Northumberland	Anna Eva Larkins, New Jersey
12/11/1859	Philips, Benjamin	"	Harriet Rothemel (Charles)
8/29/1854	"　　Elias	"	Kate Krissinger (John)
5/8/1866	Pierce, Everitt	Northumberland	Sarah Campbell (Isaac)
1/14/1743	Pontius, John	Union	Anna Catherine Zellers
1814	"　　Philip	"	Abigail Thompson (Benjamin)
9/11/1832	"　　J. Frederick	"	Mary Ann Larrabee (Dr. John)
9/5/1862	"　　John N.	"	Sarah J. Dreisbach
4/15/1792	Priestly, Joseph, Jr.	Northumberland	Elizabeth Ryland, England
4/22/1817	"　　Joseph R.	"	Frances Dundas
3/4/1847	"　　Dr. Joseph	"	Hannah Taggart
2/16/1843	Prish, Gideon	(New York)	Matilda Arnold (Peter)
12/19/1861	Purdy, Truman H.	Union	Mary E. James (Robert)

-11-

1/15/1839	Rank, Joseph L.	Lycoming	Maria Carpenter (John)
1/7/1840	Reber, David	Union	Margaret Musser (John)
2/8/1736	Reber, John	Berks	Joanna Magdalene Hahn
2/5/1853	Reber, William H.	Northumberland	Hannah Gasser (John)
1/29/1809	Redcay, Elias, Jr.	Berks	Sarah Harner, 1st wife
7/16/1826	" "	"	Elizabeth Strouse, 2nd wife
1834	Reed, Jesse	Northumberland	Charlotte Farley (Joshua)
7/12/1866	Reen, Frederick A.	"	Sarah Knight (Richard)
4/23/1865	Reichley, Frederick	Snyder	Esther Hummel (Jacob)
9/25/1852	Reiley, John A.	Dauphin	Catherine Clewine (George)
1838	Roimensnyder, John J.	Northumberland	Susan Bryan (Benjamin)
1817	Rengler, Daniel	Union	" Dunkle, 1st wife
2/20/1851	" "		" Royer (Israel), 2nd wife
1750	Renick, Henry		Martha Wilson
10/—/1797	Reynolds, John	Northumberland	Hester Foster
11/30/1837	Richter, Frederick, Jr.	Snyder	Elizabeth Seebold
8/21/1750	Roan, Rev. John	Lancaster	Mrs. Ann Cochran Lecky
10/10/1853	Robins, Dr. Edwin S.	Northumberland	Matilda Gulick (William)
4/—/1859	" Harvey S.	"	Elizabeth Heffley (Charles)
12/10/1811	Robbins, John		Jane McWilliams
7/15/1855	Robinson, James	Lycoming	Martha Missimer (Aaron)
1808	Rohrer, John	(Kentucky)	Barbara Dillman (Andrew)
1822	Ross, Rev. Joseph		Catherine Kunkle
1833	" Robert J.	Dauphin	Mary Haldeman (Jacob M.)
1708	Rothermel, John		Sybilla Zimmerman
5/11/1837	Rothrock, Abraham	Mifflin	Phoebe Brinton (Joesph)
3/27/1798	" John	Berks	Elizabeth Angst
2/15/1848	" Joseph	Juniata	Elizabeth Sieber (Samuel)
8/4/1852	" Dr. Roswell	Clarion	Catherine Mohney
3/17/1840	Rowe, Frederick	Perry	Mary Barner (George)
3/22/1853	Royer, George M.	Union	Caroline Kleckner (Eli)
9/25/1843	Rudy, Joseph	Dauphin	Hettie Landis (Abraham)
11/3/1864	Russell, Charles M.	Northumberland	Mary Ann Koch (Jonas)
2/28/1839	Rutherford, Abner	Dauphin	Ann Espy (William)
3/19/1833	" John B.		Keziah Parke (Col. James)
2/8/1771	Sallado, John	Dauphin	Margaret Everhart (George)
12/27/1881	Sampsel, Dr. J. W.	Snyder	Henrietta Spangler (George)
9/19/1819	Sassaman, Jonas	"	Fannie Kline (Barnhart)
3/12/1820	Schaffle, Charles F.	Union	Marie C. Dickes
1/23/1845	Schaffle, Charles W.	"	Mary Wykoff (Peter)
4/20/1881	" Samuel W.W.	"	Margaret B. Hutchinson (Charles)
3/14/1818	Schneider, George	Northumberland	Catherine Wagner (Jacob)
9/23/1841	Schnure, George	Snyder	Cordelia Davis (James K.)
12/2/1830	Schoch, John A.	"	Lydia Houtz (Christian)
2/23/1864	" Martin L.	Union	Anna Kleckner (Michael)
2/1/1831	Scholl, Elias	Snyder	Elizabeth Haines (Peter), 1st wife
12/—/1841	" "	"	Catherine " " 2nd wife
12/6/1846	Schuyler, Dr. Jacob	Union	Margaret Lawson (Joseph)
5/8/1864	Scott, David S.	Lycoming	Mary C. Missimer (Aaron)
11/15/1798	" John	Union	Margaret Clingan
1824	Sechrist, Jacob	Snyder	Elizabeth Herrold (Frederick)
9/22/1857	Sees, Oliver W.		Caroline Buehler (Charles)
4/19/1855	" William E.	Dauphin	Mary Kunkle, 1st wife
9/13/1857	" " "	"	" E. Chandler (Jonathan),2nd wife
3/23/1833	Seiler, Dr. Christian	"	" Hayes (William)
3/19/1842	" Jeremiah	"	Anna E. Stigelman (John)
8/26/1810	Selin, Anthony, Jr.	Snyder	Catherine Yoner, Sunbury, Pa.
11/8/1853	Sergeant, William	Dauphin	Eliza Espy (James)
11/7/1797	Shadel, Michael	"	Anna Maria Weise (Adam)
1/11/1838	Shaffer, Abraham	Union	Elizabeth Hummel (John)

11/12/1861	Shaffer, Dr. J. C.	Snyder	Sarah E. Moyer
5/8/1771	Shaffer, Jacob	Northumberland	Catherine Fossinger
12/8/1864	" John W.	Union	Angeline Schrack (John)
4/5/1795	" Philip	Dauphin	Anna Weise (Adam)
12/29/1856	Shammo, William	"	Catherine Beam (John)
9/—/1822	Sharp, James		Isabel Stockman
2/16/1802	Sharrett, Rev. Frederick	Snyder	Catherine Geugler (Nicholas)
10/30/1782	Shearer, Robert	Northumberland	Margaret Hutchison (Joseph)
11/20/1838	Sheetz, Henry	"	Margaret Hummel
1774	Shelly, Daniel	Lancaster	Catherine ————
1776	" "		Elizabeth ————
1794	" "		Barbara ————
3/25/1873	Sherwood, Henry	(Tennessee)	Lydia Fisher (Daniel), Union Co.
9/27/1860	Shimer, Samuel J.	Northumberland	Catherine Stout
9/—/1833	Shindle, Rev. J. P., Jr.	"	Sophia Young
1/18/1855	" " "	Snyder	Sallie Gobin
1/18/1842	" J.G.L.	"	Abigail Hathaway
1856	" Dr. John Y.	"	Sarah J. Motz
12/31/1863	Shipe, Moses	Northumberland	Rebecca Clark, (John)
2/1/1800	Shipman, Abraham	"	Mary Eckman
2/14/1837	" "	"	Elizabeth Yoxtheimer
178—	" William	"	Catherine Campbell, Sussex Co., N.J.
11/9/1732	Shoemaker, J. George	Northampton	Catherine Trexler
1/4/1854	Shoop, Levi	Northumberland	Lydia Hepler (Rev. John)
11/6/1808	" Michael	Dauphin	Anna Margaret Weise (Adam)
3/23/1848	Shriner, Joseph W.	Union	Elizabeth Kremer (Abraham)
5/9/1818	" Samuel	"	Ann Wheeler
1791	Sigler, George Jr.	Mifflin	Elizabeth Bun, New Jersey
1836	Simmons George W.	Dauphin	Elizabeth Bates
3/2/1843	Simonton, John W.	Union	Sarah H. Irwin
10/15/1849	Singer, Dr. Joshua	Perry	Mary Whiteside (John)
1751	Slear, J. Michael	Berks	Mary Juliana Haefle
1840	Slifer, Eli	Union	Catherine Frick
9/19/1833	Sloan, Alexander	Dauphin	Mary Todd (James)
8/28/1827	Smith, Jacob W.	Snyder	Mary Straub (Andrew), Milton, Pa.
11/25/1845	" Oliver P.	Mifflin	Margaret Taylor (John)
1828	Snyder, Charles A.	Dauphin	Barbara Keller (John)
12/25/1856	" David H.	Northumberland	Mary J. Campbell (Nicholas)
3/28/1822	" George A.	Snyder	Ann Ellen Duncan (Stephen)
10/18/1845	" John A.	Cumberland	Catherine S. Egolf (Valentine)
6/11/1818	" " "	Snyder	Mary Kittera (John)
1/1/1857	" " B.	Northumberland	Mary Lowrey (Daniel)
9/2/1860	" Samuel	"	———— Wynn
1865	" Silas R.	"	Lydia H. Shipman
6/12/1796	" Gov. Simon	Snyder	Catherine Antes
6/4/1865	" Solomon S.	Northumberland	Rebecca Bohner (Henry)
3/15/1856	Springman, Augustus	Snyder	Josephine Bard (Joseph)
6/10/1824	Stackpole, Thomas	Mifflin	Elizabeth Steese
4/12/1814	Stadden, John	Union JJ	Jane Sample (John)
4/14/1836	" "	"	Mrs. Nancy (Fowler) Van Wagoner
2/4/1841	" William	"	Sarah Ireland (David)
5/2/1843	Stahl, George	Northumberland	Maria Elizabeth Doshler (Jacob)
9/26/1846	Stauffer, Daniel	Snyder	Amelia Good (Adam)
5/—/1825	Stewart, David	Perry	Ann C. Shuman
5/22/1822	Stewart, David	Dauphin	Sarah Walker (John)
1750	" Hugh	"	Hannah Dallas, 1st wife
1764	" "	"	Nancy Moore, 2nd wife
1736	" John	"	Frances ————
?	" Capt. Lazarus	"	Martha Espy
1809	" Robert T.	?	Mary Dunlop (James)
1789	" Samuel	Dauphin	Agnes Calhoun (William)

-13-

7/11/1861	Stine, George W.	Dauphin	Anna Noff (Dr. John)
7/4/1820	Stockman, John		Hanna Dryden .
11/29/1866	Storey, J. Wilbert	Dauphin	Ada V. Adams (W. O.)
11/29/1821	Straub, Abraham	Northumberland	Nancy Balliet
4/19/1864	" Jacob	"	Araminta Schlebby
10/18/1863	Strawser, Jonathan S.	Snyder	Sallie Steffen (George)
11/5/1861	Strickler, Dr. M. B.	Perry	Anna Halbert (John)
9/12/1850	Stroh, Solomon	Northumberland	Mary Zimmerman (George)
8/6/1862	Stroup, David A.	Mifflin	Mary E. Kerns (Thomas)
1817	" John	"	" Bair
5/15/1838	Swineford, Absolom	Snyder	" A. Leshells (John)
5/5/1848	Taggart, David	Northumberland	Anna Cowden (John)
7/9/1838	Tate, Levi	Lycoming	Susan Carpenter (John)
12/22/1836	Taylor, Henry P.	Mifflin	Elizabeth Forsyth (Robert)
6/17/1794	Teitsworth, Robert	Northumberland	Elizabeth Taylor, 1st wife
3/27/1817	"	"	" Andrew (Philip), 2nd wife
3/20/1841	Thompson, James M.	"	Susan A. Campbell (Robert)
12/30/1843	" John S.	"	Elizabeth " "
1852	" James B.	Dauphin	Emily J. Black (Joseph), 1st wife
11/26/1867	" " "	"	Martha M. Reiley (William), 2nd wife
11/6/1835	Till, John	"	Rebecca Rutter, Philadelphia, Pa.
2/1/1844	Toomey, Emanuel	Perry	Margaret Earnest (Conrad)
1826	Tressler, John	"	Elizabeth Loy (George)
177~	Trexler, Col. Peter	Northampton	Catherine Grimm (Henry)
12/18/1812	Ulrich, Benjamin	Snyder	Elizabeth Houseworth (John)
1/26/1751	" J. George, Sr.	" or Berks	Anne Catherine ~~~~~~~
2/12/1824	Vandling, John	Northumberland	Susan Douty
10/9/1844	Van Valzah, John A.	Union	Sarah Barber (Thomas)
2/3/1820	" Dr. Thomas		Harriet Howard
4/8/1802	Vastine, Jeremiah	Northumberland	Elizabeth Reader
12/1/1733	Vincent, John	(New Jersey)	" Doremus
3/5/1778	" Daniel	Northumberland	Angelicia Huffe
3/24/1812	" Isaac	"	Rebecca Comly (or Conly)
3/14/1854	Voris, Gilbert	"	Harriet McWilliams
3/25/1861	Wagenseller, Dr. Benj. F.	Snyder	Maria Schoch (Jacob Jr.)
7/19/1854	" Dr. P. Richter	"	Catherine Chritsman, Adams County
3/26/1839	" William F.	Snyder	Amelia Bergstresser (Peter)
12/29/1863	Wagner, George A.	Perry	Mary E. Sheibley (John)
1830	" Samuel		Elizabeth Tressler (Andrew)
1841	Waldron, William	Northumberland	Ann Hilgert (Philip)
1803	Wallace, William	Dauphin	Rachael Forest (Dr. Andrew), 1st wife
1804			Eleanor Maclay (Hon. Wm.), 2nd wife
9/25/1832	Walls, Hon. John	Union	Margaret Green (Gen. Abbott)
5/21/1840	Walter, Geo. Henry	"	Rebecca Gemberling (Samuel)
10/27/1807	" Rev. J. Conrad	Snyder	Catherine Ulsh
3/12/1862	" Jacob	"	Ellen Fisher (George)
3/24/1861	Waugh, Beverly R.	Dauphin	Sarah Beatty (George)
8/20/1861	Weaver, George P.	Center	Catherine Mots
8/26/1843	" William H.	Northumberland	Lydia Smith (John)
11/1/1859	Weidenhamer, J. Adam	"	Sarah A. Deitsman
12/11/1864	Weist, James M.	"	Elmira Wald (John)
7/8/1856	Weist, John	Snyder	Emma J. Boyer (Isaac)
6/7/1801	Weise, John	Dauphin	Elizabeth Bordner (Michael)
1801	" J. Adam		Eva "
1808	" J. George		Charlotte Moore
11/22/1720	Weiser, Col. J. Conrad	Berks	Ann Eva Feg
8/26/1810	" J. Conrad	Snyder	Elizabeth Snyder
1832	Weitzel, Joseph	Northumberland	Sarah Woodruff (John)

2/2/1796	Wenrich, Peter	Dauphin	Susan Umberger (John)
5/—/1840	White Ebenezer	Lycoming	Elizabeth Massimer (Aaron)
11/26/1821	White, Samuel	Dauphin	Sarah Hills (Stephen)
6/23/1831	Wiestling, Dr. Benjamin	"	Matilda Ross (Andrew)
1/22/1824	" Joshua M.		Catherine Youse (George)
6/8/1862	Wilkinson, Peter	Northumberland	Mary J. Malick (Henry)
6/25/1859	Williams, Benjamin	Northumberland	Catherine Morgan
1/16/1843	Williams, Gen. Edw. C.	Snyder	Selina Hetzel (John), 1st wife
6/5/1873	" " " "		Mrs. A. E. Hetzel, 2nd wife
1804	Willard, George	Perry	Susan Culler (Michael)
10/—/1841	" Rev. Philip	"	Margaret Chritzman (George)
12/12/1839	Wilson, Abraham S.	Mifflin	Harriet Norris (John)
2/22/1821	" George	"	Nancy Taylor (Robert)
3/20/1825	" James		Margaret Wilson (John)
12/22/1831	" " Jr.	Philadelphia	Sarah Geiger, Dauphin County
10/2/1865	" John	Union	Margaret Barber
5/6/1824	" Thomas L.	Dauphin	Juliana M. Bender
1/21/1823	" William	Mifflin	Eleanor Bailey
11/20/1865	Wingert, Jesse	Dauphin	Barbara Blust (Dr. Joseph)
6/17/1857	Winters, Benjamin F.	Clinton	Catherine Woodling (Joseph)
10/11/1866	Witman, Henry	Dauphin	Fredrica Krause (David)
3/23/1865	Wolverton, Simon P.	Northumberland	Elizabeth Hendricks (Benjamin)
8/26/1877	Woodling, Henry David	(Iowa)	Ella F. Smith
6/—/1826	" William	Snyder	Anna Maria Gilbert (Adam)
10/18/1836	Wright, Pascal	Union	Jane Lawson (Joseph)
6/6/1793	Wyeth, John	Dauphin	Louisa Weiss (Lewis)
5/29/1829	Wyeth, Francis	"	Susan Maxwell (William)
4/17/1828	Witman, Dr. John	"	Caroline Orth (Henry)
5/19/1863	Yeager, John G.	Mifflin	Sophia Stroup (John)
1834	Yoder, Moses		Elizabeth Ranck
7/28/1854	" "		Mrs. Nancy Van Wagner
12/25/1849	" Nathaniel	Northumberland	Mary Fisher
9/21/1843	Young, Josiah C.	Dauphin	Catherine M. Kinter (George)
8/1/1813	Youngman, John G.	Northumberland	" Bright "
12/3/1835	Zearns, Levi	Snyder	Esther Gemberling (Philip)
6/4/1744	Zerbe, John	Berks	Catherine Stupp
7/28/1861	" Thomas	Northumberland	" Messer (Philip)
6/22/1862	Zimmerman, Peter	"	Rachael Kebach
2/23/1851	" Sebastian	"	Elizabeth Schlappig (Benjamin)

9/9/1817	Alter, Jacob	Anna Kessler
1/18/1825	Amberg, Hezekiah, New Berlin	Elizabeth Brooks
10/6/1825	Apple, Daniel	Susanna Orwig, Mifflinburg
11/14/1826	Alsbach, William	Catherine Shively
2/27/1829	Amberg, Abraham	Charlotte Brooks, Chillicothe, Ohio, formerly of New Berlin
6/11/1829	Anrand, George	Mrs. Mary Royer

9/27/1801	Breyvogel, Jacob D., Printer, Sunbury, Pa.	Susanna, dau. Christoph. Baldy, Buffalo Twp.
6/21/1807	Billmyer, Martin	Margaret Himmelreich
12/10/1807	Burnside, Thomas	Mary Fleming, Bellefonte, Pa.
12/26/1807	Brobst, John	Lydia Marriner
7/5/1808	Brown, Peter	Catherine Kantz, sister of Peter
6/11/1809	Baldy, Gen. Christopher	Eve Metzger, widow of
6/28/1809	Bower, Joseph	Susanna Machamer
3/13/1810	Bower, Moses	Catherine Moyer, daughter of Philip
5/27/1810	Bower, George	Polly Smith, daughter of Michael, deceased
2/2/1812	Black, David	Catherine Berrey
3/26/1812	Barber, Thomas	Betsy Clingan
1/24/1813	Billman, Jacob	Charity, daughter of Caleb _____
8/1/1813	Burd, Levi	Eve, daughter of Henry Winegarden
2/22/1814	Boeber, John	Anna Baker
9/3/1815	Barry, Elisha	Elizabeth, daughter of Henry Herbst
6/5/1825	Bonner, Mathias(SanduskyCo.,Ohio)	Elizabeth Overmire, (David)
5/31/1829	Bonner, Henry	_____ Moyer, Union Twp.

1/2/1806	Coasin, Ludwig	Susanna Oliphant
12/26/1811	Cochran, John, Jr.	Anna M., Daughter of Adam Grove
2/11/1812	Chamberlain, Aaron	Betsy Dale
2/24/1825	Candor, Thomas, Kelly Twp.	Margaret, John Montgomery
11/3/1825	Chestney, Jacob G., Mifflinburg	Juliana, dau.,John Cummings, Hartley Twp.
2/2/1826	Chamberlain, John	Elizabeth, daughter of Wm. Hayes, Lewisburg
2/21/1826	Caldwell, James, Lewisburg	Isabella,dau. of Jas. Duncan, Center Co.
11/20/1828	Chamberlin, Joseph,	Nancy Deal
5/20/1829	Charles, C. H., Hartley Twp.	Juliette Mann, Tioga County
8/11/1839	Christ, L. B.	Esther Bogar

11/19/1801	Dreisbach, Daniel, Merchant, Lewisburg	Kate Dreisbach, Lewisburg
12/13/1810	Dunn, Washington, Lycoming County	Betsy Musser, White Deer Twp.
10/7/1811	Davis, William	Catherine, daughter of George Derr
2/11/1813	Dickson, Jesse	Polly, daughter of Christian Morkel
4/4/1813	Donachy, Alexander	Fanny, daughter of George Seitz
5/16/1813	Dereham, Samuel	Susanna Shadel
2/24/1818	Dale, James	Eliza Bell, Dauphin County
10/14/1824	Dreisbach, Martin, Jr.	Elizabeth, daughter of Solomon Kleckner
3/15/1825	Duncan, James Aaronsburg, Pa.	Mrs. Sophia Maxwell, New Berlin, Pa.
10/31/1826	Devling, John	Mary, daughter of Judge Hugh Wilson
1/16/1828	Derr, Jacob	Isabel Hunter
12/9/1828	Duncan, David, Center County	Susanna Hayes, New Berlin
1/20/1829	Devling, Walter	Eliza, daughter Judge Hugh Wilson

4/4/1805	Epler, Peter	Eva Christ
1/12/1811	Evans, Evan Rise	Mrs._____Forrest
2/12/1812	Engleman, Michael	Barbara, daughter of Jacob Gilman
3/22/1808	Freedly, John	Elizabeth Lehman
11/29/1808	Freedly, George	Catherine Frantz
1/8/1809	Frederick, Philip	Christina Brown
2/25/1812	Fruit, Robert	Maria Nevius
6/23/1816	Francis, William widower	Catherine Gettig, widow
11/11/1828	Forster, John	Margaret, dau. of Dr. Robt. Van Valzah
2/__/1829	Forster, Robert	Jane Rutherford, Harrisburg, Pa.
1/4/1809	Grove, Henry (bro. of John, Sam, Frank, Betsy and Sarah)	
		Hannah Leisering, Lewisburg, Pa.
11/1/1812	Grove, John	Sarah, daughter of John Montgomery
2/2/1812	Goodlander, Paul	Rachael, daughter of Andrew Heckel
3/18/1823	Gutelius, John P.	Maria Aurand, Lebanon, Pa.
4/10/1823	Grove, Conrad, merchant, New Berlin, Pa.	Mary Gingrich, Juniata Co., Pa.
8/17/1826	Grier, Thomas	Mrs. Rachael Stratton, New Berlin, Pa.
2/17/1829	Grier, Dr. Joseph T.	Margaret, daughter of A. Graham
4/28/1829	Grove, Simon	Mary Miller, Reading, Pa.
2/9/1797	Howard, Thomas	Elizabeth, Dau., Widow Mary Harris
10/9/1810	Highland, William	Mary, widow of Christian Gann
12/18/1810	Hutchinson, Samuel, Dorry,	Mrs. Jennie Wallace, dau., Capt. Tm. Gray of White Deer Township
12/25/1811	Hopburn, Samuel	Anna Clay, Montgomery County
6/6/1816	Hayes, John	Jane, daughter of John McFadden
11/4/1818	Hammond, Lt.R.H.,5thU.S.Infantry	Eliza C. Gloninger, Lebanon, Pa.
7/31/1823	Hoffman, Michael, White Deer Twp.	Lydia Wagner, White Deer Twp.
5/10/1827	Housel, John	Margaret, daughter of Jacob Musser
3/13/1828	Haus, John	Margaret Roush, Mifflinburg, Pa.
5/28/1829	Hayes, Robert	Emily Fields
7/2/1829	Hill, Daniel K.	Barbara A. Musser, Lewisburg, Pa.
8/12/1813	Jodon, Francis	Elizabeth, daughter of Charles Cherry
8/--/1816	Johnson, John, painter, NewBorlinPa	Elizabeth Kress
7/22/1824	Jordon, Nathaniel, merchant, W.D.Twp	Hannah Smith, White Deer Township
11/19/1801	Kirk, William, Turbot Township	Jane Knox, Lewisburg, Pa.
5/11/1807	Kroechbaum, Peter, Jr.	Eliza Davis
11/13/1807	" George	Polly, daughter of George Keller
10/31/1809	Knox, George, Lewisburg, Pa.	Jane McIlroy, Pine Creek
3/1/1812	Kelly, James	Hannah, daughter of George Seitz
4/6/1813	Keenly, Daniel	Maria, daughter of John Richter
6/23/1816	Kemp, Titus	Betsy Huntington
12/22/1825	Kelly, William, Union County	Margaret Allison, Center County
9/8/1805	Lawshe, John	Polly Sites
3/19/1812	Lawson, James	Nancy Clingan
4/1/1813	Lesher, Philip	Polly, daughter of Andrew Billmayer
2/20/1817	Long, Peter	Sarah, daughter of Jacob Moore
10/14/1824	Linn, William, Kelly Township	Jane Morrow, Franklin County
4/28/1825	Linn, John	Mary F. Chamberlin
5/5/1825	Ludwig, Daniel	Sarah Hoffman
7/20/1826	Linn, James F., Lewisburg, Pa.	Margaret, daughter of Hugh Wilson, Buffalo

5/4/1808	Myers, Peter	Sophia Nixon
7/25/1809	Martin, Lawrence	Polly Juge
8/31/1809	Montgomery, Robert	Nancy, daughter of George Knox
11/11/1810	Mayer, Michael	Sarah Kelly
2/11/1812	Maclay, John	Anna Dale
10/12/1815	Mook, George	Julia, daughter of Adam Fasnacht
11/7/1816	Moyer, Henry	Polly Strickland
10/24/1817	Mitchell, George	Elisa Anderson
6/ /1822	Moore, Lewis	Dorothy Smith
8/26/1824	Magee, Capt. James	Elisabeth Strayhorn, West Buffalo Twp.
5/5/1825	Maclay, Robert P., East Buffalo Tp.	Margaret C. Lashels, New Berlin, Pa.
5/20/1825	Mussena, Henry B.	Elisabeth Winter, New Berlin, Pa.
10/9/1825	Maize, John	Elisabeth Jones, Jifflinburg, Pa.
11/3/1825	Mook, Daniel	Mary Dieffenbach
11/20/1825	Hauck, David	Nancy Shriner
10/19/1826	Morrill, James, New Berlin	Sarah Hopburn, Northumberland, Pa.
10/22/1826	Hauck, Jesse, New Berlin, Pa.	Catherine Crotzer, Mifflinburg, Pa.
8/30/1827	Magee, John	Susan Struble
1/3/1828	Miller, William, New Berlin	Elisabeth Myers
4/8/1828	Mackey, ------	Abigail, widow of Isaac Iddings
5/28/1828	Metzger, Abner	Eleanor Lawshe
8/4/1829	Myers, Henry	Hannah Walter
8/26/1813	McLaughlin, Hugh	Elisabeth McClister
5/22/1817	McBeth, Andrew	Ann Linn
6/5/1827	McCormick, Saul	Catherine, Daughter of Rev. Thos. Hood
11/5/1828	McLaughlin, Hugh	Frances, daughter of George Derr
3/24/1808	Nesbit, Wm., Chillisquaque Twp.	Nancy Musser, East Buffalo Township
2/10/1825	Nesbit, David	Mary, daughter of Jacob Musser
4/7/1825	Orwig, John, Mifflinburg, Pa.	Maria Bright
8/24/1824	Pontius, Conrad, of Ohio	Mary Seebold, (Christopher Junior)
10/31/1824	Peters, Isaac	Susanna Miller, New Berlin, Pa.
4/7/1806	Renner, Fred, brother of Jac.&Ben	Magdalene, Dau. Christian Krause, deceased
4/13/1809	Ranck, John	Nancy Luther
3/15/1810	" Joel	Sarah, daughter of Joseph Long
4/2/1815	" Johathan	Catherine " " " "
6/25/1815	Rees, Jacob	Elisabeth, sister of Gideon Williamson
6/19/1817	Roush, Samuel	Elisabeth Dunkle
12/26/1825	Row, John	Rachael Kinkle, Dry Valley
4/11/1826	Reedy, Jonathan	Amelia Buchner
12/16/1795	Sheckler, Tobias	Catherine daughter of George Fredericks
6/12/1796	Snyder, Simon, later Governor of Pa.	Catherine, daughter of Col. Fred Antes of Northumberland, Pa.
6/12/1806	Sergeant, John	Catherine Beyer
11/16/1806	Stromb, Michael	Sarah Grove
10/12/1809	Sierer,John,aged65years,Buff.Twp.	Louisa McMillan, aged 19 yrs., Buffalo Twp.
8/26/1810	Selin, Anthony C, Selinsgrove,Pa.	Catherine Yoner, Sunbury, Pa.
10/7/1810	Stahl, Philip	Susanna Spotz
2/23/1815	Shannon, Daniel	Christena Pross
3/23/1815	Strickland, Samuel	Elisabeth Turner
1/17/1816	Shriner, Daniel	Catherine,daughter of William Funston
12/31/1816	Strayer, Jacob	Rachael Harmony, New Berlin, Pa.
5/11/1818	Snydor, John	Mary, daughter of Hon. John W. Kittera
3/28/1822	Snyder, George A.	Anna Ellen, dau., Stephen Duncan, deceased

12/16/1824	Stedman, Wm. C.	Elizabeth, dau., Judge Hugh Wilson
10/13/1825	Strawbridge,————,ColumbiaCo.,Pa.	Louisa, daughter of Charles Mans
————1826	Snyder, John	Margaret Hammond
2/——/1829	Strayborn, Peter	————daughter of James Cornelius
6/23/1829	Shaw, John	Margaret Baker
3/27/1804	Thompson, William	Susanna, daughter of John Linn
5/15/1806	Troxel, George	Mary Hoffman
9/8/1811	Updike, Elijah	Elizabeth, daughter of Martin Snook
4/11/1809	Vandyke, John, White Deer, Twp.	Margaret Adams, White Deer Township
9/22/1829	Van Valzah, John A.	Rebecca Chambers
8/26/1810	Weiser, Conrad	Elizabeth Snyder
5/30/1815	Wehr, Jacob	Margaret Sassaman
12/19/1816	Walter, John	Susanna, daughter of John Moyer
9/25/1823	Wagoner, Jacob	Rachael, daughter of Thos. McGuire,WhiteDeer
11/2/1825	Wetsel, Jonathan	Hetty Hoff, Union Township
4/19/1827	Wilson, Thomas, Kelly Township	Mrs. Drake
1/17/1829	Wilson, Wm.,sonofJudgeHughWilson	Ruth Waddell, Center County
7/2/1829	Woods, Christopher, Jr.	Maria Little, Lewisburg, Pa.
12/26/1826	Yost, John, New Berlin, Pa.	Sarah Shaffer, Buffalo Township
2/13/1827	Yarger, John	Margaret Kelly, Hartley Township
5/17/1808	Zerbe, Henry	Susanna Heckel
7/14/1829	Zentmoyer, Israel	Eva, daughter of John Snook, West Buffalo, Twp.

END.

DATE	MAN	RESIDENCE	WOMAN	RESIDENCE
2/4/1836	Angstadt, Benjamin	Lewisburg, Pa.	Wilhant, Caroline	E. Buffalo Twp.
2/28/1839	Adams, Isaac	E. Buffalo Twp.	Marts, Elizabeth	Kelly Twp.
3/21/1846	Arbogast, Henry	------------	Gottshall, Hannah	Buffalo Twp.
8/9/1832	Beckley, Daniel	Mifflinburg, Pa.	------Elizabeth	Hartley Twp.
3/13/1832	Bub (Boop), Adam	------------	------Susanna	''
5/12/1832	'' '' Michael	------------	Marts, Maria	''
2/7/1839	Betz, Frank	Lewisburg, Pa.	Dreisbach, Maria	Mifflinburg, Pa.
6/13/1839	Brunner, Frederick	------------	Godder, Rachael	------------
10/1/1839	Bentz, John	------------	Baker, Eliza	Lewisburg, Pa.
10/12/1839	Barkelow, John	------------	Wherley, Catherine	W. Buffalo Twp.
3/5/1840	Benfer, Elias	Union Twp.	Quinn, Sarah	''
7/18/1841	Badger, John	Huntingdon Co.	Klingman, Hetty	''
8/19/1841	Barkelow, William	------------	Klingman, Lydia	''
4/18/1844	Beaver, John	Lewisburg, Pa.	Shively, Ann	''
10/24/1844	Boop, Joseph	------------	------Maria	Mifflinburg, Pa.
11/14/1844	Bender, William	------------	Frane, Rebecca	E. Buffalo Twp.
10/14/1841	Bolick, Andrew	------------	Shiffer, Lucetta	New Berlin, Pa.
1/13/1848	Bogenrief, David	------------	Kinney, Margaret	Mifflinburg, Pa.
12/31/1839	Chambers, Joseph	W. Buffalo Twp.	Shadel, Rosannah	Union Twp.
9/3/1845	Coombs, George	------Ohio	Smith, Catherine	Union County
5/9/1850	Crotser (Kratzer) Dr.And.	------------	Schoch, Catherine	Mifflinburg, Pa.
1/27/1846	Cornelius, John	------------	Moyer, Elizabeth	W. Buffalo Twp.
7/8/1832	Dunkel, Jacob	------------	Wilhand, Anna	E. Buffalo Twp.
9/7/1845	Diehl, George	Hartleton, Pa.	Stein, Catherine	Hartley Twp.
8/20/1839	Diehl, John	''	Smith, Susannah	''
10/20/1840	Diehl, Henry	New Berlin, Pa.	Bower, Eliza	Union Twp.
11/3/1840	Dorr, Levi	W. Buffalo Twp.	Weil, Elizabeth	''
6/2/1842	Dorr, Philip	Union County	Shell, Catherine	Northumberland Co.
6/13/1844	Dersham, Lewis	------------	Yoder, Anna	------------
2/5/1835	Egan, Daniel	Northumberland	Witman, Leah	E. Buffalo Twp.
1/7/1841	Englehart, David	------------	Boyer, Maria	W. Buffalo Twp.
2/26/1846	'' John	W. Buffalo Twp.	Morris, Jane	Lycoming Co.
12/31/1831	Foote, Ellis	------------	Reichley, Hannah	Mifflinburg, Pa.
9/18/1834	Feltz, Jonathan	------------	Wolf, Elizabeth	------------
12/8/1836	Fiess, Jacob	------------	Peters, Matilda	Hartleton, Pa.
2/23/1841	Frane, Jacob	Lewisburg, Pa.	Bohn, Maria	New Berlin, Pa.
2/28/1843	Fillman, David	------------	Shively, Barbara	Hartley Twp.
11/25/1846	'' Jacob	Hartley Twp.	Anderson, Elizabeth	W. Buffalo Twp.
3/12/1835	Gembel, John	Mifflinburg, Pa.	Kanz, Susannah	W. Buffalo Twp.
1/14/1836	Glover, William	Hartleton, Pa.	Sipher, Eliza	Hartley Twp.
1/21/1836	Groet (Grove?), John M.	Lewisburg, Pa.	Weyer, Hannah	Kelly Twp.
10/19/1837	Grove, David	Kelly Twp.	Gemberling, Maria	Buffalo Twp.
4/19/1838	Gansel, John	Center County	Maddon, Margaret	Hartley Twp.

Date	Groom	Location	Bride	Location
10/30/1838	Garber, August,	-----------	Klingman, Anna	W. Buffalo Twp.
2/14/1839	Gettys, William	-----------	Katherman, Barbara	Hartley Twp.
7/14/1839	Gemberling, Samuel	-----------	Kline, Matilda	New Columbia, Pa.
4/25/1844	Guyer, Peter	-----------	Grove, Louisa	Kelly Twp.
12/26/1844	Gemberling, Christopher	-----------	Nestor, Louise	-----------
10/27/1831	Hironimus, Jacob	-----------	Burd, Hannah	Hartley Twp.
2/9/1832	Hummel, Elias	Dry Balley	Brenner, Sarah	Union Twp.
2/7/1833	Huff, Peter	Kelly Twp.	Knoll, Sarah	-----------
2/28/1833	Herbst, Josiah	-----------	---------- Leah	Buffalo Twp.
5/6/1834	Herman, Simon	-----------	---------- Anna	Union Twp.
8/14/1834	Hoffman, William	-----------	Beter, Maria	E. Buffalo Twp.
1/7/1836	Haas, George	Kelly Twp.	Frey, Anna	" " "
4/3/1836	Hartman, Henry	-----------	Kniss, Susan	Centerville, Pa.
10/13/1836	Heintzelman, Wm.	E. Buffalo TP.	---------- Maria	W. Buffalo Twp.
3/20/1838	Haas, Abraham	-----------	Klingler, Elizabeth	-----------
9/26/1838	Hauck, Andrew	-----------	Buff (Puff), Maria	-----------
12/11/1838	Hoy, Benjamin	-----------	---------- Nancy	W. Buffalo Twp.
4/1/1839	Hindin, Emanuel	-----------	Engleman, Hasel	-----------
7/28/1839	Hartman, Jacob	-----------	Weigle, Priscilla	Kelly Twp.
2/13/1842	Haffer, George	-----------	Matthews, Catherine	E. Buffalo Twp.
11/19/1842	Haffer, Jacob	-----------	Hensel, Sarah	-----------
3/25/1841	Hoffer, William	-----------	Hanger, Catherine	Lewisburg, Pa.
6/3/1841	Hoffman, David	-----------	Huntginton, ----------	Hartley Twp.
11/18/1841	Heinly, John	-----------	Anderson, ----------	Buffalo Twp.
10/29/1841	Hoffman, Enoch	-----------	Grove, Esther	-----------
12/5/1844	Hollenbach, Isaac	-----------	Heinly, Catherine	Kelly Twp.
2/24/1846	Herbst, David	E. Buffalo Twp.	Stahl, Sabina	" "
2/21/1839	Irwin, James	-----------	Pontius, Amelia	Buffalo Twp.
2/28/1833	Johnson, Jonathan	-----------	Miller, Mary	W. Buffalo Twp.
10/20/1831	Kunkel, Benjamin	Kelly Twp.	Edman, Barbara	Union Twp.
11/10/1831	Knobes, Joseph	-----------	Parmer, Eliza	Buffalo Twp.
2/21/1833	Katherman, David	-----------	---------- Jane	Hartley Twp.
6/10/1834	Katherman, Charles	-----------	Troutman, Elizabeth	" "
8/14/1834	Kuhns, Josiah	-----------	Highland, Margaret	" "
4/23/1835	Kleckner, Peter	E. Buffalo Twp.	Wolf, ----------	E. Buffalo Twp.
1/12/1836	Kohl, Henry	-----------	Ludwig, Maira	Lycoming County
3/17/1836	Kauffman, Jacob	-----------	Zeller, Amelia	Buffalo Twp.
3/22/1836	" David	-----------	---------- Sarah	W. Buffalo Twp.
11/8/1836	Kline, Joel	-----------	Knib, Maria	-----------
2/9/1837	Kniss, William	-----------	Heimbach, Maria	E. Buffalo Twp.
3/26/1837	Kepler, Daniel	-----------	Sall, Maria	Union Twp.
6/20/1837	Kamp, George	Mifflinburg, Pa.	Essel, Susanna	Selinsgrove, Pa.
12/28/1837	Knoll, John, Jr.	-----------	Katherman, Sophia	W. Buffalo Twp.
6/14/1838	Kaler, David	-----------	Person, Jane	Hartley Twp.
10/12/1838	Koney, Henry	Lycoming Co.	Bastian, Sarah Ann	-----------
11/20/1838	Kline, Samuel	-----------	Kline, Sarah	Northumberland Co
5/2/1839	Knoll, John	-----------	Meixell, Leah	Kelly Twp.
4/9/1840	Kaler, Michael	-----------	Dennis, Elizabeth	Hartley Twp.
6/30/1840	Keister, Peter	-----------	Royer, Mary	" "
11/5/1840	Konz, William	Center County	Klingman, Maria	W. Buffalo Twp.
1/28/1841	Koser, Solomon	-----------	Noess, Ketty	-----------
11/11/1841	Knoll, Elias	-----------	Smith, Maria	E. Buffalo Twp.

-21-

Date	Name	Place	Spouse	Township
10/13/1842	Kosser, John	———	Englehart, Lydia	W. Buffalo Twp.
10/12/1845	Kline, Elias	———	Miller, Catherine	Hartley Twp.
6/13/1833	Long, Henry	———	Kline, Anna	White Deer Twp.
3/19/1835	Long, Daniel	New Berlin, Pa.	Waters, Maria	Mifflinburg, Pa.
1/26/1837	Libby, William	E. Buffalo Twp.	——— ———	Hartley Twp.
3/7/1837	Long, Ephrism	———	Smith, Sarah	E. Buffalo Twp.
12/14/1837	Ludwig, Arthur	———	Kaub, Katherine	White Deer Twp.
5/6/1840	Lasholls, George	———	Aurand, Magdalene	Mifflinburg, Pa.
8/17/1831	Mackay, Martin	———	Seeny, Catherine	White Deer Twp.
12/2/1832	Moser (Musser), Henry	Center Twp.	Wilhand, Hannah	W. Buffalo Twp.
11/6/1834	Moyer, John	Kelly Twp.	Meixell, ———	Kelly Twp.
10/29/1835	McCauley, Alexander	———	Sheckler, Susanna	E. Buffalo Twp.
10/29/1835	Maize, Jacob	———	Wolf, Maria	" " "
12/15/1835	Mensh, Benjamin	———	Rocksy, Sarah	W. Buffalo Twp.
4/28/1836	" Charles	———	McPherson, Elisabeth	Union Twp.
11/24/1836	Miller, Samuel	———	Snyder, Rebecca	Hartley Twp.
1/4/1838	" Joseph	Hartley Twp.	Knouse, Anna	
12/27/1838	" Henry	———	Badey, Esther	Hartley Twp.
5/27/1841	" Andrew	Hartley Twp.	Gerber, Hannah	———
9/22/1842	" George	Buffalo Twp.	Bickel, Sarah	White Deer Twp.
1/11/1844	" Peter	———	Weiss, Elizabeth	Buffalo Twp.
11/30/1845	" Louis	———	Seebold, Sarah	Union Twp.
1/29/1046	" John	———	Diefenderfer, Susan	Kelly Twp.
12/29/1835	Meixell, Jeremiah	Kelly Twp.	Moyer, Harriet	" "
3/5/1840	" George	" "	Reber, Susan	Buffalo Twp.
12/14/1837	Moyer, David	" "	Bucher, Maria	White Deer Twp.
12/8/1846	" Daniel	———	Harrison, Catherine	———
1/9/1838	Mather, Jacob	———	Ruff, Susanna	Penn Twp.,SnyderCo
10/22/1839	Maize, Elias	Mifflinburg, Pa.	Mohn, Maria	Hartley Twp.
2/16/1841	Montelius, Charles	———	Piper, Rebecca	Mifflinburg, Pa.
4/13/1843	Noll (Mull), Henry	———	Steese, Elvina	W. Buffalo Twp.
5/7/1844	Manck, Jacob	New Berlin, Pa.	Van Buskirk, Rachael	Mifflinburg, Pa.
12/24/1844	Mockley, David	White Deer Twp.	Sterner, Maria	E. Buffalo Twp.
10/21/1847	Mensch, Christian	———	Beichler, Maria	Hartley Twp.
12/11/1845	Nagel, William	———	——— Maria	Kelly Twp.
3/15/1838	Navil, George	White Deer Twp.	Bettelyon, Maria	Lebanon County
12/7/1831	Nead, David	———	Spade, Elizabeth	Center County
12/24/1835	Neihard, Jacob	———	Klingman, Margaret	E. Buffalo Twp.
9/1/1835	Newman, Peter	Lewisburg, Pa.	Filman, Hannah	Lewisburg, Pa.
12/25/1834	Oldt, Benjamin	———	——— Catherine	Union Township
5/11/1840	" Simon	Beaver Twp.	Morr, Rebecca	Penn Twp.,SnyderCo
11/9/1848	" David	Union Twp.	Matter, Catherine	Union Twp.
3/27/1834	Peters, Jacob	———	Dreisbach, Elizabeth	———
12/3/1835	Patterson, Samuel	———	Moyer, Rebecca	Kelly Twp.
3/10/1839	Pardoe, John	———	Spitler, Delilah	Lewisburg, Pa.
2/14/1832	Ritter, Peter	E. Buffalo Twp.	Ruff, Angeline	Kelly Twp.
12/3/1835	Rodman, Samuel	" " "	Madden, Maria	Hartleton, Pa.
2/25/1836	Rudy, Martin	———	Hunt, Maria	W. Buffalo Twp.
8/28/1838	Rishel, Benjamin	Lebanon, Pa.	——— Sarah	E. Buffalo Twp.
2/11/1840	Reish, Benjamin	———	Kling, Sarah	West Buffalo Twp.
12/24/1840	Rank, Moses	———	Newman, Catherine	
6/11/1844	Reed, George	———	Fessler, Sarah	E. Buffalo Twp.

| 10/2/1846 | Reish, George | Derr, Maria, Center Twp. Snyder County |
| 12/9/1848 | Rishel, John | Hoffman, Hannah, Columbia County |

2/9/1831	Shower, Samuel, Buffalo Twp.	Ster ———, New Berlin, Pa.
5/15/1832	Shons, Benjamin, E. Buffalo Tp.	Kniss, Elizabeth, E. Buffalo Twp.
5/21/1833	Shively, Christian	———, Sarah, W. Buffalo Twp.
1/16/1834	Snyder, Jacob, Hartley Twp.	Spangler, Elisa, Hartley Twp.
2/4/1834	Shaffer, Christian, W. Buffalo	Hironimus, Margaret, W. Buffalo Twp.
5/29/1834	Stine, Thomas, E. Buffalo Twp.	Kerstetter, Barbara, E. Buffalo Twp.
8/14/1834	Shawver, Henry	Moyer, Sarah, Hartley Twp.
8/13/1835	Stahl, John	Swartslander, Elizabeth, E. Buffalo Twp.
10/27/1835	Shower, John	Oberly, Sarah, Center Twp., Snyder Co.
12/3/1835	Snyder, Michael	Smith, Maria, Hartley Twp.
1/14/1836	Shaver, Karl, Susquehanna Valley	Strubel, Sarah, Buffalo Twp.
2/18/1836	Shans, John	Cornelius, Jane, E. Buffalo Twp.
2/25/1836	Spotzlander, Henry	Stahl, Sarah
4/3/1836	Shadel, Jacob	Shively, Maria, W. Buffalo Twp.
4/19/1836	Shans, Daniel	Kuns, Eliza, E. Buffalo Twp.
6/14/1836	Shawver, Benjamin, Lycoming Co.	Seiffer, Sarah, East Buffalo Twp.
1/26/1837	Seesholtz, Henry	Carl, Rebecca, Hartley Twp.
2/9/1837	Stein, Carl, Northampton County	Zimmerman, Maria, Hartley Twp.
4/4/1837	Shiffer, George, Kelly Twp.	Snyder, Elizabeth, Northumberland County
7/23/1837	Swineford, George	Yearick, Elizabeth, Mifflinburg, Pa.
10/31/1837	Snyder, Daniel, Ohio	Miller, Katherine, Hartley Twp.
1/11/1838	Shaffer, Ephraim, Kelly Twp.	Hummel, Elizabeth, d/o John, of Kelly Twp.
5/9/1838	Shively, John, West Buffalo Twp.	Katherman, Sarah, Hartley Twp.
11/1/1838	Sheet, Henry, Northumberland, Pa.	Hummel, Sarah, Northumberland, Pa.
12/23/1838	Solomon, John, New Berlin, Pa.	———, Anna, East Buffalo Twp.
4/25/1839	Smith Aaron	Sterner, Hetty, !!
12/24/1839	Stitzer, Samuel, Mifflinburg, Pa.	Hoy, Susan, Union Twp.
12/26/1839	Shaffer, Samuel, Lycoming County	Knauff, Catherine, Mifflinburg, Pa.
3/26/1840	Stahl, John, Kelly Twp.	Spotz, Elizabeth
5/7/1840	Stahl, Daniel	Heiges, Eliza, Kelly Twp.
9/8/1840	Shaffer, Carl	Montelius, Emily, Mifflinburg, Pa.
10/18/1840	Swartzlander, Daniel	Oldt, Susanna, Union Twp.
12/3/1840	Schoch, John, Kelly Twp.	Wolf, Sabina, E. Buffalo Twp.
2/28/1841	Seebold, John	Spangler, Elizabeth, Union Twp.
6/3/1841	Slear, Peter	Shively, Susanna, Hartley Twp.
11/25/1841	Snyder, George	Collins, Sophia, Hartley Twp.
3/10/1842	Steese, Samuel, W. Buffalo	Mensh, Nancy, Hartley Twp.
3/21/1842	Smith, John, Hartley Twp.	Rockey, Maria, E. Buffalo Twp.
1/25/1844	Spigelmire, Jacob	Huntington, Elizabeth, Hartely Twp.
2/1/1844	Swartz, Michael, Center County	Mensh, Hetty, Hartley Twp.
2/26/1846	Schoch, Samuel, New Berlin, Pa.	Kleckner, Mrs. Rebecca Ruhl, Hartely Twp.
5/12/1846	Smith, Frederick	Harrison, Mary Ann, New Berlin, Pa.
4/12/1846	Snyder, Josiah, Kelly Twp.	Sheckler, Matilda, Buff
3/25/1847	Shoemaker, Charles	Bogenrief, Sarah, Mifflinburg, Pa.
5/9/1850	Steese, Frederick, W. Buffalo	Oldt, Rachael Jane, Union Twp.

| 11/5/1835 | Thompson, Jesse, Juniata County | Thompson, Clarissa, E. Buffalo Twp. |
| 8/3/1841 | Taylor, B. C. Berks County | Reber, Matilda, E. Buffalo Twp. |

6/21/1838	Ultz, John	Klingman, Elizabeth, E. Buffalo Twp.
4/12/1842	Ulrich, J. C.	Moyer, Elizabeth, Union Twp.
3/7/1844	Ulrich, Joseph, Millheim, Pa.	Hoffman, Matilda, Hartley Twp.

| 7/30/1839 | Vandling, F. | Navil, Juliana, W. Buffalo Twp. |

Date	Groom	Bride
10/30/1832	Wales, James, Center County	Shonts, Susanna, Mifflinburg, Pa.
1/31/1833	Wolf, Michael, E. Buffalo Twp.	Engelhart, Margaret, White Deer Twp.
2/7/1833	Wagner, George, New Berlin, Pa.	Kerstetter, Susanna, Union Twp.
12/26/1833	Winters, John	Spitler, Juliana, New Berlin, Pa.
5/1/1834	Weigert, Joseph	Hackey, Nancy, Hartley Twp.
2/9/1836	Walborn, John, Mifflinburg, Pa.	Kniss, Susanna, W. Buffalo Twp.
1/19/1837	Winkleblech, Wm., Hartley Twp.	Smith, Sarah, Hartley Twp.
5/21/1840	Walter, Henry, Kelly Twp.	Gemberling, Rebecca, Penn Twp., Snyder Co.
12/26/1841	Weiser, G. W., Mifflinburg, Pa.	Kohler, Susanna, W. Buffalo Twp.
4/22/1845	Walter, Charles	Harrison, Martha, New Berlin, Pa.
9/2/1841	Yoder, Carl	Linn, Maria, E. Buffalo Twp.
3/10/1846	" Daniel	Druckenmiller, Sarah
12/19/1833	Young, John, E. Buffalo Twp.	Heimbach, Sarah, E. Buffalo Twp.
10/13/1839	" John	Yerger, Maria, Center Twp., Snyder County
2/13/1844 Or 2/3/1844	Adam Young	Swartzlander, Elsie, Buffalo Twp.
2/3/1835	Zellers, George	Kauffman, Margaret, W. Buffalo Twp.
2/13/1845	" Henry, W. Buffalo Twp.	Oberdorf, Maria, Mifflinburg, Pa.
4/19/1836	Zorbe, Thomas, West Buffalo Twp.	Heinly, Esther, Buffalo Twp.

PARTIAL DATA ONLY

Date	Groom	Bride
9/6/1832	Adam ———	Elizabeth Stahl, Kelly Twp.
11/11/1832	——— ———	Maria Zimmerman, East Buffalo Twp.
4/30/1833	Daniel ———, Dry Valley	Hetty Smith, E. Buffalo Twp.
1/5/1837	Jacob ———, Lewisburg, Pa.	Sarah Young, East Buffalo Twp.
11/16/1837	William ———	Elizabeth Criswell, Kelly Twp.
10/26/1837	David ———	Magdalene Getz, E. Buffalo Twp.
12/26/1837	John ———	Barbara Seebold, Union Twp.
12/25/1838	David ———, Center County	Sarah Huntington, Hartley Twp.
8/8/1839	Robert ———	Lavina Randenbush, W. Buffalo Twp.

PART IV

MARRIAGES OF REV. J. P. SHINDEL, JR., 1835-1887 Snyder and Union Counties, Pa.

Date	Groom	Place	Bride
9/9/1855	Abel, Frederick	Kratzerville, Pa.	Agnes Kreider, Kratzerville,Pa.
11/28/1843	Adams, Joseph	Penn Twp.	Elizabeth Smith, Penn Twp.
9/13/1840	Aigler, Joel	Middleburg, Pa.	Eliza Smith, Middlebrug, Pa.
12/3/1839	" Amos	Beaver Twp.	Amena Bobb, Beaver. Tp.
10/12/1845	" Reubern	" "	Mary Eisenhauer, Beaver Tp.
12/18/1845	" Noah	" "	Susan Grimm
10/30/1842	Alexander, John	Hartley Tp.	Mary Dorman, Hartley Tp.
11/10/1840	Alter, Isaac	W. Beaver Tp.	Henrietta Dubbs, W. Beaver Tp.
8/15/1841	" Daniel	Beaver Tp.	Salome Mattern, Beaver Tp.
12/3/1871	Amspacher, Amos	York Co.	Malinda Haines, Snyder Co.
4/20/1873	Arbogast, Albert	Selinsgrove, Pa.	Anna Schroyer, Selinsgrove, Pa.
10/5/1851	Arnold, Jacob	Center Tp.	Elizabeth Mitterling, Center Tp.
2/9/1858	" Samuel J.	Mussers Valley	Elizabeth Blouch, Mussers Valley
9/3/1861	" John H.	Middleburg, Pa.	Barbara Motz, Middleburg, Pa.
2/22/1842	Aumiller, George	New Berlin, Pa.	Sarah Hartman, Center Tp.
3/29/1840	Aurand, Enoch	Beaver Tp.	Amena Felker, Beaver Tp.
11/18/1847	" Isaac	" "	Caroline Robinson, Beaver Tp.
8/14/1851	" Samuel P.	New Berlin, Pa.	Mary Ann Heimbach, New Berlin, Pa.
10/17/1861	" Henry	Beaver Tp.	Leah Hassinger, Beaver Tp.
6/20/1867	" James	Mussers Valley	Sarah Kline, Mussers Valley
5/27/1849	Ayers, James	Beavertown, Pa.	Lydia Mitchell, Beavertown, Pa.
7/5/1840	Bachman, Israel	Selinsgrove, Pa.	Harriet Houseworth, Selinsgrove,Pa.
12/5/1848	Badger, Robert	Hartley Tp.	Elizabeth Derr, Center Tp.
5/12/1887	Baker, John R.	W. Beaver Tp.	Sophia Wagner, W. Beaver Tp.
1/2/1842	" Daniel	"	Susan Ritter "
9/17/1843	" Frederick	"	Sarah Smith "
1/21/1845	" Tobias	"	Elizabeth Manbeck "
4/1/1849	Bartley, John	Laurelton, Pa.	Sophia Brouse, Laurelton, Pa.
9/12/1844	Bastian, Jonathan	Sunbury, Pa.	Mary Bachman, Middleburg, Pa.
11/11/1855	Baum, William B.	Mussers Valley	Sarah Jane Troxel, Mussers Valley
9/27/1852	Bause, Michael	Indiana	Malinda Swengle, Center Tp.
9/14/1843	Baush, Henry E.	New Berlin, Pa.	Maria Fry, New Berlin, Pa.
11/26/1844	" David		Lucetta Musser (Widow), Beaver,Pa.
5/13/1849	Beachel, Reuben	Center Tp.	Amelia Erb, Center Tp.
4/19/1855	" John	Franklin Tp.	Sarah Ritter, Jackson Tp.
8/30/1883	" Job	"	Mary Alice Moyer
1/5/1847	Bear, Michael	W. Beaver Tp.	Elizabeth Spigelmire, W.BeaverTp.
12/13/1840	Beaver, John	Jackson Tp.	Susan Derk, Jackson Tp.
12/22/1842	" Elias	"	Sarah Bower, Union Tp.
7/23/1843	" Michael	Beaver Tp.	Amelia Dreese, Beaver Tp.
12/3/1843	" William	"	Savilla Smith "
12/9/1845	" Nathan	Kratzerville, Pa.	Elizabeth Walter, Kratzerville,Pa.
2/19/1846	" John	Beaver Tp.	Amanda Bear, Beaver Tp.
11/4/1852	" John S.	Union Tp.	Mary Ann Bolig, Union Tp.
11/8/1855	" Isaac	Middlecreek, Tp.	Maria Hummel, Middlecreek Tp.
6/11/1857	" Edward	Beavertown, Pa.	Mary Weirick, Beavertown, Pa.
6/18/1857	" Simon	Jackson Tp.	Barbara Herman, Jackson Tp.
8/14/1862	" Jacob	"	Polly Pontius "
6/12/1856	Benfer, Reuben	Kratzerville, Pa.	Esther Herman, Kratzerville, Pa.
10/29/1857	" Isaac	"	Susan Herman "
10/16/1838	" Lewis	"	Christina Beaver
8/9/1840	" Paul	Beaver Tp.	Leah Bingaman, Beaver Tp.
10/24/1843	" Edward	"	Susan Klose "
1/18/1844	" Levi	Union Tp.	Elizabeth Confer, Union Tp.
10/15/1845	" Samuel	New Berlin, Pa.	Harriet Bowersox, Middleburg, Pa.
7/29/1847	" Andrew	Union Tp.	Catherine Krouse, Middlecreed, Tp.
6/17/1858	" David	W. Beaver Tp.	Matilda Dreese, Beaver Springs, Pa.
10/21/1858	" Simon	Mussers Valley	Mary Aurand, Mussers Valley
9/8/1863	" William (widower)	Franklin Tp.	Mrs. Susan Bowersox Hackenberg

Date	Name		Township	Spouse
11/2/1865	Benfer, G. W.		W. Beaver Tp.	Elvina Middlesworth, W. Beaver Tp.
5/21/1871	"	Amos	Mussers Valley	Amanda Kline, Mussers Valley
12/6/1874	"	William	Center Tp.	Jane E. Long, Center Tp.
10/9/1836	Berger, Daniel			Rachael Freed
12/5/1841	"	Amos	Beaver Tp.	Matilda Herbster, Beaver Tp.
9/3/1843	"	Stephen	Center Tp.	Julia Ann Woelfley, Center Tp.
8/13/1844	"	Joseph	Beaver Tp.	Eva Horlacher, Beaver Tp.
10/29/1848	"	Simon	Middlecreek, Tp.	Rosanna Courtney
5/8/1838	Bergstresser, Daniel		Selinsgrove, Pa.	Rebecca Baker, Selinsgrove, Pa.
11/18/1841	Bertch, John		Perry Co.	Phrena Basom, Perry Co.
12/26/1861	"	Isaac	Freeburg, Pa.	Carrie Kouts, Center Tp.
3/17/1867	Bickhart, Henry		Washington Tp.	Sarah Roush, Washington Tp.
5/2/1878	"	Robert	Franklin Tp.	Sadie Earnest, Franklin Tp.
11/26/1840	Bickle, Jacob		Washington Tp.	Louisa Ortz, Washington Tp.
10/22/1863	"	"	Beaver Tp.	Amanda Helfrich, Beaver, Tp.
8/30/1866	"	Aaron	"	Maranda Mattorn, W. Beaver Tp.
4/20/1848	Bickley (Beckley), Dan.		Penn Tp.	Elizabeth Boop, Mifflinburg, Pa.
2/16/1840	Bigler, Frederick		Union Tp.	Amelia Pennichoff, Union Tp.
2/9/1841	Bingaman, Frederick		Beaver Tp.	Mrs. Mary Swineford,Middleburg, Pa.
1/1/1843	"	John F.	"	Hannah Mengle, Beaver Tp.
6/8/1848	"	Noah	"	Mary Dreese "
8/31/1848	"	William	"	Elizabeth Huffnagle, Beaver Tp.
9/4/1849	"	Jackson	"	Susan Hook (Hooch?), "
11/3/1850	"	Reuben	Jersey Shore, Pa.	Lovina Muthart, Jersey Shore, Pa.
2/9/1851	"	Jacob (Wdr.)	Center Tp.	Mary Ann Koister, Center Tp.
12/23/1852	"	Jacob	Mussers Valley	Catherine Fotterold,MussersValley
6/1/1854	"	John	Beavertown, Pa.	Rebecca Benfer, Beavertown, Pa.
8/9/1855	"	Frederick	Hartley Tp.	Elizabeth Heeter, Mussers Valley
5/23/1856	"	Daniel	Center Tp.	Clarissa Snook, Center Tp.
5/26/1861	"	" (Wdr.)	Franklin Tp.	Susan Kaley, (widow)
8/6/1865	"	Josiah	Mussers Valley	Elora Middlesworth,MussersValley
3/25/1866	"	Samuel	Franklin Tp.	Susan Bobb, Franklin Tp.
10/17/1867	"	Robert J.	Mussers Valley	Lovina Hendricks, Mussers Valley
12/18/1870	"	James H.	Beaver Tp.	Amelia Howell, Beaver Tp.
2/26/1871	"	Christian A.	Franklin Tp.	Mary M. Bobb, Franklin Tp.
4/21/1887	"	Charles W. T.		Amelia Ray
12/21/1852	Blett, Daniel		Milroy, Pa.	Catherine Reigle, Center Tp.
12/18/1845	Bobb, Jacob		Beaver Tp.	Rachael Shilling, West Beaver Tp.
5/20/1847	"	Reuben	"	Lucinda Engle, Beaver Tp.
8/10/1848	"	Jacob	Center Tp.	Elizabeth Klose, Center Tp.
5/17/1849	"	Reuben	Selinsgrove, Pa.	Mary C. Ulrich, Selinsgrove, Pa.
8/23/1849	"	Samuel	Chapman Tp.	Sarah Klose, Center Tp.
4/11/1861	"	Franklin	Middlecreek Tp.	Harriet Dunkleborger,MiddlecreekTp.
4/14/1864	Bogenrief, William		Union Co.	Elizabeth J. Moyer, Mussers Valley
8/9/1840	Bolig, Jacob		Middlecreek Tp.	Christina Brill, Middlecreek Tp.
10/20/1853	"	William	"	Elizabeth Dean "
8/26/1860	"	Frederick B.	"	Anna Maria Ranch "
12/25/1866	"	Samuel	"	Polly Zieber "
2/22/1855	Bollender, Daniel		Franklin Tp.	Sabina Shuman, Franklin Tp.
6/10/1866	Bollinger, William		Middlecreek Tp.	Lydia Erdley, Penn Tp.
12/24/1846	Boney, Isaac		Center Tp.	Sarah Beachel, Center Tp.
11/20/1849	"	Levi	"	Lydia " "
9/12/1843	Bower, Frederick		Middleburg, Pa.	Malinda J. Smith, Middleburg, Pa.
12/17/1840	Bowersox, Reuben		Center Tp.	Sarah Raish, Center Tp.
8/24/1845	"	David	"	Lucy Ann Yerger, "
10/8/1846	"	John	Center Co.	Mary Frederick, Hartley Tp.
12/29/1846	"	John	Mifflin Co.	Elizabeth Goss, Mifflin Co.
1/22/1850	"	Isaac	Center Co.	Mary Frederick, Hartley Tp.
1/13/1856	"	Franklin	Franklin Tp.	Maria Ocker, Center Tp.
6/9/1859	"	Washington	"	Susan Hackenberg, Franklin Tp.

10/27/1867	Bowersox, George	Center Tp.	Ada Herman, Center Tp.
2/10/1867	Bowersox, George A	Franklin Tp.	Margaret Renniger, Franklin Tp.
6/3/1860	Bowersox, Andrew	Center Tp.	Harriet Yeisley, Franklin Tp.
12/6/1860	" Samuel P.	Middleburg, Pa.	Elizabeth Swinefore, Middleburg,Pa.
11/16/1862	" William	Franklin Tp.	Margaret Beachel, Franklin Tp.
5/1/1864	" Jacob	Center Tp.	Esther Napp, Center Tp.
10/20/1864	" Jackson	Mifflin Co..	Rebecca Gibbony, Mifflin Co.
6/30/1867	" Harry	Center Tp.	Rachael Walter, Center Tp.
1/19/1868	" Solomon	Franklin Tp.	Lydia Kerr, Franklin Tp.
11/10/1872	" Cyrus	Center Tp.	Juliana Bingaman, Center Tp.
6/28/1874	" Gabriel	W. Buffalo Tp.	Ida M. Hertz, W. Buffalo Tp.
10/17/1854	Bowes, Dr. George	Middleburg, Pa.	Amelia Smith, Selinsgrove, Pa.
1/30/1840	Boyer, Isaac	Freeburg, Pa.	Caroline Boyer, Freeburg, Pa.
3/31/1844	" John (Mr)		Mrs. Sarah Musselman (Widow)
8/26/1845	" Jacob	Center Tp.	Elizabeth Yeisley, Center Tp.
11/25/1852	" Isaac	W. Buffalo Tp.	" Musser, Center Tp.
4/3/1855	" John	Mussers Valley	Hannah Gerhart, Mussers Valley
12/27/1881	" Allen	Snyder Co.	Clara Bolig, Snyder Co.
9/5/1847	Brack Adam	Mifflin Co.	Maria Steffen, Mifflin Co.
5/30/1848	Braucher, Jacob	Hartley Tp.	Mrs. Sophia Smith, Hartley Tp.
1/1/1856	" John		Cecelia Kauffman
8/9/1840	Breon, David	Middlecreek Tp.	MaryDinius(d/oJacob),MiddlecreekTp.
7/12/1839	Breininger, John	W. Beaver Tp.	Julia Ann Smith, W. Beaver Tp.
9/5/1848	" Samuel	Mussers Valley	Sarah Zartman, New Berlin Pa.
10/31/1858	" Ephraim	Franklin Tp.	" Heimbach, Franklin Tp.
5/12/1844	Brouse, Andrew	Kratzerville, Pa.	Elizabeth Derk, Kratzerville, Pa.
3/30/1848	" Samuel		Hannah Weaver "
10/26/1865	Brower, John L.	Mifflin Co.	Mollie Shirey, Snyder Co.
5/22/1838	Brown, Samuel T.	Sunbury, Pa.	Elizabeth Young, Sunbury, Pa.
8/28/1864	Brua, Jacob	BeaverSprings;Pa.	Elizabeth Shirey, BeaverSprings,Pa.
7/31/1859	Brubaker, Dr. D. M.	Middleburg, Pa.	Eveline Bibighaus, Middleburg, Pa.
8/23/1885	Bruff, Charles		Ellen Spangler
10/25/1841	Brunner, Peter	Mussers Valley	Sarah Musser, Mussers Valley
8/31/1847	" Moses	Center Tp.	Catherine Gilbert, Center Tp.
11/16/1856	" Joseph	Mussers Valley	Lovina Bingaman, Mussers Valley
8/27/1857	" Abner	BeaverSprings,Pa.	Emeline Kinney, Beaver Springs, Pa.
12/31/1857	" Moses	Franklin Tp.	Eliza Etsler, Franklin Tp.
11/16/1873	Bubb, W. C.	Snyder Co.	Elizabeth Ingram, Mifflin Co.
4/29/1849	Buffington, James	Middleburg, Pa.	Mary Damberman, Middlecreek Tp.
1/6/1852	" "	"	Eliza Zechman, Middleburg, Pa.
4/6/1856	" Edward	"	Amelia Weller, "
2/5/1871	Burgess, Samuel	Beavertown, Pa.	Sarah Jane Felmly, Beavertown, Pa.
3/19/1850	Burry, Simon	Limestone Tp.	Catherine Crossgrove, LimestoneTp.
6/4/1851	Camp, John L.	Beavertown, Pa.	Margaret Weirick, Beavertown, Pa.
7/29/1866	Carpenter, A. M.	Beavertown, Pa.	Sarah E. Feese, Beavertown, Pa.
4/12/1874	Castor, James H.	Paxtonville, Pa.	Catherine V. Fike, Paxtonville,Pa.
2/1/1844	Catherman, Timothy	Hartley Tp.	Susan Brouse, Hartley Tp.
10/2/1844	" Tobias	Mussers Valley	Margaret Fuhrman, Mussers Valley
12/17/1846	" John	Hartley Tp.	Susan Williams, Hartley Tp.
9/17/1857	" William	Union Co.	Barbara Oldt, Union Co.
8/21/1859	" A. J.	Lewis Tp.	Mary Ann Yeisley, Lewis Tp.
8/29/1869	" Joseph	Laurelton, Pa.	Christiana Bearick, Laurelton,Pa.
4/8/1877	" Oliver J.	Union Co.	Sarah E. Catherman, Union Co.
3/7/1880	" Perry	"	Mary Whatmore, Snyder Co.
12/24/1842	Caveny, Reuben	McAllisterville,Pa	Mary Crozier, McAllisterville, Pa.
5/28/1850	Cawley, John	Hartley Tp.	Mary Ruhl, Hartley Tp.
3/6/1846	Charles, Samuel	Laurelton, Pa.	Maria Smith, Laurelton, Pa.
10/25/1849	Childs, Charles W.	Danville, Pa.	Mary Super, Kratzerville, Pa.
11/29/1883	Clellan, Joseph		Mary E. Spade
10/28/1845	Comfort, Nathaniel	Lewistown, Pa.	Sarah C. Kulp, Lewistown, Pa.

Date	Name	Place	Spouse
10/17/1837	Conrad, Henry	Northumberland Co.	Elinor Lytle, Northumberland Co.
4/10/1856	Courtney, John F.	Middlecreek Tp.	Elizabeth Gift, Franklin Tp.
4/10/1870	Cramer, John	Franklin Tp.	Amanda Shaffer, Franklin Tp.
4/16/1836	Cressinger, Bernard	Augusta Tp.	Elizabeth Wilhelm, Augusta Tp.
6/22/1873	Cromley, P. F.	Union Co.	Maria Rummel, Snyder Co.
1/1/1867	Crossgrove, Aaron	''	Sally Steel, Union CO.
3/4/1855	Culbertson, John	Mifflin Co.	Polly Yetter, Mifflin Co.
12/21/1845	Daniels, Jacob		Elizabeth Breon, Middlecreek, Tp.
12/24/1837	Dawson, Thomas	Augusta Tp.	Susan Dreher, Augusta Tp.
3/18/1886	Daubert, David F.	W. Beaver Tp.	Sarah Weiand, W. Beaver Tp.
8/17/1854	Dauberman, Jacob	Middlecreek Tp.	Esther Yerger, Middlecreek Tp.
1/29/1857	'' Sam E.	Buffalo Tp.	Rebecca Heimbach, Buffalo Tp.
10/1/1883	'' Theodore	New Berlin, Pa.	'' Spade, Snyder Co.
9/19/1843	Dauberman, John	Middlecreek Tp.	Sarah Sauers, Middlecreek Tp.
10/5/1843	'' Lewis	Selinsgrove, Pa.	Eliza McKee, Selinsgrove, Pa.
5/22/1849	'' Mathias	Middlecreek Tp.	Hannah Erdly, Middlecreek Tp.
8/30/1868	Dean, Isaac H.	Mifflin Co.	Amelia Snook, Mifflin Co.
6/20/1873	'' William W.	Philadelphia, Pa.	Mary Bower, Franklin Tp.
4/7/1875	'' Harrison	Mussers Valley	Mary Werhood, Mussers Valley
12/6/1841	Decker, George		Susan Eberhart
10/12/1854	'' Reuben	Center Tp.	Amelia Reitz, Center Tp.
11/21/1856	'' Peter (wdr.)	Franklin Tp.	Catherine Felty (wid.), FranklinTp.
8/10/1858	'' Levi	''	Barbara Sanders ''
2/15/1866	'' Jesse	Mussers Valley	Julia Kline, Mussers Valley
10/7/1851	Derk, John	Kratzerville, Pa.	Mary Kline, Kratzerville, Pa.
12/19/1843	Derr, Daniel	Center Tp.	Lucy Ann Meister, Center Tp.
4/30/1868	'' Calvin L.	Franklin Tp.	Lydia Moyer, Franklin Tp.
4/11/1858	Diebler, Nathaniel	''	Angeline Hoffman, ''
2/20/1872	'' Zachariah	Snyder Co.	Lizzie Catherman, Union Co.
2/22/1872	'' Daniel	Center Tp.	Matilda Bishop, Center Tp.
3/6/1851	Diemer, John D.	W. Beaver Tp.	Mary Oldt, W. Beaver Tp.
6/18/1857	'' John	E. Buffalo Tp.	Amelia Smith, E. Buffalo Tp.
12/16/1858	'' Isaac	Middlecreek Tp.	Catherine Sholley, Chapman Tp.
8/12/1877	Dill, Samuel O.	Lewistown, Pa.	Anna Berger, Snyder Co.
11/20/1856	Dillman, Philip L.	Franklin Tp.	Barbara Gift, Franklin Tp.
1/30/1844	Dinius, John	Middlecreek Tp.	Esther Breon, Middlecreek Tp.
11/19/1868	Dobson, Alfred	Franklin Tp.	Sarah Eisenhauer, Franklin Tp.
10/31/1841	Doebler, Jacob	Center Tp.	Amelia Bowersox, Center
4/7/1844	Dorman, Lewis	Hartley Tp.	Catherine Dinius, Hartley Tp.
9/3/1848	Dorn, John	Beavertown, Pa.	Sarah Kline, Beavertown, Pa.
7/15/1843	Dreese, Isaac	Beaver Tp.	Mary Ann Beaver, Beaver Tp.
11/20/1838	'' John	''	Hannah Wagner ''
12/10/1857	'' Philip	''	Mary Kiddlesworth, ''
1/31/1851	'' Joseph	Beavertown, Pa.	Amelia Freed, Beavertown, Pa.
7/28/1854	'' John	Center Tp.	Sarah Bowersox, Middlecreek Tp
10/5/1873	'' Peter	Snyder Co.	Amanda Hanes, Union Co.
12/19/1843	Dobbs, Henry	Lewistown, Pa.	Elizabeth Rauch, Beaver Tp.
10/16/1830	'' Emerson S.		Sadie Reigle, Snyder Co.
3/7/1844	Duck, Emanuel		Polly Schluttcry
8/17/1851	Dufford, Samuel	Center Co.	Matilda Steininger, Laurelton, Pa.
7/24/1845	Dunkelberger, Benj.	Washington Tp.	Catherine Straub, Washington Tp.
8/18/1853	'' William	Middlecreek Tp.	Elizabeth Hare, Middlecreek Tp.
3/17/1839	Durst, William	Sunbury, Pa.	Rebecca Guss, Sunbury, Pa.
12/25/1851	Earnest, John	Beaver Tp.	Rachael Reigle, Beaver Tp.
1/26/1841	Eberhart, Daniel	Mifflin Co.	Christina Robinson, Washington Tp.
8/25/1842	'' Frederick	Selinsgrove, Pa.	Mary Brewer, Selinsgrove, Pa.
2/25/1852	Eby, John	Union Co.	Caroline Treaster, Mifflin Co.
1/6/1848	Ehrhart, Daniel	Middlecreek Tp.	Rebecca Stock, Middlecreek Tp.
6/23/1840	Eichman, Michael		Appolonia Menges

MARRIAGES OF REV. J. P. SHINDEL, JR., 1835-1877, Snyder and Union Counties, Pa.

Date	Name	Place	Spouse
1/31/1841	Eisenhamer, Abe. (wdr.)	Center Tp.	Catherine Royer (wd.), Center
12/25/1842	" Jacob	New Berlin, Pa.	Susan Rushong, New Berlin, Pa.
11/12/1857	" Jacob	Franklin Tp.	Mrs. Catherine Rearick,FranklinTp.
12/27/1859	Emerson, J. M.	Independence,Ohio	Catherine Ewig, Solinsgrove, Pa.
7/6/1865	Emmons, Franklin	Beavertown, Pa.	Elizabeth Erb, Beavertown, Pa.
10/30/1848	Emerick, John	Center Co.	Mary Huggins, Middleburg, Pa.
12/26/1843	Engle, Lewis	Middlecreek Tp.	Rebecca Oldt, Beaver Tp.
3/13/1845	" Amos	Penn Tp.	Rachael Hassinger, Center Tp.
10/31/1851	" Joseph	Kratzerville, Pa.	Anna Lepley, Kratzorville, Pa.
6/17/1852	" William C.	Beaver Tp.	Margaret Kloso, Beaver Tp.
6/25/1854	Erb, Jacob	W. Beaver Tp.	Elizabeth Hartley, W. Beaver Tp.
10/5/1873	" Robert E.	Franklin Tp.	Catherine Reich, Franklin Tp.
7/18/1875	" Franklin W.	Paxtonville, Pa.	Sallie Frantz, Paxtonville, Pa.
3/28/1878	" Samuel	"	Mary E. Earnest, "
10/26/1845	Erdly, Levi	Kratzerville, Pa.	Elizabeth Mathias, KratzervillePa
9/15/1872	" Elias J.	Snyder Co.	Susan Boyer, Snyder Co.
8/9/1855	Ettinger, William	Mussers Valley	Mary Fetterolf, Mussers Valley
9/3/1865	" Paul	Beaver Tp.	Matilda Kiester, Hartley Tp.
2/28/1841	Etzler, Benj. (wdr.)	"	Catherine Heckley, Beaver Tp.
8/3/1848	" Franklin	Center Tp.	Sarah Pontius, Center Tp.
8/13/1844	Evans, Samuel O.	Juniata Co.	Amelia Kramer, Middleburg, Pa.
2/27/1839	Ewig, Levi	"	Esther Hummel, Beavertown, Pa.
2/20/1868	" George	Beaver Tp.	Susan Erb, Beaver Tp.
1/3/1867	Ewing, William H.	Perry Co.	Elmira Middlesworth,MussersValley
6/17/1856	Eyster, Isaiah	Middlecreek Tp.	Catherine Ann Weider, MiddlecreekTp.
1/29/1852	Fassick, George	Richfield, Pa.	Hanna Shellenberger, Richfield,Pa.
8/22/1871	Feese, Robert	Beavertown, Pa.	Susan Frood, Beavertown, Pa.
5/2/1869	" Jacob H.	"	Mary Ann Conrad, Beaver Tp.
1/30/1868	" Henry	Ohio	Sabilla Aigler, Franklin Tp.
2/22/1846	" Zeno	Beavertown, Pa.	Lovina Gift, Beaver Tp.
8/23/1840	Felker, Joseph	Beaver Tp.	Louisa Feese, Beaver Tp.
10/2/1855	" John	West Beaver Tp.	Delilah Middlesworth, W. Beaver Tp.
7/1/1849	Fertig, John	Kratzerville, Pa.	Eve Horman Kratzerville, Pa.
7/27/1384	Fossler, Franklin	Center Tp.	Lovina Benfor, Center Tp.
9/6/1840	Fetter, Jacob	Kratzerville, Pa.	Mollie Herman, Kratzerville, Pa.
12/26/1844	" Jeremiah	Penn Tp.	Elizabeth Kreider, Penn Tp.
3/4/1843	" Conrad	Middlecreek Tp.	Catherine Dunkelberger,MiddlecreekTp
6/27/1843	Fetterolf, Frederick	Beaver Tp.	Elizabeth Kerstetter, Beaver Tp.
9/5/1850	" Elias	Hartley Tp.	Rachael Weiand, Hartley Tp.
6/14/1855	" Philip	Mussers Valley	Fayette Weaver, Mussers Valley
6/29/1856	" Nathaniel	"	Harriet Moyer "
9/9/1858	" Robert	"	Mary C. Ettinger "
1/7/1877	" John E.	Snyder Co.	Sarah Jane Berge, Snyder Co.
8/20/1843	Fidler, Reuben	Middleburg, Pa.	Caroline Swineford, Middleburg, Pa.
4/30/1843	Fike, Israel	Beaver Tp.	Anna Mitchell, Beaver ...
7/3/1847	" John	"	Leah Dreese "
1/26/1875	Fink, John M. (wdr.)	Ohio	Amelia Lopley (wd.), N. Berlin, Pa.
11/12/1843	Fisher, Levi	Penn Tp.	Elizabeth Aigler, Beaver Tp.
1/23/1849	" Isaac	Selinsgrove, Pa.	Lovina Kantner, Selinsgrove, Pa.
8/11/1344	Fogle, John	Beaver Tp.	Catherine Beidler, Beaver Tp.
12/16/1843	" Martin	"	Mary Swartslander, "
11/5/1843	Fogleman, Daniel	West Beaver Tp.	Maria Kerstetter, West Beaver Tp.
2/25/1351	Folk, Aaron	"	Sophia Speigelmire, "
6/18/1835	Follmer, Simon	Milton, Pa.	Margaret Zohler, Milton, Pa.
9/27/1860	Frood, Henry	Beavertown, Pa.	Sabina Feese, Beavertown, Pa.
5/11/1848	Freuse, Daniel	West Beaver Tp.	Elizabeth Baker, West Beaver Tp.
2/19/1850	" Abraham	"	Susan Moyer "
2/25/1837	Frey, John	Augusta Tp.	Mary Cressinger, Augusta Tp.
8/21/1852	Frock, Michael	Limestone Tp.	Mary Rearick, Center Tp.

Date	Name	Residence	Spouse
9/20/1849	Fry, Jonas	Center Co.	Catherine Smith, Lauralton, Pa.
8/13/1858	Fuller, William	Beavertown, Pa.	Anna Lepley, BeaverSprings,Pa.
6/6/1843	Garman, George	Washington Tp.	Leah Fisher (d/o Jacob), Penn Tp.
5/1/1838	Geiger, Jacob	Pottsgrove, Pa.	Rachael Quinn, Sunbury, Pa.
3/14/1847	Geise, Henry	Kratzerville, Pa.	Susan Brouse, Kratzerville, Pa.
3/6/1864	" "	Union Co	Eliza J. Moyer, Kratzerville, Pa.
11/22/1865	Geiswite, William H.	Center Co.	Abigail Snyder, Union Co.
3/28/1847	Gerhart, George	Mussers Valley	Polly Brunner, Mussers Valley
3/18/1858	" Frederick	" "	Esther Herman " "
1/14/1862	" George	Beaver Tp.	Elizabeth Kramer, Beaver Tp.
12/28/1866	" William	"	Rebecca " "
9/25/1887	" " H.	Mussers Valley	Elvesta Hackenberg
1/7/1845	Getz, David	Beaver Tp.	Mary Ann Lepley
6/2/1853	" Henry	Mussers Valley	Caroline Berger, Mussers Valley
12/22/1868	Gibbons, James H.	Northumberland Co.	" Garman, Freeburg, Pa.
7/2/1837	Gibson, Daniel	Sunbury, Pa.	Harriet Weaver, Sunbury, Pa.
1/12/1845	Gift, Levi	Center Tp.	Matilda Feese, Center Tp.
6/6/1868	" Austin J.	Franklin Tp.	Savilla Thomas, Franklin Tp.
12/27/1849	Gilbert, Jacob		Judith Rauch, Middleburg, Pa.
1/3/1858	" John	Franklin Tp.	Susan Gill, Franklin Tp.
1/1/1871	" John S.		Jane Stahlnecker, Franklin Tp.
1/3/1859	Gilham, Benj. F.	Beaver Tp.	Emeline Gift, Beaver Tp.
6/22/1847	Gill, Benjamin	W. Beaver Tp.	Elizabeth Spigelmire, W. Beaver Tp.
8/25/1853	" Edward	"	Sophia Ritter "
11/27/1864	" John G.	Franklin Tp.	Sarah Platt, Franklin Tp.
11/16/1865	" Levi	Mussers Valley	Catherine Shrader, Mussers Valley
12/26/1841	Gingrich, John		Eliza Eisenhauer, Middleburg, Pa.
11/21/1844	"	Washington Tp.	Elizabeth Graybill, Perry Tp.
10/20/1864	Glase, Henry B.	Chapman Tp.	Fianna Specht, Middlecreek Tp.
8/21/1866	Glass, Francis	Freeburg, Pa.	Elizabeth Bittinger, Freeburg, Pa.
10/1/1872	" Charles H.	Snyder Co.	Elnora Wolf, Snyder Co.
4/26/1841	Glueck, Jacob	W. Beaver Tp.	Mary Ann Weidner, W. Beaver Tp.
4/13/1836	Gobin, Samuel	Sunbury, Pa.	Susan Shindel, Sunbury, Pa.
7/30/1840	Good, Adam	Union Tp.	Mary Slear, Union Tp.
1/4/1842	Goss, Henry		Rebecca Goss, W. Beaver Tp.
9/8/1844	" Simon	W. Beaver Tp.	Hannah Kemberling, W. Beaver Tp.
2/22/1846	" Peter	"	Catherine Gross "
5/18/1846	" Reuben	"	Leah Smith "
1/24/1850	" Joseph	"	Elizabeth Gerhart "
3/9/1865	" David	"	Rebecca Knepp "
3/--/1835	Gottshall, Henry		Sarah Yeager, Augusta Tp.
3/24/1842	Goy, David	Perry Tp.	Mary Ann Swineford, Center Tp.
9/11/1845	Greenhoe, Samuel	Beaver Tp.	Amelia Engle, Beaver Tp.
5/20/1845	Grimm, Reuben (wdr.)	"	Elizabeth Klose (wd.), Beaver Tp.
11/30/1865	" Henry M.	Freeburg, Pa.	Elizabeth Roush, Freeburg, Pa.
11/6/1870	" Jacob		Lucy Ann Bowersox, Snyder Co.
8/9/1853	Gross, John, Jr.	Beaver Tp.	Catherine Kitterling, Beaver Tp.
10/30/1856	" Isaac	"	" L. Smith
2/13/1845	Grubb, Henry	Kratzerville, Pa.	Nancy Klingler, Kratzerville, Pa.
11/25/1863	" "	Beaver Tp.	Amanda Smith, Beaver Tp.
10/15/1837	Guss, Joseph		Harriet Eileman
4/23/1859	Hackenberg, John	Mussers Valley	Susan Stock, Mussers Valley
1/1/1857	" Amos	Beaver Tp.	Sarah Mitchell, Beaver Tp.
5/13/1864	" Hiram	Mussers Valley	Malinda Kline, Mussers Valley
9/15/1866	" Jesse	Center Tp.	Sarah Ann Motter, Center Tp.
12/13/1865	" Daniel	"	Susan Thomas "
2/24/1857	" Michael	Franklin Tp.	Mary Jane Walter, Franklin Tp.
9/12/1869	" Daniel	Center Tp.	Margaret Leader, Center Tp.
12/12/1869	" Isaac		Mary A. Swartz, Mussers Valley
5/16/1850	" Joseph E.		Eve Herman

MARRIAGES OF REV. J. P. SHINDEL, Jr., 1835-1887, Snyder and Union Counties, Pa.

5/25/1882	Hackenberg, A. K.		Mary Ann Duck
11/19/1882	" Emanuel	Center Tp.	Sarah J. Smith, Center Tp.
12/2/1883	" Hiram W.		Alice Stroub
6/9/1844	Hain, Casper	Kratzerville, Pa.	Sarah Kreider, Kratzerville, Pa.
2/22/1846	Haines, Joseph	Beaver Tp.	Harriet Rauch, Beaver Tp.
11/16/1854	" Lewis R.	BeaverSprings,Pa.	Louisa Stltzman, BeaverSpringsPa.
5/31/1860	" Paul	Beaver Tp.	Emeline Howell, Franklin Tp.
10/25/1860	" Joseph N.	West Beaver Tp.	Mary J. Shout, West Beaver Tp.
12/29/1867	" William		Elizabeth Wolf, Freeburg, Pa.
3/18/1869	" Michael	Washington Tp.	Rachael Craig, Washington Tp.
4/30/1843	Hare, Frederick	Middlecreek Tp.	Elizabeth Hummel, Middlecreek Tp.
9/19/1847	" Perry	"	Mary Jane Courtnay "
9/1/1866	" Henry V.	Franklin Tp.	Emma Rauch, Franklin Tp.
6/9/1885	" Herbert	Middleburg, Pa.	Lizzie Eikhoff, Manch Chunk, Pa.
9/27/1885	" R. W.	Snyder Co.	Laura Eisenhauer
3/21/1886	" Frank F.	"	Rebecca Catherman, Union Co.
3/7/1875	Hartley, John	Center Tp.	Jennie Swarm, Center Tp.
3/18/1858	" Daniel W.	Mifflin Co.	Sophia Poter, Mifflin Co.
5/21/1840	Hartman, John		Mary Keefer
2/25/1866	" Jacob	Center Tp.	Catherine Stine, Center Tp.
8/16/1863	" Henry		Susan Benfer "
10/5/1884	" Martin	Snyder Co.	Sarah Frock, Union Co.
9/10/1850	Hassenplug, Dr. Jacob H.	New Berlin, Pa.	Priscilla Kleckner, New Berlin, Pa.
11/29/1853	Hassinger, John S.	Center Tp.	Margaret Klockner, Mifflinburg, Pa.
1/1/1854	" William	"	Amelia Arbogast, Center Tp.
12/17/1854	" Aaron	Mussers Valley	Lucy Ann Snook, Mussers Valley
1/10/1856	" Jacob C.	Franklin Tp.	Jane Wittenmire, Franklin Tp.
4/5/1857	" Samuel	"	Catherine Breininger "
11/1/1860	" Levi	Beaver Tp.	Lydia Weiand, Beaver Tp.
11/3/1864	" Robert	"	Hetty Herman, Center Tp.
9/24/1865	" Elias	"	Catherine Brunner, Center Tp.
12/5/1867	" Daniel I.	"	Sabilla Norman, Franklin Tp.
4/10/1870	" Samuel	Franklin Tp.	Jane Moyer, "
8/23/1874	" Samuel	Middlecreek Tp.	Sarah J. Hummel, Middlecreek Tp.
7/37/1853	Heckendorn, David		Mary Ann Rearick
11/22/1885	Hedding, Warren	Northumberland Co.	Lydia Specht, Snyder Co.
9/21/1847	Heimbach, John S.	Mifflinburg, Pa.	Lucy Ann Bocksy, Mifflinburg, Pa.
4/13/1851	" John E.	Center Tp.	Barbara Long, Center Tp.
11/12/1857	" Jonathan	Middlecreek Tp.	Harriet Seuers, Middlecreek Tp.
6/25/1865	" Benj. F.	Franklin Tp.	Alda Howell, Franklin Tp.
9/18/1870	" Edward	"	Amelia Hackenberg "
12/1/1870	" Zachrias		Malinda Dean
5/21/1871	" Franklin	Franklin Tp.	Isabel Beachel, Franklin Tp.
9/11/1881	" Clinton C.		Sarah Stahlnecker
5/22/1879	Heintzelman, Uriah	Washington Tp.	Emma Snoke, Washington Tp.
2/18/1838	Heiser, Jacob		Zetty Boyer
11/18/1852	" Henry	Kratzerville, Pa.	Sarah E. Miller, Kratzerville, Pa.
10/8/1857	" John	"	Sarah Heim "
8/26/1858	Helfrick, Charles W.	Beaver Tp.	Mary Ann Oldt, Beaver Tp.
11/9/1841	Hendricks, George	Middlecreek Tp.	Phoebe Kantz, Middlecreek Tp.
6/10/1845	" John	Mussers Valley	Susan Fetterolf, Mussers Valley
5/2/1850	" Hiram P.	Kratzerville, Pa.	Lydia Kreider, Kratzerville, Pa.
5/51/1843	Herbst, Henry	East Buffalo Tp.	Mary Swarts, Center Tp.
3/27/1845	Herbster, Thomas	West Beaver Tp.	Mary Baker, West Beaver Tp.
12/31/1847	" George	Beaver Tp.	Sophia Meckley, Beaver Tp.
4/13/1848	" Philip	Center Tp.	Malinda Kline, Center Tp.
5/16/1848	" Adam	West Beaver Tp.	Delilah Freese, West Beaver Tp.
6/6/1853	" Hiram	"	Elizabeth Krebs "
8/21/1870	" Ammon H.	Beaver Tp.	Angeline Klose Beaver Tp.
11/18/1845	Herner, Daniel	Kratzerville, Pa.	Molly Fetter, Kratzerville, Pa.
8/16/1855	" Richard A. M.	Beaver Tp.	Catherine Benfer, Beaver Tp.

-31-

```
3/26/1839  Herman, Jacob          Kratzerville, Pa.  Nancy Breon, Kratzerville, Pa.
11/14/1850    "    Benjamin              "            Lydia Jarrett,    "
4/14/1853     "    Jacob                 "            Sarah Smith       "
8/6/1854      "    Henry           Center Tp.         Susan Bilger, Middlecreek Tp.
12/6/1855     "    Joel            Penn Tp.           Lovina Hendricks   "
4/6/1858      "    Philip          Kratzerville, Pa.  Elisabeth Ritter, Kratzerville,Pa.
11/1/1863     "    Enos            Mussers Valley     Margaret Kline, Mussers Valley
9/10/1848  Hettrick, J. Penrose                       Mary Shannon, Middleburg, Pa.
9/14/1851      "    J.     "                           Amelia    "       "
2/18/1845  Hilbish, George        Freeburg, Pa.      Harriet Schoch, Center Tp.
8/10/1845  Hoch, David            Center Tp.         Mary Ann Klose, Center Tp.
2/24/1870  Hoefflich, John        Mussers Valley     Elizabeth Reigle, Mussers Valley
2/13/1844  Hoffman, Elijah        Penn Tp.           Jane Hoff, Penn Tp.
11/3/1846     "    Daniel         Mifflin Co.        Sarah Rager, Mifflin Co.
6/24/1847     "    George         Hartley Tp.        Hannah Fetterolf, Mussers Valley
12/4/1838  Hollenbach, Daniel                         Louisa Benfer
6/24/1847     "    John           Kratzerville, Pa.  Catherine Kline, Kratzerville, Pa.
3/28/1865  Hooven, Conrad         Beaver Tp.         Adeline Decker, Beaver Tp.
3/14/1843  Horlacher, David           "             Elizabeth Snook    "
6/26/1842  Hosterman, Peter       Penn Tp.           Catherine School, Penn Tp.
6/20/1839  Houseworth, John       Selinsgrove, Pa.   Elizabeth Staley, Selinsgrove,Pa.
11/19/1854 Houts, Henry           Center Co.         Rebecca Kline, Mussers Valley
12/26/1861    "    Philip         Mussers Valley     Harriet Fuhrman, Mussers Valley
1/24/1864     "    Albert M.      Middlecreek Tp.    Susan Dunkelberger, Middlecreek Tp.
5/18/1869     "    Jackson                            Molly Shellenberger, Juniata Co.
4/27/1845  Howell, Jackson        Center Tp.         Mary Reigle, Center Tp.
5/30/1850     "    John C.        W. Beaver Tp.      Barbara Weller, W. Beaver Tp.
10/31/1858    "    Abner          Franklin Tp.       Catherine Bowersox, Franklin Tp.
4/12/1838  Huber (Hoover), Jonathan                   SarahKeiser(dau.ofHenry)AugustaTp.
12/3/1867  Hufnagle, Mark         Beaver Tp.         Elvina Boush, Beaver Tp.
2/23/1840  Hummel, George         Center Tp.         Anna Ringert, Center Tp.
10/27/1842    "    Jacob          Kratzerville, Pa.  Susan Beaver, Kratzerville, Pa.
8/28/1842     "    George         Penn Tp.           Sarah Hix, Penn Tp.
4/13/1845     "    Henry          Middlecreek Tp.    Elizabeth J. Zellner, Juniata Co.
5/27/1847     "    Lewis R.       Penn Tp.           Eliza Hummel, Penn Tp.
11/14/1848    "    Andrew         Middlecreek Tp.    Barbara Moyer, Middlecreek Tp.
1/4/1849      "    Simon                              Catherine Alspach, Schuylkill Co.
8/23/1849     "    Aaron          Kratzerville, Pa.  Susan J. Beaver, Kratzerville, Pa.
2/20/1862     "    Elias          Franklin Tp.       Susan Bollender, Franklin Tp.
12/25/1862    "    William        Beaver Tp.         Elizabeth Aigler, Beaver Tp.
3/26/1871     "    John           Middlecreek Tp.    Sabilla Bowersox, Beaver Tp.
4/15/1873     "    Aaron          Franklin Tp.       Amanda Steininger, Franklin Tp.
2/14/1841  Huth, Isaac            Beaver Tp.         Lydia Fahl, Beaver Tp.

5/6/1842   Jarrett, Jacob         Penn Tp.           Mary Ann Engle, Penn Tp.
6/2/1853      "    Hiram P.       Selinsgrove, Pa.   Rebecca Musselman, Selinsgrove, Pa.
6/15/1876  Jordan, Enoch          Center Tp.         Kate Moyer, Center Tp.
6/27/1882     "    David                "            Amanda Koons,    "

10/6/1840  Kaley, Charles         Beaver Tp.         Elizabeth Ulsh, Beaver Tp.
12/16/1845    "    John                "            Susan Rearick, Center Tp.
4/21/1846     "    Henry                "            Sarah Dreese, Beaver Tp.
12/29/1844 Kalpetzer, Andrew (wdr) W. Beaver Tp.     Esther Heeter (wd,) W. Beaver Tp.
6/6/1843   Keeler, Eli            Washington Tp.     Matilda Bickel, Penn Tp.
12/4/1851  Keiser, Philo          Mifflin Co.        Rebecca Baum, Mifflin Co.
2/4/1869      "    William        Union Co.          Alice Yerger, Union Co.
4/18/1837  Keller, Henry          Shamokin, Pa.      Hester Lancius, Shamokin, Pa.
2/27/1844     "    George W.      Selinsgrove, Pa.   Harriet Singer, Selinsgrove, Pa.
12/16/1864    "    James F.       Beaver Tp.         Susan Smith, Beaver Tp.
8/4/1867      "    Thomas J.           "            Elizabeth Specht, Beaver Tp.
```

Date	Groom	Residence	Bride
3/20/1849	Kerchner, George	Perry County	Mrs. Mary Ann Kunkle, Juniata Co.
12/28/1866	Kern, I. Jefferson	Mussers Valley	Elizabeth Weaver, Mussers Valley
6/9/1850	Kerstetter, William	W. Beaver Tp.	Leah Speiglmire, W. Beaver Tp.
4/12/1849	Kidder, John F.	Middleburg, Pa.	Jane Shannon, Middleburg, Pa.
1/6/1850	Kiester, Samuel	Hartley Tp.	Margaret Dangenbaugh, Hartley Tp.
1/7/1856	" John	Union Co.	Sarah Long, Center Tp.
2/15/1859	" Phares	"	Susan Paul, Hartley Tp.
9/6/1885	" Abraham	Snyder Co.	Clara J. Thomas, Snyder Co.
5/9/1848	King, Lewis	New Columbia, Pa.	Lydia Hilbish, Middleburg, Pa.
2/18/1851	" Amos	W. Beaver Tp.	Sarah Speigelmore, W. Beaver Tp.
12/22/1870	" John S.	Juniata Co.	Tillie Kerschner, Juniata Co.
9/29/1839	Kinney, Edward	Beaver Tp.	Leah Grimm, Beaver Tp.
1/23/1840	Klockner, Charles	Center Tp.	Mary Gift, Center Tp.
6/2/1861	" Daniel	Union Co.	Agnes Hilbish, Union Co.
3/7/1872	Klick, H. C.	Ohio	Susan Diobler, Center Tp.
1/30/1842	Kline, John	W. Buffalo Tp.	Elizabeth Valentine, Beaver Tp.
2/27/1842	" Samuel	Beaver Tp.	Hannah Huffnagle, Beaver Tp.
10/21/1844	" Jesse	"	Catherine Miller "
3/11/1847	" John	Mussers Valley	Leah Fotterold, Mussers Valley
8/3/1848	" George	Beavertown, Pa.	Sarah Pontius, Beavertown, Pa.
11/12/1849	" Aaron	Mussers Valley	Catherine Bingaman, Mussers Valley
4/25/1850	" Barnhart	Kratzerville, Pa.	Hannah Herman Kratzerville, Pa.
6/5/1850	" Solomon	Mussers Valley	Catherine Reish, Mussers Valley
3/18/1851	" William	Beaver Tp.	Matilda Aigler, Beaver Tp.
2/19/1852	" Michael	Mussers Valley	Rachael Thomas, Mussers Valley
10/25/1853	" Emanuel	"	Esther Hackenberg, "
11/6/1856	" Michael	Beaver Tp.	Eliza Hassinger, Beaver Tp.
4/15/1859	" Joseph	Mussers Valley	Harriet Ocker, Mussers Valley
8/28/1860	" Harrison	"	Hannah Shawver "
1/14/1864	" John W.	"	Elizabeth Lepley "
7/6/1864	" John S.	"	Barbara Kline,
2/22/1866	" James	W. Beaver Tp.	Mary Ann Romig, W. Beaver Tp.
4/5/1866	" Robert	Mussers Valley	Elizabeth Dreese, Mussers Valley
10/6/1846	Klingler, John	Kratzerville, Pa.	Lucy Ann Leitzel, Kratzerville, Pa.
5/25/1848	" Reuben	"	Hannah Kratzer, "
4/16/1882	Klock, Edward B.	Northumberland Co.	Lydia Ann Weaver, Snyder Co.
11/13/1824	Klose, John Jacob	W. Beaver Tp.	Sarah Musser, Center Tp.
9/3/1844	" Reuben	Beaver Tp.	Sarah A. Middlesworth, Beaver Tp.
11/15/1849	" "	"	Susan Kline, Beaver Tp.
7/1/1860	Knauer, Nathaniel	Union Co.	Harriet Hilbish, Union Co.
3/28/1841	Knopp, Henry	Beaver Tp.	Barbara Stock, Beaver Tp.
11/26/1844	" William	W. Beaver Tp.	Sophia Peter, W. Beaver Tp.
2/13/1851	" Andrew	Beaver Tp.	Malinda Klose, Beaver Tp.
3/9/1854	" Reuben	Mifflin Co.	Maria Diemer, W. Beaver Tp.
12/4/1856	" Joseph	Mussers Valley	Barbara Stock, Mussers Valley
5/2/1867	" Paul H.	W. Beaver Tp.	Catherine Smith, W. Beaver Tp.
11/25/1883	" John	Snyder Co.	Ellen Shrader, Snyder Co.
3/3/1844	Knittle, Joseph	Center Tp.	Elizabeth Krick, Center Tp.
3/24/1846	" Abraham	Mussers Valley	Amelia Moyer, Mussers Valley
2/11/1840	Knouse, David	Union Tp.	Sarah Maurer, Union Tp.
10/9/1845	" John	Kratzerville, Pa.	Elizabeth Herman, Kratzerville, Pa.
11/10/1839	Koch, Reuben	Beaver Tp.	Susan Goss, Beaver Tp.
8/12/1845	" Elijah	"	Maria Bingman, "
12/13/1849	" Franklin	W. Beaver Tp.	Elizabeth Bonfer, W. Beaver Tp.
2/25/1836	Kohler, J. William		Mary Goss, Augusta Tp.
8/20/1867	Koser, Samuel	Union Co.	Catherine Burns, Middlecreek Tp.
12/17/1840	Kratser, Jacob	Kratzerville, Pa.	Rachael Klingler, Kratzerville Pa.
11/16/1841	" John	"	Polly Bonfer "
1/21/1845	" Henry, Jr.	Beaver Tp.	Amelia Oldt, Beaver Tp.
2/11/1847	" John	Penn Tp.	Susan Klingler, Penn Tp.
12/21/1847	" Andrew	Kratzerville, Pa.	Catherine Breuse, Kratzerville Pa.
4/5/1849	" Philip	"	Elizabeth Kershner "

10/1/1876	Kratzer, George W.	Snyder Co.	Kate Pick, Union Co.
6/13/1853	Kramer, Frederick E.	Middleburg, Pa.	Elmira Smith, Selinsgrove, Pa.
3/23/1845	Krebs, Jacob	West Beaver Tp.	Elizabeth Oldt, West Beaver Tp.
5/27/1852	" William	Mussers Valley	Maria Esther Swartz, MussersValley
4/10/1840	Kreider, Jacob	Penn Tp.	" Kessler, Penn Tp.
9/14/1843	" Joel	"	Elizabeth Haines, "
12/9/1851	" Franklin	"	Mary Oplinger, "
5/31/1855	Kreisher, Jacob	Buffalo Tp.	Regina Leitzel, Middlecreek Tp.
9/22/1853	Krick, William	West Beaver Tp.	Malinda Ritter, West Beaver Tp.
1/31/1843	Krouse, Samuel	Kratzerville, Pa.	Molly Kratzer, Kratzerville, Pa.
7/24/1851	" Lewis	"	Rebecca Klingler "
10/7/1852	" Charles	Middlecreek Tp.	Hannah Yerger, Middlecreek Tp.
8/7/1856	" Henry	Kratzerville, Pa.	Mary Leitzel, Kratzerville, Pa.
3/25/1860	Kuhn, George	Center Tp.	Barbara Rearick, Center Tp.
2/18/1862	" Samuel	"	Rebecca Stock, Mussers Valley
3/16/1851	Kuhns, Isaiah	Beaver Tp.	Catherine Mitchell, Beaver Tp.
9/7/1851	" Daniel	Center Tp.	Amelia Decker, Center Tp.
5/11/1856	" John	"	Elizabeth Stock, Center Tp.
10/20/1867	" Isaac	Mussers Valley	Catherine Hendricks, MussersValley
2/2/1869	" George	Center Tp.	Amelia Bobb, Center Tp.
5/26/1878	" Henry W.	Mussers Valley	Eve Shipe, Mussers Valley
8/19/1849	Kutz, David	Hartley, Tp.	Leah Kiester, Hartley Tp.
2/16/1842	Laber, Joseph	Center Tp.	Lydia Husser, Center Tp.
4/21/1844	" George	West Beaver Tp.	Sophia Krick, West Beaver Tp.
6/8/1865	Laub, Henry H.	"	Louisa Shout, West Beaver Tp.
2/7/1869	Lauber, John	Juniata Co.	Catherine Wertz, Snyder Co.
11/5/1836	Laudenslager, Valentine		Elizabeth Berger
10/18/1849	Lehr, Aaron	West Beaver Tp.	Lucetta Houtz, West Beaver
9/4/1881	Leister, Henry A.	Snyder Co.	Angeline Snyder
8/11/1840	Leitzel, Daniel	Kratzerville, Pa.	Sarah Snyder, Kratzerville, Pa.
8/26/1845	" Joel	"	Rebecca Klingler "
11/11/1858	" Frederick	"	Lydia Herman "
9/9/1841	Lenig, John	Perry Co.	Mary Ann Lose
6/9/1861	" Peter	Washington Tp.	Jemima Roish, Center Tp.
5/2/1880	" H. J.	"	PriscillaHinkle,UnionTp.,SnyderCo.
12/15/1842	Lepley, Joseph	Kratzerville, Pa.	Sarah Oldt, Kratzerville, Pa.
2/24/1846	" Jacob	Beaver Tp.	Rebecca Lash, Beaver Tp.
10/9/1851	" "	West Beaver Tp.	Sophia Hook, West Beaver Tp.
2/22/1855	" Wallis	"	Elizabeth Kalpetzer, W. Beaver Tp.
1/18/1838	Lloyd, James		Elizabeth Slear
5/11/1859	Logan, Robert	Juniata Co.	Elizabeth Miller, Middleburg, Pa.
1/13/1846	Lomison (Lamison), David		Caroline Youngman, Beaver Tp.
12/12/1844	Long, George	Beaver Tp.	Sophia Oberdorf, Beaver Tp.
11/14/1848	" William	Center Tp.	Polly Hartman, Center Tp.
9/19/1841	" Peter	"	Sarah Long, "
7/15/1851	" Josiah B.	Beaver Tp.	" Aigler, Beaver Tp.
12/31/1867	" Samuel B.	Philadelphia, Pa.	Magdalene Hoch, Middleburg, Pa.
12/25/1873	" James H.	Center Tp.	Martha Sanders, Center Tp.
10/25/1849	Lose, Benjamin	"	Elizabeth Shambach, "
12/19/1850	" David	"	Harriet Leitzel, Kratzerville, Pa.
12/26/1850	" Joel	"	Elizabeth Bowersox, Center Tp.
9/3/1882	" James	Snyder Co.	Henrietta Hackenberg
6/26/1849	Louder, Joseph	Limestone Tp.	Margaret Badger, Hartley Tp.
8/31/1849	" Henry	West Beaver Tp.	Mary Ann Shilling, West Beaver Tp.
9/25/1859	" Theodore	Franklin Tp.	Sarah Snyder, Franklin Tp.
10/5/1873	Lower, John	Jackson Tp.	Jane Brunner, Jackson Tp.
12/11/1856	Lowmiller, Thomas	Lewistown, Pa.	Barbara Specht, Beavertown, Pa.
6/19/1866	Lumbard, Joseph A.	Middleburg, Pa.	Sarah Scharf, Middleburg, Pa.
5/3/1887	Lutz, Charles E.	Selinsgrove, Pa.	Anna E. Erdly, Middleburg, Pa.

MARRIAGES BY REV J. P. SHINDEL, JR., 1835-1887, Snyder and Union Counties, Pa.

Date	Name	Place	Spouse
4/24/1836	Magurn, Thomas	Sunbury, Pa.	Elizabeth Mantz, Sunbury, Pa.
1/28/1845	Manbeck, Joseph	Beaver Tp.	Caroline Rauoh, Beaver Tp.
12/6/1849	" Harrison	West Beaver Tp.	Rebecca Goss, West Beaver Tp.
12/9/1858	" Lewis	Beaver Tp.	Louisa Aurand, Beaver Tp.
9/8/1864	" Isaac I.	BeaverSprings,Pa.	Lovina Dreese,BeaverSprings,Pa.
10/15/1839	Margerits, Edward	West Beaver Tp.	Magdalene Bear, West Beaver Tp.
12/25/1883	Makle, William H.	"	Mary Speiglemire "
12/27/1868	Martin, Thomas	Mussers Valley	Mary Musser, Mussers Valley
2/26/1861	" John H.	Union Co.	Hannah Schoch, Snyder Co.
9/29/1867	Martz, William	Selinsgrove, Pa.	Malinda Heimbach, Selinsgrove, Pa.
2/2/1863	Mathias, Henry W.	Middleburg, Pa.	Emma Bollender, Middleburg, Pa.
3/26/1846	Mattern, John Jacob	West Beaver Tp.	Mary J. Stoll, West Beaver Tp.
12/8/1853	" Charles	Mussers Valley	Catherine Ocker, Mussers Valley
4/15/1849	Maurer, Joseph	Beaver Tp.	Amelia Swanger, Beaver Tp.
8/14/1851	" Harrison	West Beaver Tp.	Delilah Breiner, West Beaver Tp.
9/12/1844	May, William J.	Beaver Tp.	Leah Klose, Beaver Tp.
8/20/1882	McAfee, O. P.	Paxtonville, Pa.	Jane M. Gill, Paxtonville, Pa.
1/1/1885	" William	Snyder Co.	Emma K. Marks, Snyder CO.
4/29/1852	McClintock, Mathias	West Beaver Tp.	Mary A. Lash, West Beaver Tp.
5/22/1851	Menges, Conrad	Washington Tp.	Mary Ann Erdly, Buffalo Tp.
7/25/1850	Mengle, Elias	Mifflinburg, Pa.	Jemima Lose, Center Tp.
12/9/1883	" Gustavus	Washington Tp.	Izora Bickhart, Franklin Tp.
4/14/1839	Mertz, George	Beaver Tp.	Rachael Keller, Beaver Tp.
11/2/1838	Metzger, Jacob L.	Union Co.	Hester Long, Union Co.
2/28/1843	Middlesworth, Jacob	Beaver Tp.	Sarah Bobb, Beaver Tp.
6/3/1845	" Aaron (wdr)	"	Elizabeth Dreese (wid), Beaver Tp.
2/19/1852	" John F.	"	Lydia Beaver "
10/16/1859	" Joseph	"	Sarah Kern "
9/6/18--	" John	"	Elizabeth Bingaman "
4/24/1861	" Jacob	"	Matilda Fahl, "
10/17/1861	" Henry	Mussers Valley	Amanda Bingaman "
11/14/1861	" Isaac	Beaver Tp.	Mary Specht "
8/20/1864	" Nor B.	West Beaver Tp.	Amelia Dreese, BeaverSprings, Pa.
9/8/1867	" James	Mussers Valley	Sarah Bigaman, Mussers Valley
2/17/1839	Miller, Peter	Selinsgrove, Pa.	Lydia Houseworth, Selinsgrove, Pa.
12/22/1840	" Jacob	Hartley Tp.	Catherine Ritter, Penn Tp.
12/25/1842	" John	Middleburg, Pa.	Elizabeth Froad, Middleburg, Pa.
5/2/1844	" John	Mifflin Co.	Mary Kalay, Beaver Tp.
12/29/1844	" Jeremiah	Beaver Tp.	Susan Landis "
1/27/1853	" Adam	Penn Tp.	Amelia Smith, Penn Tp.
1/17/1856	" Jacob	Union Co.	Sarah Spangler, Jackson Tp.
2/8/1857	" George	Washington Tp.	Isabelle Dreese, Beaver Tp.
12/25/1860	" Lewis	Freeburg, Pa.	Sarah Stahlnecker, Middleburg, Pa.
5/15/1870	" Daniel J.	Washington Tp.	Susan Kiester, Penn Tp.
12/8/1870	" Jonathan D.	Union Co.	Lydia Reigle, Union Co.
8/13/1881	" Charles C.	Danville, Pa.	Margaret Haines, Danville, Pa.
12/12/1881	" George W.	Union Co.	Kate Kohler, Snyder Co.
3/2/1865	Minium, Jacob	Perry Co.	Catherine Botteiger, Middleburg, Pa.
3/23/1847	Mitchell, Henry	Middlecreek Tp.	Barbara Berger, Middlecreek Tp.
1/9/1859	" James J.	Beaver Tp.	Mary Carroll, Beaver Tp.
6/19/1866	" David	Union Co.	Emma Walter, Jackson Tp.
12/27/1868	" Charles	Beaver Tp.	Sarah Smith, Middleburg, Pa.
3/7/1881	" Kop	Center Tp.	Amelia Kratzer, Center Tp.
8/21/1838	Moll (Mull), Isaac	Shamokin, Pa.	Catherine Persing, Shamokin, Pa.
7/8/1844	Molts, Solomon	Lewistown, Pa.	Margaret Kemberling, Beaver Tp.
5/15/1850	Montgomery, John	Beaver Tp.	Mary Ann Engle, Beaver Tp.
11/17/1839	Moyer, Thomas	West Beaver Tp.	Leah Klose, Beaver Tp.
3/1/1842	" George C.	Freeburg, Pa.	Elizabeth Fisher, Penn Tp.
5/22/1842	" Henry	Beaver Tp.	Sarah Platt, Beaver Tp.
6/26/1842	" "	Center Tp.	Leah Walter, Center Tp.
12/15/1846	" John	Beaver Tp.	Sarah Dreese, Beaver Tp.
12/10/1850	" Jacob	"	Magdalene Long, Center Tp.

-35-

3/30/1854	Moyer, Daniel	Mussers Valley	Lydia Gerhart, Mussers Valley
12/21/1854	" Henry	Beaver Tp.	Amelia Hassinger, Franklin Tp.
8/5/1856	" William	Center Tp.	Sarah Beachel, Center Tp.
10/2/1856	" Henry H.	Mussers Valley	Appolonia Weaver, Mussers Valley
6/11/1857	" Hezriah	Union Co.	Elizabeth Hoffman, Union Co.
2/15/1859	" Samuel S.	Ohio	Mary Kramer, Franklin Tp.
3/17/1859	" Henry	Beaver Tp.	Lydia Knepp, Beaver Tp.
6/19/1859	" Harrison	Beavertown, Pa.	Rebecca Musser, Beavertown, Pa.
12/22/1859	" Uriah	Mussers Valley	Lucy Ann Musser, Mussers Valley
2/9/1860	" Archibald	Beaver Tp.	Elizabeth Stout
12/30/1860	" Daniel	Middleburg, Pa.	Hannah Hartley King, Middleburg,Pa.
5/29/1862	" John	Mussers Valley	Mary Kline, Mussor Valley
3/22/1863	" Jesse	Franklin Tp.	Catherine Hartman, Franklin Tp.
10/6/1864	" Jesse	Mussers Valley	Leah Kline, Mussers Valley
8/13/1868	" Jackson	"	Catherine Brunner "
10/8/1868	" Boswell	Center Tp.	Amelia Moyer, Center Tp.
12/12/1869	" Jeremiah	"	Elizabeth Shrader, Center Tp.
1/19/1871	Moyer, Aaron	West Beaver Tp.	Sarah Wagner, West Beaver Tp.
3/19/1871	" Joseph M.	Center Tp.	Ellen Dean, Center Tp.
9/21/1871	" Franklin	Ohio	Emma Nerhood, Franklin Tp.
7/14/1872	" George	Dauphin Co.	Rachael Bolig, Snyder Co.
9/1/1872	" Irwin J.	Mussers Valley	Ellen Wittenmire, Mussers Valley
3/2/1886	" Zacharias	Snyder Co.	Laura E. Seebold, Snyder Co.
4/8/1847	Mull, Conrad	West Beaver Tp.	Mary Ann Yetter, West Beaver Tp.
10/17/1869	" William	Freeburg, Pa.	Catherine Houser, Freeburg, Pa.
1/1/1867	" Robert H.	Union Co.	Mary Smith, Middleburg, Pa.
10/25/1855	Musselman, Jacob	Penn Tp.	Susan Oplinger, Penn Tp.
8/30/1840	Musser, George	Mussers Valley	Sarah Swartz, Mussers Valley
1/19/1841	" Jeremiah		Mary Dinius, Hartley Tp.
12/11/1842	" Valentine	Beaver Tp.	Lucetta Kern, Beaver Tp.
11/21/1850	" Philip	Center Co.	Mary Catherman, Union Co.
4/1/1858	" Element	Center Tp.	Sarah Yeisley, Center Tp.
1/22/1860	" Archibald	Beaver Tp.	Louisa Kinney, Beaver Tp.
8/23/1868	" Jonathan	Conter Tp.	Catherine Woelfley, Center Tp.
1/21/1869	" Joseph	Mussers Valley	" Kratzer, Mussers Valley
4/13/1873	" Edward	"	Amanda Moyer "
6/15/1873	" John H.	Snyder Co.	Margaret P. Kratzer, Snyder Co.
10/1/1878	" George	Jackson Tp.	Elizabeth Lose, Jackson Tp.
10/17/1841	Nerhood, Amig		Barbara Landis
7/16/1844	" Jesse	Mussors Valley	Catherine Knittle
11/9/1865	" Jacob	"	Laura Heeter
4/10/1870	" Nathaniel J.	Franklin Tp.	Susan Heimbach, Franklin Tp.
8/10/1876	" Josiah	Mussers Valley	Amanda Ettinger, Mussers Valley
2/11/1837	Oberdorf, George	Augusta Tp.	Charity Souders, Augusta Tp.
8/1/1841	Oberlin, John	Middleburg, Pa.	Rebecca Swenk, Middleburg, Pa.
2/24/1842	" Michael	West Buffalo Tp.	Leah Valentine, West Buffalo Tp.
10/7/1858	Ocker, Stephen H.	West Beaver Tp.	" E. Knepp, West Beaver Tp.
11/8/1859	" William F.	Mussers Valley	Sarah A. Fetterolf, Mussers Valley
12/24/1861	" Josiah H.	Snyder Co.	" Havice, Mifflin Co.
8/31/1858	Oldt, George	Beaver Tp.	Mary Klingler, Beaver Tp.
9/6/1870	Osbun, John	Union Co.	Ellen Ray, Union Co.
5/25/1847	Pawling, Levi	Penn Tp.	Margaret Weaver, Penn Tp.
6/7/1863	" Lewis E.	Middlecreek Tp.	Amanda Schoch, Middlecreek Tp.
10/11/1842	Peters, Henry	West Beaver Tp.	Maria Smith, West Beaver Tp.
3/6/1851	Peters, John	Mifflin Co.	Mary Ann Stout, West Beaver Tp.
11/27/1879	" Charles W.	Middleburg, Pa.	Maria Hummel, Middlecreek Tp.
8/23/1872	Pick, Samuel	Union Co.	Ellen Wertz, Snyder Co.
5/30/1843	Platt, George	Beaver Tp.	Susan Musser, Beaver Tp.
4/19/1877	" Levi	Franklin Tp.	Sarah J. Moore, Middlecreek Tp.

6/10/1866	Pontius, Samuel	Middlecreek Tp.	Mary Ann Courtney
12/14/1854	Price, Frederick	West Beaver Tp.	Catherine Fessler, West Beaver Tp.
12/4/1873	Rager, William	Paxtonville, Pa.	Hattie Howell, Paxtonville, Pa.
10/30/1845	Ramsey, Chas. O. P.	West Beaver Tp.	Amelia Margorits, West Beaver Tp.
11/30/1852	Rahmstine, John	Beavertown, Pa.	Elizabeth Jane Specht,BeavertownPa
6/3/1841	Rauch, James		Caroline Hartman, Hartley Tp.
9/16/1886	" William	Franklin Tp.	Cora Hartman, Franklin Tp.
3/31/1856	Ray, Henry	Center Tp.	Susan Gerhart, Center Tp.
11/13/1856	Ream, Jacob	Mifflin Co.	Susan Yetter, Mifflin Co.
10/9/1842	Rearick, Reuben	Middleburg, Pa.	Sarah Moyer, Middleburg, Pa.
8/2/1849	" Jacob	Beaver Tp.	Catherine A. Walter, Center Tp.
6/12/1856	" Samuel	"	Mary Haines, Beaver Tp.
1/19/1860	" Henry	"	Martha Middlesworth, Beaver Tp.
4/12/1835	Reed, Casper J.	Shamokin, Pa.	Alice Barrett, Shamokin, Pa.
5/24/1885	Reichenbach, Milton	Freeburg, Pa.	Kate Shamory, Freeburg, Pa.
5/14/1846	Reichley, Jacob	Mifflinburg, Pa.	Elizabeth Frederick, Mifflinburg,Pa.
5/23/1840	Reigle, Michael		Anna E. Bigaman
1/10/1843	" Jacob	West Beaver Tp.	Sophia Wagner, West Beaver Tp.
3/33/1847	" Peter	Center Tp.	Matilda Middlesworth, Beaver Tp.
6/12/1849	" John	Mifflin Co.	Susan Keller, Beaver Tp.
8/14/1864	" Daniel	Snyder Co.	Caroline Houtz, Union Co.
10/8/1837	Reimert, Abraham	Shamokin, Pa.	Catherine Glass, Shamokin, Pa.
8/3/1841	Reish, Daniel	Center Tp.	Elizabeth Swartz, Center Tp.
7/31/1851	" David	Mussers Valley	Jullia Ann Kline, Mussers Valley
3/16/1854	" Solomon	"	Lucinda Sanders "
4/30/1848	Reitz, Isaac	Center Tp.	Lydia Klose, Center Tp.
9/24/1857	" John	Franklin Tp.	Elizabeth Renninger, Franklin Tp.
9/2/1857	Renn, John	Augusta Tp.	Margaret Frey, Augusta Tp.
10/4/1855	Renninger, John	Franklin Tp.	Eve Bollender, Franklin Tp.
12/9/1866	" Adam	Middlecreek Tp.	Catherine Herman, Middlecreek Tp.
3/29/1869	" Wm. H.	Franklin Tp.	Barbara E. Bowersox, Franklin Tp.
11/25/1869	" Adam	"	Lovina Jane Bilger "
7/18/1854	Ressler, Amos	Juniata Co.	Albertina Margaritz, WestBeaverTp.
11/23/1865	Rhodes, Daniel T.	Middleburg, Pa.	Mary Ann Swineford, Middleburg, Pa.
6/12/1886	Rhodes (Rhoads) David	Washington Tp.	Amelia Ettinger, Washington Tp.
6/5/1849	Rine, Benjamin	"	Susan Hummel
4/26/1840	Ritter, Jacob	Beaver Tp.	Sarah Treaster, Beaver Tp.
12/28/1843	" Elias	Penn Tp.	Eve Herman, Penn Tp.
1/19/1845	" Amos	"	Lydia Reachner, "
12/2/1845	" Samuel	West Beaver Tp.	Catherine Gill, West Beaver Tp.
12/25/1845	" Samuel	Penn Tp.	Leah Probst, Penn Tp.
8/14/1856	" Jacob	West Beaver Tp.	Elizabeth Hecter, WestBeaverTp.
6/12/1851	Ritzman, William	Illinois	Mary Mitterling, Center Tp.
6/4/1845	Rockey, John L.	Union Co.	Mary Ann Ruhl, Union Co.
10/5/1856	Rohback, James H. C.	"	Elizabeth Heimbach, Snyder Co.
1/29/1843	Romig, Andrew, Jr.	West Beaver Tp.	Sarah Kerstetter, West Beaver Tp.
2/11/1845	" Levi	"	Sophia " "
8/6/1857	" Daniel	Beaver Tp.	Elizabeth Ulsh, Beaver Tp.
9/18/1864	" Alex. A.	West Beaver Tp.	Lucy Ann Nerhood, West Beaver Tp.
11/24/1864	" Noah R.	Beaver Tp.	Elizabeth Oldt, Beaver Tp.
6/2/1844	Rossman, Aaron	Hartley Tp.	----- Braucher, Hartley Tp.
6/3/1841	Roth, George	West Beaver Tp.	Sophia Baker, West Beaver Tp.
2/13/1844	" Frederick	Beaver Tp.	Elizabeth Romig, Beaver Tp.
6/6/1869	" "	"	Sarah J. Pontius, "
5/9/1858	Roush, Henry	Middlecreek Tp.	Eliza Dauberman, Middlecreek Tp.
3/23/1865	" Philip	Washington Tp.	Mary Ann Freyman, Middlecreek Tp.
11/21/1867	" Daniel	Freeburg, Pa.	Elisabeth Rine, Freeburg, Pa.
2/27/1874	" George (wdr)	Washington Tp.	Elizabeth Bolig(vid),WashingtonTp.
4/26/1855	Row, Simon	Penn Tp.	Sarah Specht, Penn Tp.
6/30/1849	Ruhl, David	Middlecreek Tp.	Angeline Schock, Middlecreek Tp.
10/10/1850	" Henry	Laurelton, Pa.	Nancy Grove, Kelly Tp.

Date	Name	Location	Spouse
2/4/1844	Sassaman, Lewis	Kratzerville, Pa.	Sarah Super, Kratzerville, Pa.
3/19/1846	" Simon	Center Tp.	Ann Hasslinger, Center Tp.
10/1/1843	Sauers, Adam	Middlecreek Tp.	ElizabethSwartzlander,MiddlecreekTp
2/9/1845	" John	"	Dianna Engle, "
10/10/1853	Schnee, John	Freeburg, Pa.	Lydia Swangle, Center Tp.
3/12/1840	Schoch, David		Maria Pawling, Penn Tp.
8/19/1841	" Emanuel	Middlecreek Tp.	Susan Kline, Middlecreek Tp.
2/11/1845	" Frederick	Penn Tp.	Jane Pawling, Penn Tp.
5/22/1849	" Levi K.	Hartley Tp.	Catherine Yerger, Hartley Tp.
4/25/1850	" Charles	New Berlin, Pa.	Amelia Klose, New Berlin, Pa.
5/18/1857	" George	Selinsgrove, Pa.	ElvinaSmith,BeaverSprings,Pa.
12/25/1862	" Michael K.	Middlecreek Tp.	Sallie Bickel, Middlecreek Tp.
12/4/1866	" Sephares S.	Franklin Tp.	Maggie Walter, Winfield, Pa.
1/14/1851	Searer, Jacob	West Beaver Tp.	Nancy Shilling, West Beaver Tp.
1/14/1841	Sechrist, John	Chapman Tp.	Anna Fisher, Chapman Tp.
4/29/1845	Seebold, Jacob	New Berlin, Pa.	Christiana Bolig, New Berlin Pa.
10/22/1881	" J. W.	Union Co.	Phoebe Felty, Paxtonville, Pa.
11/17/1844	Seesholtz, Samuel	Selinsgrove, Pa.	Catherine Ramstein, Center Tp.
1/24/1843	Seib, Peter	West Beaver Tp	Elizabeth Goss, West Beaver Tp.
9/13/1855	Shaaf, Frederick	Mifflin Co.	Sarah Bassler
11/3/1850	Shaffer, Henry K.	Center Tp.	Mary Bowersox, Center Tp.
5/14/1859	" John W.	Union Co.	Anna Ware (Wehr)
3/26/1860	" Isaac	Center Tp.	Polly Sanders, Center Tp.
6/5/1854	Shambach, George	"	Sarah Hassinger, "
9/28/1873	Shamory, John	Franklin Tp.	Rachael Diebler, Center Tp.
5/8/1870	Shannon, Newton	"	Amanda Rearick, Franklin Tp.
4/15/1849	Shawver, Reuben	West Beaver Tp.	Rebecca Oldt, West Beaver Tp.
4/27/1852	" Daniel	Mussers Valley	Matilda Fotterolf, Mussers Valley
12/20/1860	" John	"	Eva A. Erb "
11/1/1864	Sheffley, John	Mifflinburg, Pa.	Agnes Bickel, Beaver Tp.
12/3/1843	Shilling, William	West Beaver Tp.	Esther Felmly, West Beaver Tp.
10/5/1847	Shipman, Abraham	Hartley Tp.	Mary Cherry, Hartley Tp.
2/8/1842	Shipton, Thomas		Catherine Snook, Beaver Tp.
5/5/1852	Shindle, Martin L.	Sunbury, Pa.	" Young, Sunbury, Pa.
6/15/1853	" Philip M.	"	" Haas, "
8/2/1863	Shibkle, John	Center Tp.	Mary Showers, Center Tp.
12/4/1838	Shirer, John	Beaver Tp.	Catherine Aurand, Beaver Tp.
5/23/1844	Shiveley, Levi	West Buffalo Tp.	Elizabeth Smith, Hartley Tp.
5/1/1859	" O. P.	Lewisburg, Pa.	Elizabeth J. Baker
2/4/1844	Sholler, John	Kratzerville, Pa.	Catherine Herman, Kratzerville,Pa.
10/6/1877	Sholter, William	Union Co.	Mary S. Specht, Middleburg, Pa.
9/14/1852	Showers, George W.	Center Tp.	Mary Ann Yerger, Center Tp.
12/24/1844	Shrader, Jacob	Mussers Valley	Maria C. Swartz, Mussers Valley
7/30/1851	" Solomon	Mifflinburg, Pa.	Catherine Catherman, MifflinburgPa
2/17/1859	" Samuel	Center Tp.	Anna C. Hartman
10/5/1865	" Frederick	Mussers Valley	Maria E. Fottorolf, Mussers Valley
12/23/1858	Shultze, Rev. G. W. M.	West Beaver Tp.	Mary Ann Steininger
6/27/1837	Simpson, Bloomfield	Sunbury, Pa.	Sarah Millett, Sunbury, Pa.
4/16/1835	Slack, Henry	Augusta Tp.	Mary Sampsell, Augusta Tp.
2/8/1844	Slear, Charles	Kratzerville	Elizabeth Smith, Kratzerville, Pa.
12/7/1854	Smull, John	Clearfield Co.	Elizabeth Hackenberg, Union Co.
10/3/1840	Snyder, John	Middleburg, Pa.	Maria Sampsell, Center Tp.
11/15/1840	" Aaron R.	"	" Shambach, Middleburg, Pa.
11/21/1858	" Charles S.	Franklin Tp.	Sarah Steininger, West Beaver Tp.
8/17/1861	" David A.	Perry Co.	Margaret Foster
5/31/1866	" Samuel	Middlecreek Tp.	Henrietta Beaver, Jackson Tp.
6/11/1882	" Edwin	Washington Tp.	Medora Roush, Washington Tp.
3/15/1858	Spade, Philip	Middleburg, Pa.	Catherine Smith, Beavertown, Pa.
9/13/1855	Spangler, William	BeaverSprings,Pa.	Amanda Mitchell
4/21/1839	Specht, Moses	Beaver Tp.	Rachael Bingaman, Beaver Tp.
7/31/1851	" Henry	Middlecreek Tp.	Caroline Bolig, Middlecreek Tp.
8/5/1866	" Jacob F.	Middleburg, Pa.	Amanda Dorr

Date	Groom	Place	Bride
3/27/1839	Smith, Jacob J.	Beaver Tp.	Catherine Kerstetter, Beaver Tp.
7/24/1840	" Samuel	Center Tp.	Elizabeth Bollender, Center Tp.
10/27/1840	" John A.	Middleburg, Pa.	Catherine " Middleburg, Pa.
1/31/1841	" Henry, Jr.	" "	Diana Aigler, Beaver Tp.
8/3/1841	" Levi	West Beaver Tp.	Eva Kerstetter, West Beaver Tp.
1/29/1843	" John	Beaver Tp.	Martha Hiddlesworth, Beaver Tp.
8/6/1843	" " "	" "	Anna Baker, " "
3/25/1845	" Samuel	Penn Tp.	Juliana Bingaman, Penn Tp.
4/23/1845	" James	Center Tp.	Margaret Dreese, Center Tp.
5/1/1849	" Reuben	West Beaver	Mary Ann Mattern, West Beaver Tp.
9/15/1851	" John M.	Middleburg, Pa.	Elizabeth Schoch, Middleburg, Pa.
2/21/1856	" George O.	Beavertown, Pa.	Mary Ann Kern, Beavertown, Pa.
4/20/1858	" Edward	West Beaver Tp.	Matilda Baker, West Beaver Tp.
9/13/1860	" Robert	Beaver Tp.	Malinda Gross, Beaver Tp.
4/3/1862	" Michael	Mussers Valley	Susan Middlesworth, Mussers Valley
6/18/1865	" Alfred	Beavertown, Pa.	Mary Ann Freed, Beavertown, Pa.
12/8/1867	" William A.	Franklin Tp.	" " Shambach, Franklin Tp.
7/12/1868	" William	Mussers Valley	Alvilda Fetterolf, Mussers Valley
2/9/1869	" Charles L.	Middleburg, Pa.	Harriet Wittenmeyer, Middleburg, Pa.
5/9/1869	" Albert M.	Beavertown, Pa.	Alvilda Stettler,
11/22/1874	" J. Allen	Washington Tp.	Mary E. Reich, Franklin Tp.
4/4/1878	" John P.	Perry Co.	Carrie Patton, Perry Co.
9/28/1884	" William	Union Co.	Anna Bolig, Center Tp.
2/25/1886	" J. D.	Kansas	Ida Heckendorn, BeaverSprings, Pa.
3/21/1847	Snook, Isaac	Beaver Tp.	Sophia Swanger, Beaver Tp.
10/16/1851	" John P.	West Beaver Tp.	Caroline Koch, West Beaver Tp.
8/22/1861	" David A.	Mifflin Co.	Amanda J. Goss, West Beaver Tp.
6/21/1868	Specht, James V.	Beaver Tp.	Ellen Bobb, Beaver Tp.
3/13/1869	" George E.	Middleburg, Pa.	Rose E. Smith, Middleburg, Pa.
6/6/1869	" Arthur B.	Beavertown, Pa.	Amanda Moyer, Beavertown, Pa.
7/25/1869	" H. D.	Beaver Tp.	Harriet, J. Long, Beaver Tp.
3/5/1876	" Charles F.	Middleburg, Pa.	Mary E. Rearick
5/10/1877	Spencer, Charles H.	Elk Co.	Susan Bickhart, Snyder Co.
5/7/1839	Speigelmire, Valent.	Mifflin Co.	Sophia Knopp, Mifflin Co.
3/1/1840	" Benjamin	Beaver Tp.	Elizabeth Young, Beaver Tp.
12/17/1850	" Daniel	West Beaver Tp.	Isabel Weiand, West Beaver Tp.
9/16/1851	" Samuel	Beaver Tp.	Catherine Weiand, Beaver Tp.
7/1/1855	" Levi	BeaverSprings, Pa.	Amelia Haines, BeaverSpring, Pa.
6/16/1872	" Henry S.	West Beaver Tp.	Lydia Bear, West Beaver Tp.
11/8/1874	Springer, Christ. H.	Montour Co.	Mary J. Dreese, Snyder Co.
3/24/1868	Stahlnecker, Daniel	Northumberland Co.	Eliza Stahlnecker, Middleburg, Pa.
7/30/1845	Stembach, John	Beaver Tp.	Mary Ann Long, Beaver Tp.
10/29/1843	Stauffer, Samuel F.	Selinsgrove, Pa.	Sophia Walter, Selinsgrove, Pa.
2/15/1849	Steese, Joseph	West Buffalo Tp.	Sarah J. Mensch, West Buffalo Tp.
10/19/1853	Steimling, Henry	Franklin Tp.	Christiana Long, Franklin Tp.
8/14/1865	" Benj. F.	" "	Amanda Musser, " "
11/23/1847	Steininger, Joseph	West Beaver Tp.	Salome Knepp, West Beaver Tp.
1/3/1856	" Elias	Franklin Tp.	Mary Ann Stahlnecker, Franklin Tp.
11/2/1865	" Henry	Middleburg, Pa.	Malinda Bowersox, Middleburg, Pa.
1/18/1844	Sterner, Daniel	Washington Tp.	Sarah Rummel, Washington Tp.
5/13/1847	Stettler, Aaron	Middleburg, Pa.	Mary Walter, Middleburg, Pa.
11/30/1848	" George	Beaver Tp.	Malinda Kaley, Beaver Tp.
5/17/1855	" Amos	Franklin Tp.	Amelia Gift, Franklin Tp.
10/1/1857	" Daniel	" "	Mary Heimbach, " "
3/11/1851	Stock, Simon	Mussers Valley	Delilah Kline, Mussers Valley
9/16/1858	" Jesse	" "	Elizabeth Wagner, " "
3/17/1859	" Anthony	West Beaver Tp.	Lydia Goss, West Beaver Tp.
12/8/1861	" David	Center Tp.	Margaret Trutt, Center Tp.
12/25/1884	" Henry	" "	Laura P. Stine, " "
12/26/1844	Stringer, Christian	Union Co.	Sarah Lepley, Fratzerville, Pa.
6/12/1851	Strohecker, Thomas S.	Beavertown, Pa.	Catherine Backman, Beavertown, Pa.

1/16/1858	Stroup, John W.	Freeburg, Pa.	Sallie Berry, Freeburg, Pa.
10/17/1869	" Philip	"	Emma Shoemaker, "
5/30/1868	Strouse, Elias	Washington Tp.	Sarah Shaffer, Monroe Tp.
1/9/1849	Stump, Samuel	West Beaver Tp.	Rachael Bowersox, West Beaver Tp.
8/28/1851	" Edward	"	Agnes Dreese, "
9/11/1843	Swarts, Elias	Beaver Tp.	Rebecca " Beaver Tp.
5/4/1852	" Samuel	Mussers Valley	Jemima Hare, Mussers Valley
2/9/1854	" Harrison	West Beaver Tp.	Matilda Wagner, West Beaver Tp.
6/18/1871	" J. Wilson	Troxelville, Pa.	Catherine Earnest, Beaver Tp.
4/21/1872	" A. Howard	Mussers Valley	Mary Middlesworth, Mussers Valley
12/14/1843	Swengle, John	Center Tp.	Sarah Frantz, Center Tp.
2/7/1856	" William	Union Co.	Catherine Bingaman, Mussers Valley
5/13/1838	Swineford, Emanuel	Center Co.	Margaret Hamilton, Union Co.
2/9/1840	" Henry	Center Tp.	Amelia Klose, Center Tp.
9/22/1872	" Henry C.	Union Co.	Caroline Shively, Union Co.
5/10/1836	Swinehart, Daniel	Augusta Tp.	Judith Hileman, Augusta Tp.
10/21/1847	" John	Beaver Tp.	Barbara Reachner, Beaver Tp.
11/17/1842	Stroup, William F.	West Beaver Tp.	Albertina Margertis, WestBeaverTp.
2/22/1885	Tharp, L. V.	Perry Co.	Mary Lebkichler, Perry Co.
6/16/1853	Thomas, Samuel	Mussers Valley	Sarah Hartley, Mussers Valley
9/6/1868	" B. Franklin	Beaver Tp.	Elizabeth Fike, Beaver Tp.
3/16/1845	Thompson, Emanuel	Penn Tp.	Catherine Laudenslager, Penn Tp.
5/1/1849	Treaster, Henry	West Beaver Tp.	Sophia Goss, West Beaver Tp.
2/11/1858	" Joseph	"	Sarah Gross, "
11/15/1842	Trexler, Willoughby	Monroe Tp.	Amelia Filbert, Monroe Tp.
11/20/1838	Troxel, John	Center Tp.	Lydia Hassinger, Center Tp.
7/2/1843	Try, Benjamin	Laurelton, Pa.	Lydia Smith, Laurelton, Pa.
10/29/1839	Ulrich, Daniel C.	Selinsgrove, Pa.	Mrs. Fannie Fisher, Selinsgrove,Pa.
8/30/1842	" George	"	Cordilla Genglor, Selinsgrove, Pa.
8/5/1845	" Samuel	Kratzerville, Pa.	ElizabethHollonbach,KratzervillePa.
11/25/1845	" John	"	Eve Benfer "
1/1/1839	Ulsh, Andrew, Jr.	Beaver Tp.	Catherine Miller, Beaver Tp.
8/3/1847	" Joseph	West Beaver Tp.	Christina Moyer, Mussers Valley
4/3/1851	" John, Jr.	Perry Co.	Susan Reber, Union Co.
2/11/1858	" Henry M.	West Beaver Tp.	Louisa Smith, West Beaver Tp.
11/29/1849	" Isaac	"	Christina Troxol, Mussers Valley
1/2/1842	Vail, William	Center Tp.	Hannah Lose, Center Tp.
4/3/1849	Valentine, John	"	Mrs. Susan Schnee, Mifflin Co.
3/16/1854	" George	Kratzerville, Pa.	Eva Hartley, Kratzerville, Pa.
8/5/1845	Vanatta, Henry	Hartley Tp.	Mary Hartman, Hartley Tp.
6/30/1861	Van Ormer, G. W.	West Beaver Tp.	Malinda Bobb, West Beaver Tp.
9/8/1839	Vogel, Martin	Beaver Tp.	Leah Kern, Beaver Tp.
2/18/1886	Wagner, Andrew (wdr)		Mary Mattern (wid), W. Beaver Tp.
12/13/1866	" "	Beaver Tp.	Sarah Kratzer, Beaver Tp.
1/23/1846	" George (wdr)	West Beaver Tp.	Mary Phillips (wid)
2/3/1847	" Isaac	"	Elizabeth Shilling, W. Beaver Tp.
1/22/1850	" Adam	"	Maria Goss "
6/6/1850	" Daniel	"	Matilda Erb "
8/31/1851	" Isaac	Beaver Tp.	Catherine Swinehart, Beaver Tp.
1/19/1854	" John	"	Matilda Long, "
5/3/1855	" Solomon	West Beaver Tp.	Sarah Maurer, West Beaver Tp.
8/30/1855	" Abraham	"	Sabina Tittle "
12/18/1855	" William	Mussers Valley	Mary Bingaman, Mussers Valley
1/29/1856	" Reuben	West Beaver Tp.	Susan Moyer, Franklin Tp.
5/29/1856	" Franklin	Middlecreek Tp.	Mary M. Gilbert, Middlecreek Tp.
2/3/1859	" Henry (wdr)	Beaver Tp.	Sarah Long (wid), Beaver Tp.
5/22/1859	" George	West Beaver Tp.	Amanda Benfer, West Beaver Tp.
11/26/1861	" Henry	"	Caroline Speigelmire "

5/31/1875	Walker, Josiah	Union Co.	Matilda Peters, Middleburg, Pa.
12/25/1842	Walter, Samuel	Kratzerville, Pa.	Catherine Long, Kratzerville, Pa.
8/15/1845	" Daniel	Beaver Tp.	Elizabeth Renninger, Beaver Tp.
8/10/1845	" Jacob	Center Tp.	Catherine Eisenhauer, Center Tp.
11/25/1845	" Benjamin	Kratzerville, Pa.	Hannah Geise, Kratzerville, Pa.
1/30/1849	" Isaac	Center Tp.	Lucinda Renninger, Center Tp.
8/19/1849	" Solomon	"	Mary Ann Derr, Center Tp.
9/20/1849	" John	"	Amelia Rearick, Beaver Tp.
12/13/1849	" Jacob	Franklin Tp.	Sarah Rauck, Franklin Tp.
3/18/1852	" Samuel	Center Tp.	Mary Ann Renninger, Center Tp.
10/20/1853	" Henry	Kratzerville, Pa.	Sarah Jane Neitz, Kratzerville,Pa.
6/23/1855	" William	Franklin Tp.	Barbara Heimbach, Franklin Tp.
10/25/1855	" Joseph	"	Susan Hassinger, Franklin Tp.
1/8/1857	" Solomon	Center Tp.	Delilah Louder, Center Tp.
3/17/1863	" David	Franklin Tp.	Jane Hackenberg, Franklin Tp.
1/11/1866	" Enoch	West Beaver Tp.	Susan Goss, West Beaver Tp.
11/22/1866	" Adam	Franklin Tp.	Mary Walter, Franklin Tp.
10/14/1865	" Job	Franklin Tp.	Catherine Bingaman, Franklin Tp.
7/17/1870	" Jefferson	Center Tp.	Harriet Jordan, Center Tp.
6/18/1870	" Jeremiah	Snyder Co.	Susan Yeisley, Snyder Co.
12/10/1882	" Abner	"	Ada Gift, "
4/22/1860	Wayne, Jacob	Franklin Tp.	Ada Wittes, Franklin Tp.
5/14/1837	Weaver, Charles	Sunbury, Pa.	Elisabeth Hileman, Sunbury, Pa.
2/15/1842	" Jacob	Center Co.	Amelia Botdorf, Freeburg, Pa.
12/13/1860	" George Z.	Mussers Valley	Catherine Hackenber, Mussers Valley
12/18/1870	Weiand, John	Beaver Tp.	Savilla Smith, Beaver Tp.
11/16/1841	" Michael	Center Tp.	Polly Dreese, Center Tp.
4/23/1837	Weidensaul, Jacob	Sunbury, Pa.	Catherine Kiehl, Sunbury, Pa.
5/18/1841	Weider (Woeder), Moses	West Beaver Tp.	Lydia Steininger, West Beaver Tp.
7/19/1857	Weirick, Samuel	Mifflin Co.	Elizabeth Hook, Mifflin Co.
11/3/1850	Welfley, Adam	Center Tp.	Catherine Stock, Center Tp.
5/15/1864	" Jeremiah	"	Matilda Shaffer, "
9/14/1854	Weller, Simon	Middlecreek Tp.	Elisabeth Rehrer, Middlecreek Tp.
10/11/1849	Wetzel, Henry E.	Middleburg, Pa.	Eliza Bostwick, Middleburg, Pa.
9/29/1839	" John	Beaver Tp.	Lydia Aigler, Beaver Tp.
3/9/1843	" Samuel	"	Catherine Felker, "
11/13/1866	" Jacob	"	Louisa Beaver " (d/o Jacob)
8/22/1880	Whatmore, John Z.	Paxtonville, Pa.	Ida J. Erdly, Paxtonville, Pa.
3/19/1835	Whitaker, John	Augusta Tp.	Polly Tucker, Augusta Tp.
9/27/1853	Williams, L. D.	Mifflinburg, Pa.	Mary J. Smith, Mifflinburg, Pa.
1/30/1873	Wilt, George A.	Snyder Co.	Mary Ann Heimbach, Snyder Co.
11/15/1838	Wiltz, John	West Buffalo Tp.	Catherine Romig, Beaver Tp.
10/20/1883	Wirth, James F.	Union Co.	Elizabeth Specht, Snyder Co.
1/20/1842	Wittenmeyer, Simon	Beaver Tp.	Sophia Smith, Beaver Tp.
1/22/1860	" Philip	Franklin Tp.	Louisa Kinney, Franklin Tp.
1/25/1866	" Henry	Middlecreek Tp.	Abby Yerger, Middlecreek Tp.
2/3/1885	Wohlheater, William	Union Co.	Sarah J. Bickel, Indiana
6/10/1851	Yeager, Jacob (wdr)		Mary Feirick (wid), Mifflin Co.
11/19/1850	Yearick, Samuel R.	Kratzerville, Pa.	Matilda Sassaman, Kratzerville, Pa.
7/12/1863	Yeisley, Henry	Franklin Tp.	Amelia Swineford, Franklin Tp.
5/23/1869	" Henry K.	Union Co.	Matilda Zimmerman, Union Co.
6/21/1885	Yerger, William	Middlecreek Tp.	Lizzie Hull, Middlecreek Tp.
1/26/1882	" Samuel C.	Franklin Tp.	Lydia Duke, "
2/11/1845	" John	Center Tp.	Margaret Farnsworth, Center Tp.
4/6/1845	" Israel (wdr)	"	Catherine Ungor (wid) "
4/30/1850	" John	Hartley Tp.	Lucinda Huntington, Hartley Tp.
5/15/1851	" George	Middlecreek Tp.	Mary Catherman, Mifflinburg, Pa.
1/17/1856	" David	"	Margaret Bause, Middlecreek Tp.

Date	Name		Place	Spouse
4/13/1848	Yetter,	Samuel	West Beaver Tp.	Mary Ann Youngman, W. Beaver Tp.
11/6/1851	"	Moses	Mifflin Co.	Matilda Keiser, Mifflin Co.
4/26/1855	"	Henry	West Beaver Tp.	Maria Koch, West Beaver Tp.
11/22/1866	"	Joseph	Mifflin Co.	Catherine Hackenberg, Snyder Co.
9/11/1843	Young, John		Beaver Tp.	Harriet Rudy, Beaver Tp.
2/23/1845	Youngman, Thomas		West Beaver Tp.	Catherine Lepley, West Beaver Tp.
9/28/1865	Zartman, John F.		Union Co.	Sarah Heeter, Snyder Co.
10/12/1862	Zechman, Reuben		Middlecreek Tp.	Elizabeth Wittenmeyer,Middlecreek Tp.
12/21/1869	"	Joel	Franklin Tp.	Lydia Bolig, Franklin Tp.
9/24/1882	"	John	"	Anna Swarm, "
2/24/1853	Zeiner, Gotlieb		Lewistown, Pa.	Elizabeth Bower, Lewistown, Pa.
12/30/1838	Ziebor, Philip		Union Tp.	Hannah Maurer
8/4/1859	"	Samuel	West Beaver Tp.	Caroline Potter, West Beaver Tp.
4/8/1866	"	Jacob	Juniata Co.	Adeline Margeritz
12/7/1871	"	John	West Beaver Tp.	Sarah J. Lambert, W. Beaver Tp.
1/22/1837	Zimmerman, George		Augusta Tp.	Sarah Fasold, Augusta Tp.

END

Date	Name	Place	Spouse
3/9/1854	Albert, Frederick		Catherine Doebler, New Berlin, Pa.
11/20/1849	Antes, Charles	Mifflinburg, Pa.	Mary A. Roshon, "
2/7/1839	Asper, P.		Lydia Lonhart
1/11/1852	Aumiller, Geroge		Temima Bopp, Middlecreek Tp.
12/16/1877	Aurand, Henry S.		Lydia Moser (Musser?)
5/11/1848	Bakor, Solomon	Beavertown, Pa.	Harriet Eichinger, Beavertown, Pa.
3/2/1845	Barber, John		Emily Wayne, Middleburg, Pa.
8/7/1859	Beachol, Christian		Elizabeth Showers, Center Tp.
5/1/1855	Beaver, George		Anna Fisher
2/4/1858	" Percival	Monroe Tp.	" Hummel, Penn Tp.
6/3/1858	" William	"	Lydia Walter, Union Tp., Union Co.
9/11/1864	" Absalom		Kate Beaver, Monroe Tp.
1/1/1867	" George K.	Monroe Tp.	Sarah A. Walter, Union Tp.
2/27/1851	" Daniel		Hetty Meyer
8/30/1874	Becker, Alexander		Kate Bolig
9/13/1842	Benfer, John	Union Co.	Mary Maurer, Union Co.
10/21/1847	" William	Center Tp.	Mary J. Eichinger, Beavertown, Pa.
12/4/1849	" Enos	Union Co.	Sarah Maurer, Union Tp.
5/27/1858	" George		Polly Brouse, Jackson Tp.
10/11/1860	" Benj. T.		Esther Boyer, Middlecreek Tp.
5/9/1861	" James L.	Union Tp.	Ann Amelia Beaver, Monroe Tp.
11/30/1862	" Joel		Mary Snyder Jackson Tp.
3/12/1863	" Henry	Middlecreek Tp.	Rose Ann Bilger, Jackson Tp.
11/16/1873	" Henry	New Berlin, Pa.	Louise Yeisley, Franklin Tp.
7/31/1846	Benner, William		Sarah Swarts
9/26/1849	" Edward		Sarah Weikel, New Berlin, Pa.
2/5/1846	Bennett, Samuel		Charlotte Boone, Lewisburg, Pa.
5/21/1850	Berge, Jonas	Union Tp.	Esther Smith, East Buffalo Tp.
8/28/1855	" Henry	Limestone Tp.	Sarah Sasseman, Union Tp.
4/3/1856	" Samuel		Margaret Geise, Jackson Tp.
6/22/1856	" Levi		Melinda Keller, Beaver Springs, Pa.
4/3/1842	Bilger, John		Barbara Swineford, Middleburg, Pa.
6/14/1860	" Jesse	Center Tp.	Lucinda Stock, Middlecreek Tp.
11/28/1880	Bingaman, Charles		Anna Gerhart
11/14/1843	" John	Beaver Tp.	Mary Keeter, Beaver Tp.
8/3/1879	Birl, Peter		Lydia Shannon
11/18/1860	Bishop, Alexander	Center Tp.	Mary Ann Trutt, Union Tp.
6/16/1863	" Ner		Maria Gerhart, Center Tp.
6/14/1866	Blough, Michael		Polly Leader, Beaver Tp.
7/8/1845	Bogar, John		Diana Kleckner, New Berlin, Pa.
7/21/1852	" William		Sebra Bibighaus
9/8/1844	Bolig, P.		Susan Shiffer, New Berlin, Pa.
9/11/1862	" Elias		Emeline Erb, Middlecreek Tp.
3/21/1844	Bollender, Frederick		Sarah Steese, Union Co.
12/24/1844	" Joseph	Middleburg, Pa.	Anna Boyer, Middleburg, Pa.
2/2/1864	Bollender, Wm. F. A.	Limestone Tp.	Mary Seebold, Union Co.
9/27/1849	" Michael	Center Tp.	Elizabeth Engle, Center Tp.
11/11/1852	Boop, John		Sarah Ann Beise, New Berlin, Pa.
8/3/1856	" Charles		Elizabeth Yergor, "
2/1/1857	" George	New Berlin, Pa.	Fianna Steely, Lewisburg, Pa.
11/9/1847	" Jacob		Elisa Dibons, Mifflinburg, Pa.
3/4/1845	Bower, Thomas		Catherine Kramer, Middleburg, Pa.
3/12/1843	Bowersox, Daniel	Center Tp.	Christina Long, Beaver Tp.
11/12/1850	" Andrew	"	Mary Ann Wetzel, Union Tp.
12/18/1851	" Abraham		Rebecca Getz, Union Co.
12/1/1853	" Henry		Mary Noll, "
4/27/1854	" William		Sarah Rearick, Franklin Tp.
8/9/1860	" Johathan		Harriet Maurer, Center Tp.
8/19/1860	" George		Christina Kerr, "

8/18/1872	Bowersox, Jacob	Jackson Tp.	Melinda Beaver
1/13/1877	" Phares	Center Tp.	Minerva Kleckner, Center Tp.
12/30/1856	Boyer, Henry		Elizabeth Valentine, Jackson Tp.
10/29/1857	" David		Lovina Houts, West Beaver Tp.
6/8/1858	" Leonard		Catherine Mark, Limestone Tp.
12/3/1866	" Jacob		Sarah Moll, Mifflinburg, Pa.
12/24/1871	" George	Center Tp.	Catherine Eister, Franklin Tp.
2/7/1839	Brandt, ———		——— Penny
8/18/1872	Brema, George W.		Lucinda Brouse
8/19/1852	Brouse, Joseph		Susan Young, Union Co.
8/18/1857	" Harrison		Sarah Kreider, Penn Tp.
1/28/1858	" Franklin	Penn Tp.	" A. Beaver, Union Tp.
1/13/1859	" Benjamin		Susan Mertz, Union Co.
11/17/1859	" Joel	Union Tp.	Nettie Zimmerman, New Berlin, Pa.
11/17/1867	" George	Jackson Tp.	Harriet Herman, Monroe Tp.
6/25/1865	Brown, Reuben		Minerva Stahl, Monroe Tp.
2/13/1842	Brunner, Samuel	Beaver Tp.	Elizabeth Felker, Beaver Tp.
6/7/1868	" William		Susan Rearick, New Berlin, Pa.
6/6/1867	Burns, Abraham		Sarah Wagner, Limestone Tp.
4/20/1876	Burty, "		Mary E. Leitsel, Middlecreek Tp.
8/3/1852	Cawley, Charles		Catherine Kleckner
7/29/1866	Christie, James		Mary Wagner, Limestone Tp.
11/30/1840	Cochran, Henry		Rebecca Witman, Union Co.
3/22/1855	Conley, Thomas		Harriet Clemens, Union Tp.
8/24/1865	" William	Monroe Tp.	Caroline Moase, Kelly Tp.
12/24/1874	" Jeremiah		Wilhelmina Williams
4/5/1868	Cooney, David		Julia Ann Rudy, New Berlin, Pa.
3/27/1860	Craig, John R.		Susan Long, Monroe Tp.
4/4/1878	Culp, John H.		Jane Wittenmyer, Center Tp.
7/19/1868	Dangert, Jacob		Mary Aurand, New Berlin, Pa.
2/20/1844	Danley, Charles S.		Elizabeth Bigelow
8/20/1846	Dauberman, Christian		Mary Norman
5/20/1847	Dean, Joseph		Mary Snook
2/12/1847	Decker, Simon		" Reitz, Center Tp.
6/2/1861	DeLong, Reuben	Center Tp.	Caroline Yeisley, Limestone Tp.
9/12/1867	" "	Limestone Tp.	Susan Fuhrman, Limestone Tp.
3/28/1869	" "	Center Tp.	Maria Ettinger, Beaver Tp.
12/28/1854	Derk, George		Lydia Beaver, Union Tp.
2/11/1845	Derr, John		Susan Smith
12/22/1869	Dieffenbach, Solomon		Mary Neff, Union Co.
3/1/1853	Dieffenbach, Wellophren	East Buffalo Tp.	Caroline Jarrott, Penn Tp.
1/1/1852	Dietrick, Joseph	Lycoming Co.	Sarah Ann Benner, East Buffalo Tp.
7/3/1864	Dorman, Samuel		Elizabeth Miller, Hartley Tp.
5/21/1848	Dreese, George		Gretchen Plough, Beaver Tp.
3/11/1852	" Reuben		Matilda Sabman, BeaverSprings,Pa.
6/15/1873	" Jacob		Susan Bingaman
2/7/1840	Dreifus, Marcus		Joanna Bishop
5/8/1851	Dunkle, Samuel	Union Co.	Susan Madera, Berks Co.
4/20/1862	Dunkelberger, William		Sarah Courtney, Middlecreek Tp.
1/21/1844	Eisenhauer, Reuben	Center Tp.	Rachael Deckard, Center Tp.
1/14/1847	" Henry	"	Esther Aigler, Beaver Tp.
2/9/1854	Engle Jacob	Union Tp.	Catherine Wolf, Buffalo Tp.
1/2/1855	Engle, Silas	"	Sarah Newbury, Union Tp.
7/19/1869	Erb, John	Beaver Tp.	Ada Herman, Center Tp.
4/9/1850	Erdly, Levi		Sarah Mathias, Penn Tp.
5/3/1853	" John F.		Mary A. Coleman, Union Tp.
8/22/1858	" Joseph		Margaret Beaver, Jackson Tp.

MARRIAGES OF REV. A. B. CASPER, 1839-1882, Snyder and Union Counties, Pa.

11/6/1870	Ettinger, Abraham		Lizzie Moll
1841	Eyster, Dr. ——		—— Houtz

8/5/1851	Fair, Tobias		Mary Zechman, Union Tp.
6/30/1852	Feese, John G.		Lydia Swartzlander, New Berlin, Pa.
1/15/1843	Ferster, Daniel	Middlecreek Tp.	Lydia Wagner, Middlecreek Tp.
12/28/1851	Fetter, Nathaniel	Union Tp.	Susan Wittenmeyer, Penn Tp.
6/29/1852	Fetterolf, Frederick		" Kerstetter, Mussers Valley
3/1/1843	Fogel, George	Beaver Tp.	Elizabeth Overmire
12/18/1859	Forry, Edward		Sarah A. Zodon, Limestone Tp.
8/4/1846	Frantz, John		Rachael Hefte, Center Tp.
2/3/1842	Frederick, John		" Walter
10/22/1846	" Abraham		Catherine Eschbaugh, Union Co.
10/1/1876	Frock, John	Limestone Tp.	Susan Herman, Center Tp.
3/25/1845	Fry, Henry		Matilda Knepp, West Beaver Tp.
3/9/1847	Fuhrman, Daniel	Buffalo Tp.	Sarah Bandt, Center Tp.

3/4/1851	Gemberling, Levi	Kelly Tp.	Caroline Dunkle, Buffalo Tp.
7/5/1842	Gephart, Benjamin	New Berlin, Pa.	Elizabeth Rudy, New Berlin, Pa.
2/6/1842	Gerhart, Jacob	Center Tp.	Lydia Hassinger, Beaver Tp.
2/12/1846	Getz, Henry		Catherine Romig, Buffalo Tp.
11/9/1848	Gift, Amig		Elizabeth Walter
5/22/1855	" Samuel J.	Lewisburg, Pa.	Catherine Aurand, East Buffalo Tp.
7/26/1868	Gilbert, William	Freeburg, Pa.	Mary Bowersox, Center Tp.
12/19/1848	Gill, Isaac		Malinda Band, Middleburg, Pa.
8/18/1861	Good, William	Monroe Tp.	Polly Ann Kratzer, Jackson Tp.
2/15/1842	Goss, Jacob	Beaver Tp.	Maria Stump, Beaver Tp.
11/14/1848	" Isaac		Rebecca Manbeck, West Beaver Tp.
12/21/1848	Gramley, Levi		Mary Benfer
7/8/1856	Gross, David	Selinsgrove, Pa.	Sarah Ann Walter
10/21/1875	Grubb, Daniel		Mary Hess
8/23/1853	Guyer, John		Mary Ann Snyder, Union Tp.

11/16/1847	Hackenberg, Jacob	Center Tp.	Hannah Krick, Beaver Tp.
11/28/1858	" Albert		Maria Brouse
6/2/1853	Hackman, Samuel		Lovina Kayes
2/25/1845	Hafflich, Jacob		Judith Wolf, Center Tp.
11/8/1849	Hanks, William	Union Co.	Sarah Eilert, Mifflinburg, Pa.
3/4/1853	Hane, John		Harriet Brouse (dau. of Andrew)
3/24/1861	Hanes, Daniel	Union Co.	Margaret Leibensferger, Bucks Co.
7/11/1848	Harter, Samuel	Ohio	Catherine Mertz, Middleburg, Pa.
2/9/1840	Hartman, George		Polly Bickart
10/18/1855	Hassinger, David		Louise Kinney, Middlecreek Tp.
5/12/1867	" Allen		Margaret Stroh, "
10/22/1868	Hassenplug, Samuel	Mifflinburg, Pa.	Anna Frederick, Mifflinburg, Pa.
3/5/1854	Heck, John		Jane Walters, Northumberland, Pa.
10/15/1850	Heimbach, Jacob		Lydia Weil, Union Co.
9/16/1866	" Elias	Union Co.	Amelia Ritter(Witter?), Jackson Tp.
3/22/1881	" Frank B.		Rebecca Lessman
3/21/1854	Heiser, Samuel		Mary Magd. Wagner, Penn Tp.
3/28/1847	Hendricks, Jacob	Hartley Tp.	Mabel Krebs, West Beaver Tp.
10/1/1848	" Samuel		Emily Charles(Charteris?)N.Berlin,Pa.
1/24/1861	" Hiram		Mary E. Kessler, Penn Tp.
10/14/1866	Herbster, Jeremiah		Barbara Oldt, West Beaver Tp.
8/19/1855	Herman, Jacob		Mary Slear, Penn Tp.
3/11/1860	" Phares		Margaret Klingler, Penn Tp.
12/24/1857	" George		Elizabeth Kline
5/27/1860	" Frederick		" Brouse, Penn Tp.
12/24/1863	" Joseph		Hetty A. Leitzel, "
1/14/1864	" Michael	Penn Tp.	Mary J. Klingler, Jackson Tp.
9/4/1864	" Peter	"	Catherine Ann Bengor, "
1/2/1876	Harrold, Simon I.	-45-	Barbara Leitzel, Middlecreek Tp.

Date	Name	Place	Spouse
8/17/1845	Hoch, John		Sophia Arnold, Center Tp.
10/28/1851	Hoffman, Charles		Magdalene Mathias, Penn Tp.
9/6/1853	Hollenbach, Samuel	Union Co.	Sarah E. Slear, Union Tp.
3/29/1855	" Joseph	Penn Tp.	Rebecca Kline, Jackson Tp.
11/9/1847	Hoover, David	Mifflin Co.	Susan Price, West Beaver Tp.
1/13/1861	Hottenstein, Benjamin	West Beaver Tp.	Anna Krouse, Middlecreek Tp.
3/4/1852	Houtz, Henry C.		Harriet Boop, New Berlin Pa.
8/9/1849	Hess, Thomas		Elmira Marshall, Union Co.
7/18/1859	" "	Union Co.	Catherine Brown, "
6/11/1871	" William	Union Tp.	Catherine Hummel, Monroe Tp.
12/27/1843	Huffnagle, Abraham		Elizabeth Bingaman, Musser Valley
12/1/1853	Hummel, William		Margaret Long, Union Tp.
2/15/1855	" Jonathan		Elizabeth Slear, "
1/11/1859	" Aaron		" Laundenslager
1/11/1859	" Frederic		Elsie Conley, Monroe Tp.
6/9/1859	" Conrad	Middlecreek Tp.	Magdalene Benfer, Jackson Tp.
12/4/1862	" Frank		Mary Slear, Union Tp.
6/20/1878	" Charles L.		Sarah C. Smith
11/27/1864	" Solomon		Nancy Leitzel, Middlecreek Tp.
10/17/1867	" Benjamin	Monroe Tp.	Amanda Conley, Monroe Tp.
3/23/1869	" "	Buffalo Tp.	Maria Reish, Center Tp.
5/12/1872	" Cyrus B.		Anna Trutt
3/22/1853	Hyman, L. M.	Loyalsock Tp.	Anna Miller, New Berlin, Pa.
3/22/1855	Jarrett, Daniel		Lovina Bassler, Penn Tp.
11/4/1852	Kennell, Joseph		Lydia Zechman, Union Tp.
11/13/1842	Kern, George	Beaver Tp.	Maria M. Fetterolf, Beaver Tp.
1/1/1856	Kessler, Louis		Catherine Roshong, New Berlin, Pa.
7/11/1874	" John		Louise Catherman
5/18/1840	Kinney, Henry		Eliza Eisenhauer
1/27/1842	Kleckner, Isaac		Anna Haines
1/10/1851	" Charles		Harriet A. Orwig
9/4/1851	" Solomon	Hartley Tp.	Catherine Swarm, Union Tp.
4/7/1853	Kline, Samuel	Penn Tp.	Mary Maurer, Union Tp.
4/9/1854	" George	Mifflinburg, Pa.	Caroline Benfer, Union Tp.
11/22/1855	" Joseph	Jackson Tp.	Sarah Brouse "
2/19/1857	" "	Middlecreek Tp.	Mary Ann Pawling, Penn Tp.
8/26/1858	" Solomon		Lydia Brouse, Jackson Tp.
2/13/1859	" Henry		Eve Leitzel, "
5/26/1864	" Josiah		Susan Moyer, Beaver Tp.
11/14/1844	Klingler, Elias	New Berlin, Pa.	Sarah " Union Tp.
11/4/1852	" Jacob	Penn Tp.	Amelia Walter "
2/21/1856	" Enos	"	Elizabeth Oldt, Jackson Tp.
1/21/1858	" Benjamin		Sarah Herman, Penn Tp.
8/23/1860	" Peter	Penn Tp.	Catherine Ritter, Monroe Tp.
2/25/1866	" Nathan	"	Sarah Kline, Jackson Tp.
12/20/1868	" Peter	Center Tp.	Mary Jane Koon, Center Tp.
3/30/1848	Klose, Isaac		Elizabeth Hassinger, Beaver Tp.
9/21/1847	Knepp, Isaac		Anna Peters, West Beaver Tp.
3/3/1863	Knouse, Samuel		Mary Brouse, Jackson Tp.
8/25/1872	" Jacob		Leah Cochran
9/10/1857	Koser, Levi	Buffalo Tp.	Catherine Musser, Snyder Co.
7/10/1853	Kratzer, Louis		Harriet Stettler, Penn Tp.
9/28/1854	" Joseph	Penn Tp.	Catherine Leiby, Jackson Tp.
10/6/1864	" Franklin		Susan Kratzer, Jackson Tp.
12/29/1867	" Benjamin		Eva Kline
5/10/1868	" Jacob	Jackson Tp.	Mary Ann Walter, Jackson Tp.
10/4/1874	" W. W.		Barbara Boney
2/1/1880	Krebs, James		Laura A. Pierce

4/11/1869	Krick, William	Buffalo Tp.	Mahala Edman, New Berlin, Pa.
3/31/1871	" Peter		Christine Edman
8/25/1872	" Henry		Rachael Young
11/26/1857	Krouse, Abraham		Diana Brouse
12/7/1858	" Daniel	Kelly Tp.	Catherine Frederick, Buffalo Tp.
4/21/1859	" Peter	Middlecreek Tp.	Elizabeth Leitsel, Jackson Tp.
3/23/1846	Kunkle, George		Maria Moyer, Union Tp.
11/30/1852	" Adam		Catherine Bogar, "
12/14/1856	" John		Mary Ann Fass "
6/5/1862	" John		Maria Maurer, Jackson Tp.
12/6/1840	Kuns, Daniel	Ohio	Rachael Pennichoff, Union Co.
4/27/1873	Leader, John		Harriet Wittenmayer
2/23/1868	Lee, Robert		Mary Ann Wehr
2/1/1842	Leibig, John		Catherine Weil
2/15/1844	Leiby, David	Union Tp.	Elisabeth Mayer, Kelly Tp.
1/6/1846	" Jacob		Lovina Weil
12/15/1859	Leitner, Samuel		Anna Haslot, Limestone Tp.
11/21/1854	Lepley, Isaac	Union Tp.	Elisabeth Trutt, Penn Tp.
10/13/1853	Lloyd, William		Sarah Ann Conley, Union Tp.
11/24/1859	Long, John D.	Union	Mary C. Eisenhauer
1/4/1853	" Lincoln		Mary C. Young
10/31/1854	" Frany	Franklin Tp.	Mrs. Mary Sasseman, Limestone Tp.
2/1/1855	" John	Center Tp.	Charlotte Altor, Mifflinburg, Pa.
5/3/1856	" William		Mary Doebler, New Berlin, Pa.
9/15/1859	" Henry		Elisabeth Yerger, Center Tp.
3/19/1854	Loose, William		Sarah Bonfer
9/2/1852	Luck, Jeremiah		" Hummel
3/21/1861	Maize, John	Union Tp.	Caroline Ritter, Jackson Tp.
10/13/1864	Manbeck, P. L.		Lucy Long, Beaver Springs, Pa.
8/23/1860	Markley, William		" Ann Sabyman, BeaverSprings,Pa.
4/3/1855	Maurer, Conrad		Sarah E. Pontius, Jackson Tp.
2/22/1857	" Charles		Magdalene Ulrich, Union Tp.
1/21/1858	" Peter		Mary Ann Snyder, Jackson Tp.
11/4/1858	" Daniel	Beaver Tp.	Susan Moyer, Union Tp.
5/22/1882	" Henry		CatherineHafflich, Beaver Tp.
2/23/1875	" Charles		Elisabeth Engle
6/19/1868	" Jacob		Christina Benfer, Union Tp.
5/4/1841	" John		Margaret Benfer
2/6/1844	" Samuel		Mary Ann Klingler, Penn Tp.
11/7/1844	" Isaac		Maria Pontius
1/16/1845	" Jacob		Catherine Smith
5/7/1850	" Henry	New Berlin, Pa.	Sarah E. Benfor, Union Tp.
12/5/1850	" Daniel		Hetty Erdly
12/12/1851	" Andrew		Lovina Cherry, Limestone Tp.
6/5/1842	Matter, Samuel		Elizabeth Fidler, Mifflin Co.
11/14/1854	Mason, Samuel B.		Mary Ann Shirk
2/27/1851	McCullough, Hugh		Ellen Kessler
6/30/1853	McVey, Dr. George M.		Margaret Ruffnagle, Middleburg, Pa.
10/19/1845	Mertz, John		Nancy Bonfer, Union Co.
2/25/1858	Metzger, Peter		Susan " "
5/20/1875	Miller, Philip D.		Mary Heimbach, Buffalo Tp.
11/8/1864	" Jacob D.		Mary Ann Britor, Limestone Tp.
1/1/1861	" John S.		Christine Moll, Mifflinburg, Pa.
9/11/1851	Millhoff, Benjamin		Margaret Merts
12/13/1842	Millhouse, Nicholas	New Berlin, Pa.	Lydia Neiman, New Berlin, Pa.
3/27/1860	" Daniel		Agnes Bilger, Mifflinburg, Pa.
3/29/1868	Mitchell, David		Esther Courtney, New Berlin, Pa.
2/25/1857	" Levi		Mary Gill, Center Tp.
10/13/1864	Mock, Franklin		Susan Conley, Monroe Tp.

Date	Groom	Residence	Bride
2/1/1857	Moyer, Samuel		Margaret Brown, Union Tp.
2/9/1860	" Henry		Harriet Bollender
2/29/1844	" Michael	Union Tp.	Catherine Berge, Union Tp.
1/11/1849	" John		Elizabeth Hummel
10/19/1852	" David	Buffalo Tp.	" Dubs, Union Tp.
2/11/1857	Musser, Samuel		Catherine Musser
6/9/1878	" Adam		Susan Cochran
4/30/1841	Neiman, Peter	Center Tp.	Catherine Snyder, Union Tp.
12/11/1851	" Henry		Magdalene Stock, Middlecreek Tp.
1/4/1870	" "	Kansas	Maria Hummel "
9/10/1841	Noecker, George		Catherine Orwig, Mifflinburg, Pa.
10/23/1851	Noll, John		Hannah Ritter, Union Co.
10/26/1841	Norman, John		Elizabeth Snook
6/17/1847	" Henry		Maria Kreisher
10/16/1859	Ocker, David	West Beaver Tp.	Sarah E. Maurer
11/16/1852	" William	Beaver Tp.	Catherine Spangler, Limestone Tp.
11/3/1846	Oldt, Daniel		Sarah Benfer
10/7/1855	" Reuben	New Berlin, Pa.	Amelia Bollender, Jackson Tp.
3/13/1856	" Zeno		Elizabeth Benfer, Jackson Tp.
12/12/1861	" John		Sarah E. Maurer, Limestone Tp.
10/18/1846	Peter, John	West Beaver Tp.	Elizabeth Steininger, Mifflin Co.
11/20/1846	Platt, Isaac		Susan Forger
8/4/1846	Pontius, Henry		Rebecca Mitchell
9/25/1852	" John N.		Sarah Dreisbach, Mifflinburg, Pa.
9/13/1860	Rauch, Martin T.	East Buffalo Tp.	Mary Ann Leader, West Buffalo Tp.
10/25/1859	Raudenbush, Benjamin	Schuylkill Co.	Elizabeth Wetzel, Middlecreek Tp.
2/19/1848	Reich, Frederick	Middlecreek Tp.	Sarah Breininger, Middlecreek, Pa.
12/30/1879	Reichley, William G.		Mary E. Trutt
3/15/1846	Reichner, John		Hannah Bechtel, Middleburg, Pa.
12/31/1876	Reigle, William	Adams Tp.	Mary Maurer, Adams Tp.
12/16/1845	" Frederick		Mary Ann Weil
12/12/1880	" Albert		Emma Hummel
3/1/1840	Reim, Joseph	Union Co.	Maria Schoch, Union Co.
4/18/1868	Reitmire, George		Harriet Shiffer, New Berlin, Pa.
4/1/1869	Remmell, Charles	New Berlin, Pa.	Anna Black, New Berlin, Pa.
12/31/1844	Renninger, Elias	West Beaver Tp.	Sarah Snook, West Beaver Tp.
7/26/1868	Rishel, John		Mary C. Spitler, New Berlin, Pa.
5/29/1856	Ritzman, Jacob		Amanda Neiman, Middlecreek Tp.
10/25/1846	Romig, Jacob		Lydia Pontius
9/5/1848	Rothermel, Amos		Anna Maurer, Middleburg, Pa.
9/17/1857	Row, John		Jane E. Winegardnor
1/28/1858	" Daniel	Union Tp.	Mary J. Loose, Limestone Tp.
7/3/1859	" George W.	Penn Tp.	Lydia Brouse, Jackson Tp.
8/14/1862	" William		Amanda Catherman
1/1/1863	" George		Diana Fetzer, Northumberland Co.
11/--/1841	Royer, -----		----- Shoemaker
10/23/1859	Sampsell, William		Sarah Kline, Center Tp.
11/14/1850	Sanders, Jacob		Hetty Miller
8/26/1847	Sassaman, Henry		Mary Borger, Union Tp.
9/6/1849	" Daniel		Eva Klingler, "
11/15/1864	" Jonas		Mary Jane Bertch, Monroe Tp.
12/4/1873	" Abraham		Elmira Soebold
3/29/1880	" Henry A.		Ann Bower
6/6/1880	Sauers, James		Christiana Oberlin
4/3/1839	Scheurer, Rev. Peter		Martha Johnson
2/10/1842	Schrack, John		Catherine Dunkle
4/25/1848	Schroyer, Henry		Maria Steininger, Mifflin Co.

MARRIAGES OF REV. A. B. CASPER, 1839-1882, Snyder and Union Counties, Pa.

Date	Groom	Residence	Bride
10/19/1854	Seebold, Christopher		Catherine Miller, Jackson Tp.
2/22/1860	" George E.		" Crossgorve, Limestone Tp.
7/8/1871	Seiffert, J.		——Musser
10/11/1843	Shambach, David	Center Tp.	Catherine Stahlnecker, Center Tp.
3/9/1846	" George	"	" Mover "
8/13/1848	Shamory, Israel		Caroline Long, Musser Valley
8/29/1852	" Jacob	Center Tp.	Mary Straub, Middlecreek Tp.
5/19/1859	Shannon, William	Union Tp.	Lucinda Zechman, New Berlin, Pa.
9/4/1873	" Joseph		Mrs. Elizabeth Super
1/31/1361	Shirk, Benjamin M.		Elizabeth Young, Center Tp.
12/25/1859	Shrader, John		" Trutt, Union Tp.
3/29/1855	Showers, Daniel	Center Tp.	Elizabeth Herts, New Berlin Pa.
5/19/1864	Shuman, James M.	Franklin Tp.	Mametta Bowersox, Center Tp.
11/11/1847	Shunkweiler, Daniel		Susan Miller
8/2/1850	Silberwood, Mathias		Mary McPherson, Union Tp.
10/27/1841	Smith, Aaron		Elizabeth Snook
7/13/1843	" Edward	New Berlin, Pa.	Emily Lehman, Mifflinburg, Pa.
12/7/1845	" John	Center Tp.	Elizabeth Troxel, Troxelville, Pa.
3/25/1847	" Daniel		Mary Saltzman, Beaver Springs, Pa.
1/30/1848	" Robert		Eliza Wittenmeyer, Middleburg, Pa.
1/4/1849	" Aaron		Sophia Stump, West Beaver
9/25/1851	" Spyker	Buffalo Tp.	Emily Benfer, Union Tp.
8/25/1853	" George		Susan Gross
4/14/1847	" Joseph		Rebecca Price, West Beaver Tp.
6/22/1862	" John	Jackson Tp.	Emma L. Wehr, West Buffalo Tp.
1/4/1870	" Robert		Mary Ann Dauberman
4/16/1874	" Henry H.		Barbara Ann Dorr
1/11/1880	" Jerome		Emma De Long
11/9/1845	Snook, Henry		Maria Bishop, Center Tp.
12/12/1847	Snyder, Absalon		Catherine Troxel
8/6/1854	" Jacob K.	Middlecreek Tp.	Martha Dauberman, Middlecreek Tp.
12/23/1859	" George W.		Catherine Wehr, Jackson Tp.
9/3/1860	Solomon, Benjamin F.		Susan Beaver, Monroe Tp.
6/9/1846	" John C.		Elizabeth Knauff (Knause?)
5/12/1853	Spade (Spaide), Isaac		Harriet Neiman
10/22/1837	" Robert	Mifflinburg, Pa.	Sarah Smith
12/18/1863	Spangler, Louis		Ann Leitner, Limestone Tp.
11/17/1864	" George		Jane " "
4/9/1843	Spigelmire, Jacob	Beaver Tp.	Leah Knepp, Beaver Tp.
12/25/1879	Stahl, Frederick		Elizabeth Dork
3/15/1853	" Philip	Buffalo Tp.	Rebecca Dubs, Union Tp.
11/29/1868	St. Clair, Samuel H.	Monroe Tp.	Jane Sandors, Monroe Tp.
8/24/1843	Steese, Carl	West Beaver Tp.	Barbara Smith, Middleburg, Pa.
6/18/1837	Stettler, Elias	Union Tp.	Susan Jarrett, Monroe Tp.
1/8/1857	" Valentine	"	Catherine A. Reichley, Monroe Tp.
12/31/1850	" Isaac		Sarah Brouse
12/1/1853	" Noah	"	Elizabeth Jarrett, Penn Tp.
2/23/1860	" John		Mahala Shannon, Union Tp.
1/1/1861	" Jacob	Union Tp.	Amanda Miller, Selinsgrove, Pa.
11/17/1859	Stocker, Mathias	"	Mary Ann Pontius, Jackson Tp.
3/31/1860	Straub, Samuel	Washington Tp.	Sophia Lenver, Center Tp.
7/16/1865	" Charles		Malinda Krouse
6/9/1867	" George P.		Mary Ann Woodling, Middlecreek Tp.
5/29/1842	Strouse, Daniel	Beaver Tp.	Louise Ann Ruffnagle, Beaver Tp.
8/12/1845	Stump, Samuel		Maria M. Krebs, West Beaver Tp.
10/21/1845	" Joseph		Sophia Ulsh "
4/29/1847	" John		Sarah Oldt
12/6/1860	Super, Andrew T.		Elizabeth Conley, Monroe Tp.
1/16/1362	" William		Sophia Sassaman, Monroe Tp.
1/27/1857	Swarm, Isaac		Susan Frock
12/8/1844	Swartz, Elias	Beaver Tp.	Maria C. Bingaman, Beaver Tp.
3/15/1846	Swengle, David	—49—	" Bogar, Middleburg, Pa.

12/17/1843	Swenk, William		Catherine Mitchell
1/15/1849	" "	Mifflinburg, Pa.	Eliza Rinehart, Center Tp.
10/2/1849	" Hiram		Emily Lauter, "
3/1/1842	Thomas, George	Beaver Tp.	Magdalene Mick, Beaver Tp.
12/17/1843	" Peter	"	Mary Arnold "
1/30/1863	" Charles		Elizabeth Ramer, Union Co.
3/10/1864	" Peter		Amanda Kratzer, Beaver Tp.
10/28/1856	Troxel, Samuel		Susan Heinly, Mifflin Co.
3/12/1854	Trutt, Daniel R.	Union Tp.	Elizabeth Kratzer, Penn Tp.
11/15/1867	" Jacob		Rebecca Sassaman, Monroe Tp.
10/9/1862	Updegrove, Daniel	Lycoming Co.	Sarah Ann Culp, Union Co.
10/3/1865	Ulsh, Joseph		Catherine Gross, Beaver Tp.
10/5/1871	" Alvin		Amanda Reigle,
11/15/1853	Ulrich, Henry	Jackson Tp.	Hetty Beaver, Union Tp.
11/18/1869	" James		Margaret Fiss, Northumberland, Pa.
3/3/1839	Van Orsdahl, Samuel		Lydia Heiges
6/1/1865	Walker, Henry		Laura J. Hunt, New Berlin, Pa.
5/3/1840	Walter, John		———— Snook
3/2/1845	" Frederick		Harriet Shannon
6/11/1848	" Daniel		Catherine Hackenberg, Beaver Tp.
1/6/1850	" William		Mary Ann Noll, Union Co.
3/9/1852	" Elias		Hannah Moyer, Union Tp.
12/23/1852	" Jesse		Rachael Long
9/16/1858	" Reuben D.		Mary Ellen Straub, Middlecreek Tp.
10/16/1870	" Isaac	Franklin Tp.	Maria Bowersox, Franklin Tp.
11/11/1852	Weaver, Bernard	Limestone Tp.	Elizabeth Hummel, Union Tp.
3/9/1848	Wehr, George		Magdalene Faust, "
5/31/1841	Weirick, Samuel		Mary Ann Seebold
1868	Werlin, J. W.	Center Tp.	Emily DeLong, Center Tp.
10/28/1848	Wetzel, Harrison		———— Duck (Dock)
6/18/1848	Wittenmeyer, Samuel	Middleburg, Pa.	Catherine Glass, Freeburg, Pa.
2/24/1842	Wittes, Isaac	Center Tp.	Ann Betzer, Center Tp.
2/19/1852	Wolf, Charles	New Berlin, Pa.	Catherine Miller, Limestone Tp.
3/1/1833	" Samuel	East Buffalo	Sabilla Engle, Union Tp.
12/13/1865	Wolfinger, Samuel		Agnes Wolf, Union Co.
1/11/1857	Yeager, John		Hannah Boyer, New Berlin, Pa.
12/31/1850	Young, Noah		Margaret Dewire
12/25/1856	" Peter		Nancy Winegardner, Union Tp.
4/28/1859	" George		Margaret Snook, Center Tp.
10/22/1859	" Israel	Center Tp.	Amanda Ewig, Beaver Tp.
10/31/1847	Yount, Michael		Mary Ann Albert, Selinsgrove, Pa.
1/1/1873	Yost, William		Isabelle Ettinger
10/3/1861	Zartman, Henry		Mary Stettler, Union Tp.
7/27/1851	Zechman, Simon		Emily Bilger, Middleburg, Pa.
8/22/1850	Zeiber, Joseph	Middlecreek Tp.	Sarah Bowersox, Center Tp.

Date	Groom		Location	Bride
11/18/1851	Acaly, Wm. B.		Mifflin Co.	Anna Lehr, Perry Co.
10/4/1855	Adams, Samuel			Elizabeth Doebler, North'd. Co.
1/3/1850	"	William	Penn Twp.	Caroline Jarrett, Penn Twp.
2/13/1872	Adie, Horace			Julia Ann Wasser, Lewisburg, Pa.
3/5/1855	Albright, Daniel			Louise Schnee, Freeburg, Pa.
5/23/1852	Allman, Adam			Louise Lawver
12/1/1857	Amig, Lewis			Julia Ann Lawver
8/8/1843	Anderson, Elias			Catherine Bordner
3/14/1843	Anspach, Rev. J. G.		Mifflinburg, Pa.	Susan Schoch
12/3/1848	Arbogast, John		Wash. Twp.	Hettie Roush, Washington Twp.
10/7/1849	"	Ludwig	Freeburg, Pa.	Mrs. Anna M. Boyer
10/3/1851	"	William		Sarah J. Cluck, Perry Twp.
11/18/1852	"	Peter P.		Sarah Holtzapple, Washington TP.
7/14/1853	"	Jacob	Perry Tp.	Catherine Shrader, Perry Tp.
10/19/1854	"	Joseph		Elisabeth Steimling, "
1/25/1855	"	David		Catherine Holtzapple, Wash. Tp.
6/14/1855	"	Jacob		Mary Ann Lahr
9/4/1855	"	Fred	Perry Tp.	Sarah Mitterling, Perry Tp.
8/3/1856	"	Philip		Sophia Spade "
7/29/1858	"	Levi	Perry Tp.	Catherine Hoot, Chapman Tp.
12/16/1858	"	Israel		Mrs. Angelina Spade, Perry Tp.
8/11/1859	"	Jacob		Abbie Roush, Washington Tp.
3/21/1861	"	John		Barbara Rine
9/26/1861	"	Philip	Perry Tp.	Sarah Angstadt, Washington Tp.
6/18/1863	"	Abraham		" Garman "
11/22/1863	"	Nathan		Phrene Stepp, Perry Tp.
4/10/1870	"	Ner		Amelia Smithe "
7/21/1870	"	Johathan B.		Julia Ann Reigle, Freeburg, Pa.
5/19/1872	"	J. D.		Susan Garman, Fremont, Pa.
9/1/1872	"	Gustavus	Perry Tp.	Sarah Yeager, Perry Tp.
2/27/1874	"	John	Wash. Tp.	Amanda J. Kants, Washington Tp.
5/23/1875	"	Henry	"	Emma Kants, Penn Tp.
10/31/1875	"	Simon		Sallie Hoffman, Perry Tp.
6/8/1852	Arker, Jonas			Elizabeth Dougherty, Lycoming Co.
10/7/1869	App, Solomon		Monroe Tp.	Sevilla Gemberling, Penn Tp.
10/19/1841	Arnold, Philip			Elizabeth Winkleman
5/18/1845	"	Peter	Chapman Tp.	Mary Ann Shaffer, Chapman Tp.
1/22/1846	"	Augustus	"	Leah Rine, Chapman Tp.
2/15/1859	"	Joseph P.		Mary Ann Fisher, NorthumberlandCo.
11/23/1871	"	Henry K.	Juniata Co.	Emma Reamer, Juniata Co.
6/30/1850	Apple, Philip		Wash. Tp.	Rebecca Himes, Washington Tp.
9/30/1852	"	Benjamin	"	Mary Ann Angstadt, "
1/15/1856	"	"		Martha Graybill, Juniata Co.
7/2/1846	Auchmuty, James		Penn Tp.	Lucy Ann Strawser, Penn Tp.
11/9/1854	"	"		" " Steffen, "
4/2/1840	Aucker, Joseph			Mary Kepner
12/19/1850	"	John S.	Perry Tp.	" Lauver, Perry Tp.
6/24/1869	"	Emanuel		Maggie Weipert, Perry Tp.
11/16/1856	"	Henry		Anna Shotzberger
2/13/1862	"	"	Perry Tp.	Elizabeth Leitzel, Jackson Tp.
1/20/1850	Ammiller, Daniel		Penn Tp.	Catherine Mull, Penn Tp.
12/30/1858	"	Jacob		Melinda Kremer, Middlecreek Tp.
1/12/1860	"	David		Leah Aurand "
4/30/1850	Aurand, Lewis		Penn Tp.	Elizabeth Ammiller, Penn Tp.
12/20/1855	"	Henry S.		Catherine Kinney, Middlecreek Tp.
12/28/1856	"	"		Maria Hoffman, Monroe Tp.
5/24/1863	"	John		Sarah Row, Penn Tp.
7/18/1840	Baabs, Michael		Halifax, Pa.	Susan Taylor, Halifax, Pa.
2/11/1840	Bachms, Jacob			Elizabeth Wagner

2/21/1865	Bachman, Frederick		Mary Bingaman, Beaver Tp.
6/17/1849	Bailey, Elias	Penn Tp.	Mary Ann Swartz, Washington Tp.
3/26/1854	Baker, George	Selinsgrove, Pa.	Mrs.MaryCath.Heim,Selinsgrove,Pa.
7/13/1862	Baney, Daniel		Amanda Dunkelberger,MiddlecreekTp.
12/6/1847	Barner, George	Juniata Co.	Catherine Arnold, Chapman Tp
12/16/1866	" " W.		Fianna Heiges, Perry Tp.
4/22/1852	Basom, Tobias	Richfield, Pa.	Caroline Van Ormer, Richfield, Pa.
4/20/1848	Batdorf, David	Freeburg, Pa.	Eliza Boyer, Freeburg, Pa.
5/19/1869	" "		Elizabeth Arnold, Chapman Tp.
9/8/1870	" George	Freeburg, Pa.	Mary Ann Goy, Freeburg, Pa.
1/9/1844	Baum, Henry		Sarah Froyer, Chapman Tp.
12/27/1853	Beachol, Jackson	Union Co.	Hetty Kantz, Penn Tp.
4/9/1854	Bear, George	Center Tp.	Susan Weller, Washington Tp.
8/19/1841	" Jacob		Sarah Rhoads
7/5/1840	Beaver, ——		Mary Shipe
3/1/1868	" Michael		Alice Hoffman, Monroe Tp.
12/19/1872	Becker, Augustus Z.	Berks Co.	Barbara E. Boyer, Perry Tp.
9/29/1860	Bender, Jacob	Perry Tp.	Mary E. Bettylon, NorthumberlandCo
11/15/1863	" John		B. Amelia Herrold, Chapman Tp.
12/26/1861	Benfer, Daniel		Cath. Marg. Pontius, Jackson Tp.
12/2/1869	" Jacob		Mrs.ChristianaBolig,MiddlecreekTp.
3/13/1873	" Joseph	Jackson Tp.	Margaret Leitzel, Jackson Tp.
2/1/1874	" Emanuel	"	Rebecca " "
5/8/1844	Benner, Samuel		Elizabeth Shadow
1/4/1846	" Daniel	Washington Tp.	Mary Lenig, Washington Tp.
10/18/1846	" Fester	"	Susan Wayne, "
6/15/1871	" Christian		CarrisGingrich,McAllisterville,Pa.
11/12/1873	" Jacob	Juniata Co.	Barbara Snyder, West Perry Tp.
5/19/1840	Bertch, Jacob		Elizabeth Moyer
10/12/1856	" William	Freeburg, Pa.	Mary Somers, Middlecreek Tp.
3/5/1848	Bickel, John	Chapman Tp.	Harriet Philips, Chapman Tp.
4/28/1858	" Philip	Freeburg, Pa.	Sarah J. Haas, Freeburg, Pa.
10/30/1875	" Charles	Penn Tp.	Agnes Donmeyer, Franklin Tp.
12/30/1875	" W. H.	Middlecreek Tp.	Mary E. Ritter, Jackson Tp.
11/18/1852	Bickhart, Henry		Adeline Herrold, Chapman Tp.
10/5/1858	" Benjamin		Elizabeth Bender, Perry Tp.
6/9/1859	" Emanuel		Hattie Thomas, Center Co.
3/17/1861	" Samuel		Sarah Steffen, Washington Tp.
10/14/1866	" Jonas		Harriot Wetsel
2/12/1850	Bidelspach, Isaac		Mary A. Hummel, Penn Tp.
1/14/1851	Biehl, James	Buffalo Tp.	Rebecca Pawling, Penn Tp.
10/28/1851	Bilger, Henry		Catherine Hoff
12/28/1854	" Frank		Anna Maria Schuman, Center Tp.
10/2/1870	" Howard		Catherine Hummel, Middlecreek Tp.
12/1/1873	" Enoch		Janetta Roush, Washington Tp.
11/24/1874	" Joel	Middleburg, Pa.	Mrs. Margaret Bitting,Liverpool,Pa.
1/11/1844	Bingaman, Frederick		Susan Swartz, Beaver Tp.
8/3/1845	" "	Center Tp.	" Houts, Center Tp.
3/31/1872	Bitner, Adam		Rebecca Sholly, Union Tp.
2/21/1843	Bitting, Joshua	Union Co.	Ann Kreisher, Union Co.
11/18/1847	" William		Eliza Loss
7/6/1873	Bittinger, David		Emma Arbogast, Freeburg, Pa.
1/20/1841	Black, Joseph		Mary Strawbridge
12/25/1859	Bobb, Benneville		Eliza Roush, Washington Tp.
5/30/1857	Bogar, Jacob		Sarah Witmer, Port Trevorton, Pa.
12/16/1845	Bolig, Henry		Mary A. Herrold
11/28/1858	" Benj. F.	Selinsgrove, Pa.	Harriet Ulrich, Selinsgrove, Pa.
6/5/1875	" Amos	Middlecreek Tp.	Amanda Wagner, Middlecreek Tp.
1/13/1842	Bonsall, Jesse	Greenwood Tp.	Margaret Smith, Greenwood Tp.
8/24/1865	Bopp, Frank		Amelia Kramer, Middlecreek Tp.

Date	Name	Place	Spouse
10/25/1855	Botteiger, James		Polly Arbogast, Perry Tp.
10/15/1857	" Johathan	Perry Tp.	Mary Ann Bender, "
10/28/1858	Bollender, Jacob		Susan Naugle, Washington Tp.
12/21/1856	Bowersox, Andrew		Polly Rine, Perry Tp.
10/11/1863	" Jackson		Elizabeth Smith, Franklin Tp.
12/11/1870	" A. W.	Middleburg, Pa.	Violetta Stauffer, Selinsgrove,Pa.
10/11/1874	" Maxwell	Franklin Tp.	Catherine Walter, Franklin Tp.
3/21/1843	Boyer, Harry	Freeburg, Pa.	Rebecca Reel, Dauphin Co.
10/12/1843	" Elias		Mary Ann Wittenmeyer
5/20/1845	" Samuel	Penn Tp.	Sophia Boyer, Penn Tp.
4/28/1846	" Franklin	"	Eliza Arnold, "
2/6/1849	" Henry		Mary Wagenseller, Selinsgrove, Pa.
2/13/1849	" John	Freeburg, Pa.	Hannah Kantz, Penn Tp.
10/19/1851	" Emanuel	Penn Tp.	Phoebe Ann Boyer, Penn Tp.
12/8/1853	" David	Freeburg, Pa.	Catherine Frederick, Freeburg, Pa.
6/8/1854	" Henry	"	Amelia Glass "
11/30/1854	" Henry S.		Sarah " "
1/11/1855	" Samuel	Perry Tp.	" Rine, Perry Tp.
8/23/1855	" Henry		" Luck, Penn Tp.
11/30/1856	" Philip	Freeburg, Pa.	" Roush, Freeburg, Pa.
12/31/1857	" Henry		Catherine Rine
4/13/1858	" Charles		Polly Rathfon, Perry Tp.
5/12/1861	" William		" Arbogast, "
1/15/1863	" "	Penn Tp.	Catherine Row, Penn Tp.
12/11/1864	" Francis		Weathy Erdly, Penn Tp.
12/15/1864	" David		Mary Diemer, Washington Tp.
2/22/1866	" Edward K.		Louisa Kantz, Penn Tp.
12/23/1866	" William		Sarah Weiss, Penn Tp.
3/17/1868	" Daniel		Mrs. Sarah Bollender, Washington Tp.
10/5/1869	" Edward		Emeline Garman, Washington Tp.
8/28/1870	" Daniel	Penn Tp.	Anna Reed, Penn Tp.
6/8/1871	" Charles H.	Selinsgrove, Pa.	Amelia Lechner, Selinsgrove, Pa.
12/—/1871	" Fred I.	Freeburg, Pa.	Mollie Fessler, Center Tp.
10/13/1872	" Reuben	Penn Tp.	Cyrene Walter, Center Tp.
12/22/1872	" Henry C.	Washington Tp.	Carrie Wise, Port Trevorton, Pa.
12/25/1873	" Francis S.		Agnes Roush, Freeburg, Pa.
1/10/1875	" " D.	Washington Tp.	Elizabeth Benfer, Middlecreek Tp.
1/2/1868	Bratton, Reuben	Mifflin Co.	Ellen Hosterman, Freeburg, Pa.
11/25/1852	Breon, David	Union Co.	Eliza Bilger, Union Co.
12/21/1873	" Henry		Sarah Spangler, Jackson Tp.
4/16/1868	Bressler, George	Perry Tp.	Susan Ancker, Perry Tp.
12/23/1852	Bretz, Abraham	Selinsgrove, Pa.	Mary Shaffer, Selinsgrove, Pa.
11/6/1840	Brink, Daniel	Liverpool, Pa.	Ann Henry, Liverpool, Pa.
7/26/1845	Brosius, Benjamin	Penn Tp.	Sarah A. Showalter, Penn Tp.
9/11/1870	" George F.	Perry Tp.	Emma Schnee, Perry Tp.
1/1/1871	" William		Martha Wagner, West Beaver Tp.
12/15/1872	" George F.	Perry Tp.	Mary Schnee, Perry Tp.
4/7/1870	Brouse, William		Rebecca Hollenbach, Jackson Tp.
5/27/1866	Brown, Edward		Mary Benfer, Penn Tp.
8/14/1870	" U. Henry	Progress, Pa.	Sarah Weaver, Freeburg, Pa.
3/18/1847	Brubaker, Davis		Susan Shettorly
11/18/1851	Brugger, Rudolph		Sophia Moyer, Center Tp.
6/19/1855	Bryan, Abraham O.	Mifflinburg, Pa.	Mary Harter, Perry Co.
10/10/1875	Bubb, Reuben		Emma Kreigbaum
1/5/1841	Buchanan, Daniel		Sarah Kepner
1/1/1852	Burkhart, Joseph B.		Margaret Law
10/23/1849	Burkwalter, John	Chapman Tp.	Mary Stricker, Chapman Tp.
1/24/1850	Bussler, Jacob	Washington Tp.	Lucetta Roush, Washington Tp.
11/28/1858	Burns, Isaac	Selinsgrove, Pa.	Mary Ann Kantz, Penn Tp.
2/22/1849	Byerly, Peter	Selinsgrove, Pa.	Sarah Hartman, Penn Tp.
10/24/1841	Byrum, William		Sarah Willis

Date	Name	Place	Spouse
2/10/1842	Camp, John	Greenwood, Tp.	Sarah Arner, Greenwood Tp.
5/25/1843	Casper, Rev. Adolph		Sarah Bogar, Middleburg, Pa.
1/32/1840	Charles, John	Liverpool, Pa.	Susan Charles, Liverpool, Pa.
7/24/1853	" Levi	Freeburg, Pa.	Amelia Keiper, Freeburg, Pa.
12/9/1866	" Henry F.	"	Elizabeth Row, Penn Tp.
12/15/1867	" "		Mary Alice Neitz, PortTrevorton, Pa.
3/2/1871	" Wilson	Selinsgrove, Pa.	Mary J. Hoff, Selinsgrove, Pa.
12/25/1862	Coffee, G. R.		Sarah Mover (Moyer?), Chapman Tp.
2/2/1869	Coleman, John J.		Ellen Bowersox, Center Tp.
8/31/1841	Collins, Thomas		Lydia Louden, Perry Co.
8/24/1865	Conley, Fred		Matilda Hummel, Monroe Tp.
5/12/1850	Cook, John	Chapman Tp.	Rachael Steffen, Chapman Tp.
12/4/1870	Courtney, Mahlon		Harriet Ferry, Middlecreek Tp.
3/20/1856	Craig, John		Mrs. Elisabeth Arnold
1/18/1856	Daubert, George		Mary Keet, Penn Tp.
4/8/1849	Deckard, William		Sarah Hettrick
7/23/1873	Derk, Samuel	New Berlin, Pa.	Sevilla Schnee, New Berlin, Pa.
4/16/1874	Dent, Charles P.		Sarah E. Erlenmeyer, Freeburg, Pa.
12/25/1855	Derr, Joseph		" Minium, Chapman Tp.
6/28/1870	" Philip	Milton, Pa.	MaryAnnHockendorf, McAllisterville,
3/5/1871	" Henry		Sarah Ann Maurer, Middlecreek Tp.
2/19/1853	Diehl, Henry	Chapman Tp.	Catherine Karstetter, Chapman Tp.
8/16/1866	" George		Amelia Martin, Freeburg, Pa.
11/26/1867	" Joseph S.		Sarah Shreffler, Northumberland Co.
2/26/1846	Dietrich, Samuel		" Giltrick
1/5/1847	" John	Penn Tp.	Polly Wittenmire, Center Tp.
12/1/1853	" Jeremiah		Sarah Rissinger, Selinsgrove, Pa.
8/31/1854	" John	Selinsgrove, Pa.	Caroline Herman, Selinsgrove, Pa.
1/14/1856	" Abraham		Sarah Fetter, Penn Tp.
3/8/1859	" Frank		Harriet Engle
4/9/1863	Dinius, Henry		Sarah J. Erdly, Middlecreek Tp.
2/22/1874	" Jacob		Hannah M. Benfer, Jackson Tp.
11/7/1843	Dresse, Jacob	Beaver Tp.	" Bingaman, Beaver Tp.
8/6/1865	Doebler, Henry J.		Isora Eyer, Selinsgrove, Pa.
2/25/1840	Duck (Dock), Jacob		Rebecca Aucker
1/15/1850	" Jacob M.	Penn Tp.	Margaret Fisher, Penn
3/7/1856	" William		SarahKeister(Kuster?), Hartleton, Pa.
8/28/1858	" Henry		" Arbogast
7/16/1867	" Frank		Rebecca Henly, Dauphin Co.
1/7/1872	" Jacob	Middlecreek Tp.	Amelia Diemer, Middlecreek Tp.
6/6/1872	" Zach.		Catherine Kuster, Penn Tp.
11/11/1852	Dunkelberger, Charles	Washington Tp.	Sarah Hoffman, Washington Tp.
2/26/1854	" Samuel		Jane Roush, Freeburg, Pa.
8/10/1871	" Daniel		Sarah Ann Maurer, Middlecreek Tp.
10/12/1875	" Oscar	Freeburg, Pa.	" Huff(Hubb?), Freeburg, Pa.
10/15/1848	" John		Susan Longenecker
1/20/1841	Ebersole, Joseph		Barbara Grubb
2/14/1841	" John		Jemima Herman
4/24/1845	Eby, Peter		Elizabeth Weller, Perry Tp.
7/13/1840	Ellig, John		Judith Smith
2/16/1840	Emig, Philip		Harriet Shambach
3/27/1841	Engle, John		Hannah Wetzel
3/20/1845	Erb, Jacob	Center Tp.	Sarah Ann Bitner, Center Tp.
7/28/1849	" John		Elizabeth Deckard
9/29/1861	Esmore, Peter	Buffalo Tp.	Sarah Lauver, Perry Tp.
12/19/1850	Erdly, Morris	Penn Tp.	Elizabeth Stettler, Penn Tp.
1/27/1853	" Enos	"	Margaret Laudenslager
5/20/1858	" William		Maria Walter, Penn Tp.
7/11/1858	" Levi	Middlecreek Tp.	Amanda Hassinger, Middlecreek Tp.

9/12/1858	Erdly, Warren	Penn Tp.	Mary Reed, Penn Tp.
4/1/1860	" Jeremiah		Sarah Jarrett, Penn Tp.
6/11/1861	" Henry		Diana Bickel, Penn Tp.
3/18/1866	" Samuel		Sarah Krouse, Penn Tp.
4/28/1867	" James		Lizzie Hendricks, Middlecreek, Tp.
11/26/1867	" Willis		Catherine Snyder, Jackson Tp.
11/1/1866	Erlenmeyer, Gustavus	Freeburg, Pa.	Malinda Houtz, Freeburg, Pa.
3/23/1848	Eshleman, Joseph	Middleburg, Pa.	Catherine Gaugler, Penn
11/22/1840	Ewig, Jacob		Barbara Dillman
7/5/1868	" George	Jackson Tp.	Amanda Dietrich, Middlecreek Tp.
9/9/1841	Fahdt, Henry		Margaret Kepler
6/28/1842	Farmer, William		Phoebe Reed
5/18/1859	Feehrer, Joseph E.	Selinsgrove, Pa.	Mary C. Gingrich, Selinsgrove, Pa.
6/30/1841	Fenstermacher, Cha.		Sarah Shoemaker, Perry Co.
6/12/1851	Felmly, John	Center Tp.	Catherine Young, Center Tp.
12/25/1873	Felty, Henry W.	Paxtonville, Pa.	Sarah Gill
12/24/1857	Feirich, John		Catherine Shamory, Chapman Tp.
5/17/1846	Fertenbaugh, ——	Dauphin Co.	Susan Stricker, Chapman Tp.
10/31/1846	Fetter, Charles	Washington Tp.	Elizabeth Fetter, Washington Tp.
5/23/1858	" James		Elizabeth A. Diemer, Washington Tp.
11/10/1840	Fisher, Jacob		Mary Wilt
3/14/1841	" John Harlan	Selinsgrove Pa.	Catherine Deckard
4/6/1845	" Moses	Penn Tp.	Hannah Musselman, Penn Tp.
8/3/1845	" Henry	" "	Sarah Ann Moody, Penn Tp.
8/4/1845	" David	Chapman Tp.	Henea Heim, Chapman Tp.
1/10/1847	" Adam J.	Penn Tp.	Barbara Woodling, Washington Tp.
11/7/1847	" Henry	Perry Tp.	Polly Rohrer, Perry Tp.
2/17/1848	" John	Chapman Tp.	Catherine Wilt, Chapman Tp.
11/19/1848	" Aaron	Penn Tp.	Sarah Lenig
1/1/1850	" Dr. Chesseldon	Selinsgrove, Pa.	Jane Wareheim, Selinsgrove, Pa.
6/16/1853	" Benjamin	Penn Tp.	Lydia Snyder, Dauphin Co.
2/23/1854	" David	Chapman Tp.	Barbara Heim, Chapman Tp.
4/27/1854	" Henry	Monroe Tp.	Harriet Harrison, Monroe Tp.
2/7/1855	" William P.	Jackson Tp.	Margaret Herrold, Chapman Tp.
11/22/1860	" Henry		Elizabeth Bickhart, Middleburg, Pa.
8/1/1865	Fisher, Henry K.	Selinsgrove, Pa.	Clarinda Parks, Selinsgrove, Pa.
7/22/1866	" " W.	Penn Tp.	Ellen Fisher, Penn Tp.
2/21/1864	" Michael	Penn Tp.	Sarah Hoot
6/10/1864	" Martin L.		Abbie Eyster, Selinsgrove, Pa.
6/26/1870	" Levi	Selinsgrove, Pa.	Alice Hoffman, Selinsgrove, Pa.
9/11/1870	" Jacob W.	Union Tp.	Mrs. Mary Thomas Grissinger
12/24/1871	" Henry R.		Martha J.Minium,MtPleasantMills,Pa.
7/22/1866	" Henry W.	Penn Tp.	Ellen Fisher, Penn Tp. (2ndcousins)
11/23/1873	Field, John	Middlecreek Tp.	Mary Bolig, Middlecreek Tp.
6/27/1854	Flanders, Isaac	Chapman Tp.	Catherine Miller
2/25/1840	Fortney, Arthur		Susan Nagle
11/15/1846	Foose, Herman		Susan Thomas
5/20/1855	Foreman, Wm.	Northumberland Co.	Elizabeth Bretz, Same County.
4/24/1859	Forry, John S.		Catherine Oté, Monroe Tp.
12/12/1861	" Jonathan		Deborah Grissinger
10/29/1874	" Calvin	Penn Tp.	Alice Daubert, Port Trevorton, Pa.
1/1/1871	Forgy, Casper D.	Selinsgrove, Pa.	Sarah Keiser, Selinsgrove, Pa.
1/4/1848	Frantz, Michael		Harriet Mitchell, Center Tp.
11/15/1853	Frederick, Jacob		Emily Brown, Washington Tp.
5/25/1856	" "		Mary Born (Burns?), Penn Tp.
3/30/1858	Franklin, I. C.		Elizabeth Rine, McKeesHalfFalls,Pa.
12/25/1859	Frymoyer, Moses		Sophia Zeller, Perry Twp.

Date	Name	Place	Spouse
11/14/1869	Freyman, Ephraim		Susan Snyder, Franklin Tp.
12/13/1866	Fryman, William		Sevilla Smith, Middlecreek Tp.
2/24/1863	Freed, John		Susan Craig, Washington Tp.
2/21/1867	" Henry M.		Louise Sechrist
4/25/1869	" Philip		Caroline Craig, West Perry Tp.
5/1/1870	" George		Ellen Roush, Washington Tp.
5/14/1872	" Abraham	Washington Tp.	Emma J. Apple, Washington Tp.
11/5/1871	Gable, John	Chapman Tp.	Amelia Boyer, Washington Tp.
4/18/1858	Gemby, George		Caroline Kerstetter
4/23/1847	Garman, William	Chapman Tp.	Leah Menges, Chapman Tp.
4/5/1849	" "		Elisa Ann Craig
11/25/1852	" Peter		Catherine Moyer, Washington Tp.
11/9/1856	" Henry		Elisabeth Freed, Perry Tp.
8/1/1857	" Jonas		Martha Lupold
2/20/1858	" Peter		Sarah Straub, Perry Tp.
1/2/1862	" David		Elisabeth Rine, "
5/17/1863	" Percival		Sarah Boyer, Perry
3/9/1869	" Henry	Penn Tp.	Catherine Jarrett, Penn Tp.
4/8/1870	" Peter M.	Perry Tp.	Mary Landis, Perry Tp.
4/21/1872	" Gustavus		Josephine Landis, Perry Tp.
12/29/1872	" Jerome		Susan Bolig, Penn Tp.
5/2/1875	" Johathan	Perry Tp.	Regina Mengle, Perry Tp.
4/1/1852	Garrett, George (Maybe Jarrett)		Anna Dietrich, Penn Tp.
5/12/1859	Gaskins, I. K.	Northumberland Co.	Lizzie Hartman, Shamokin Dam. Pa.
12/6/1849	Gangler, Daniel	Chapman Tp.	Phoebe Arnold, Chapman
5/29/1851	" "		Gemby, Susan
5/14/1865	" Jacob		Caroline Reichenbach
2/4/1845	Gebhart, Benjamin		Elisa Miller, Washington Tp.
1/1/1867	Geiselman, Jefferson		Mary Souloff, Juniata Co.
15/5/1851	Gellinger, Daniel	Washington Tp.	Mary Roush, Washington Tp.
10/23/1849	Gemberling, Lewis	Buffalo Tp.	Mrs. Jane C. Schoch, Penn Tp.
6/4/1871	" Zach. T.		Mary Wayland, Penn Tp.
6/2/1844	Gets, Solomon		Mary Fasnacht, Selinsgrove, Pa.
4/28/1846	Gilbert, Henry	Center Tp.	Anna Spade, Center Tp.
5/15/1849	" John	Washington Tp.	Anna Swarts, Washington Tp.
11/1/1851	" David	"	Sarah Shamory, "
7/29/1855	" Samuel	"	Araminta Bussler, "
12/7/1856	" Fred		Susan Reigle, "
9/5/1864	" Samuel	Philadelphia, Pa.	Rosanna Smith, Absecon, N. J.
10/29/1871	" William		Mrs. Diana Wolf, Middlecreek Tp.
1/17/1867	" "		Caroline Mains, Washington Tp.
10/29/1871	Gill, Aaron W.		Ellen B. Gemberling, Penn Tp.
1/10/1854	Gingrich, Henry		Elizabeth Garman, Washington Tp.
12/23/1855	Gise, John B.		Lilly Boyer, Gratz, Pa.
10/1/1846	Glass, Henry	Freeburg, Pa.	Elizabeth Stettler, Center Co.
5/30/1857	" John	"	Margaret Haas, Freeburg, Pa.
9/2/1857	" George	"	Sarah Schoch, Penn Tp.
1/1/1857	" Henry	"	" Boyer, Washington Tp.
3/12/1857	" Frederick	"	Susan Garman, Freeburg, Pa.
9/24/1875	" John A.	"	Mary Glass, "
12/29/1868	Glase, George W.		Susan Benner, Penn Tp.
11/13/1855	Glase, Hiram		Elvina Roush, Washington Tp.
2/5/1846	Goodling, George		Anna Goy, Perry Tp.
8/24/1858	" Adam		Catherine Gelnett, Perry Tp.
6/24/1866	" George		Caroline Garman, Perry Tp.
2/28/1869	" Lewis		Mary A. Derr, Chapman Tp.
11/16/1874	Goodwill, Andrew	Shamokin, Pa.	Cora Brown, Freeburg, Pa.
3/22/1874	Goy, David	Freeburg, Pa.	Mrs. Salome Forry, Freeburg, Pa.

Date	Name	Place	Spouse
9/28/1849	Graybill, Thomas	Richfield, Pa.	Susan Rine, Perry Tp.
2/6/1851	" John	Perry Tp.	Elizabeth Fisher, Perry Tp.
10/26/1854	" Peter	"	Polly Rine, Washington Tp.
11/20/1855	" Christian		Susan Wayne, Perry Tp.
10/8/1863	" William		Elizabeth Shelly, Richfield, Pa.
1/1/1846	Grier, Samuel	Washington Tp.	Mary Miller, Washington Tp.
9/4/1853	Greiner, Jacob		Sevilla Hartman, Shamokin Dam, Pa.
12/25/1853	" Philip		Mrs. Elizabeth Wendt, Perry Tp.
5/17/1874	" Jacob	Shamokin Dam, Pa.	Anna Mitchell, Northumberland, Pa.
10/14/1875	Grimm, Jonathan	Washington Tp.	Sarah Apple, Washington Tp.
11/16/1873	" William	Freeburg, Pa.	Clara Hosterman, Freeburg, Pa.
9/6/1857	" Daniel		Catherine Herrold, Washington Tp.
9/21/1871	Greenough, Chas. O.		Caroline Gross, Beaver Tp.
12/24/1846	Gross, Peter	Penn Tp.	Sarah Ann Wendt, Penn Tp.
9/5/1862	Grissinger, Nathan		Mary Thomas, Penn.
12/10/1840	Grubb, Henry	Perry Co.	Catherine Keagle, Perry Co.
6/27/1841	" Samuel	"	Martha Steffen (Stephen?)
6/17/1844	" Abraham	Liverpool, Pa.	Frances Hallman, Liverpool, Pa.
6/22/1845	Gundrum, William		Lucy Strayer, Freeburg, Pa.
6/25/1855	" "		Elizabeth Roush, "
5/8/1856	" John		Catherine Roush, Washington Tp.
2/28/1858	" Aaron	Selinsgrove, Pa.	Susan Gemberling, Selinsgrove, Pa.
9/3/1865	" Samuel		Amelia Roush, Freeburg, Pa.
1/2/1859	Guth (Good?), Charles		Mrs. Catherine Boyer, Selinsgrove, Pa.
3/31/1861	Haas, Elias	Freeburg, Pa.	Amanda Freyman, Freeburg, Pa.
6/14/1842	Hackenberg, John		Mary Wise
6/30/1849	"		Mrs. Hannah Metzger
9/8/1840	Hallman, Adam	Liverpool, Pa.	Sophia Hamaker, Liverpool, Pa.
11/2/1854	" John	Perry Co.	Mrs. Lydia Holtzman, Perry Co.
3/21/1848	Haldeman, Isaac	Juniata Co.	Anna Graybill, Juniata Co.
3/4/1842	Hare, John		Barbara Charles, Liverpool, Pa.
2/26/1860	Haines, Peter		Sarah Gundrum
7/29/1860	" Isaiah		Malinda Shotsberger, Chapman Tp.
1/8/1843	" Reuben		Sybilla Shadel
7/25/1845	" Marcus	Washington Tp.	Hannah Brenner, Washington Tp.
8/22/1850	" David	"	Eliza Bender, "
7/12/1855	" Christopher	"	????
8/20/1857	" William	Selinsgrove, Pa.	Elizabeth Snyder, Penn Tp.
1/3/1850	Hain, Michael		Elizabeth Landonslager
3/4/1842	Hare, John		Barbara Charles, Liverpool, Pa.
9/11/1870	" James H.		Mary Smith, Middleburg, Pa.
1/15/1854	" Fred		Mrs. Hettie Zerus
5/19/1850	Harrison, George	Penn Tp.	Lydia Millhoff, Penn Tp.
5/20/1852	Hartman, Elias	"	Catherine Keiper, Penn Tp.
10/3/1850	" Percival	"	Sarah Kreider, "
1/9/1859	" Samuel		Catherine Aurand, Monroe Tp.
7/2/1871	" Newton E.	Shamokin Dam, Pa.	Alice Lenhart, Shamokin Dam, Pa.
3/10/1853	" Percival		Margaret Hoff, Penn Tp.
2/2/1845	Hassenplug, John J.		Sarah Boyer, Freeburg, Pa.
10/31/1850	Haupt, Edward	Penn Tp.	" Long, Penn Tp.
6/14/1868	Hammaker, Samuel		Mrs. Elizabeth Strayer, Freeburg, Pa.
3/3/1875	Heckman, Jacob	Washington Tp.	Margaret Dusk, Washington Tp.
11/1/1863	" Daniel		Mary Ann Moyer, Washington Tp.
9/22/1864	" Samuel		Margaret Freed, Washington Tp.
10/26/1865	Hoiges, William		Susan Sholl, Chapman Tp.
12/11/1870	" Levi		Elizabeth Nagle, Perry Tp.
1/17/1847	Heim, John	Chapman Tp.	Catherine Sharder (Shrader), Chap. Tp.
9/15/1867	" Joseph		Melinda Hoffman, Perry Tp.

Date	Groom		Residence	Bride
12/24/1846	Heimbach, George			Elizabeth ———, Chapman Tp.
4/24/1848	"	Levi	Center Tp.	Harriet Moyer, Center Tp.
1/12/1868	"	William N.		Amanda Thomas, Selinsgrove, Pa.
3/9/1858	"	Daniel	Washington Tp.	Lucy Ann Hendricks, Washington Tp.
10/21/1852	"	Henry	"	Mrs. Mary Brown, Washington Tp.
1/12/1855	"	John		Mary Ann Bolig, Washington Tp.
11/11/1851	Heintzelman, Andrew		Chapman Tp.	Mary Nerhood, Chapman Tp.
6/3/1851	"	Daniel	Washington Tp.	Catherine Lenig, Washington Tp.
2/5/1865	"	Elias		Deborah Reichenbach, Chapman Tp.
12/5/1867	"	Jacob		Henrietta Smith, Middlecreek Tp.
1/4/1870	"	Daniel		Sybilla Heim, Union Tp.
12/11/1870	"	Jonathan		Catherine Phillips, Chapman Tp.
4/15/1875	"	Peter		Hattie Gilbert, Schuylkill Co.
4/14/1859	Heiser, Daniel		Monroe, Tp.	Martha Long, Monroe Tp.
1/24/1850	Helvig, George			Caroline Lenig
3/28/1852	Hendricks, Jacob			Susan Haggerty
7/24/1866	"	"	Monroe Tp.	Mary Schreffler, Northumberland Co.
12/31/1868	"	George R.	Washington Tp.	Matilda Boyer, Washington Tp.
7/7/1857	"	Philip	"	Elizabeth Gilbert, "
12/28/1864	"	John V.		Esther Herman, Middlecreek Tp.
6/12/1864	"	John J.		Fannie Hovis, Washington Tp.
6/18/1854	Hepner, Samuel		Northumberland Co.	Angeline Kepler
2/9/1847	Herman, Simon		Penn Tp.	Catherine Neitz, Penn Tp.
7/17/1853	"	Alfred		Sarah Miller, Selinsgrove, Pa.
9/28/1854	"	George	Penn Tp.	Elizabeth Fisher, Penn Tp.
6/13/1871	"	Jacob K.		Matilta Fettor, "
5/17/1842	Herrold, Abraham		Chapman Tp.	Mary Anderson, Chapman Tp.
1/31/1843	"	John George	"	Christina Walter, Union Co.
2/15/1844	"	William	"	Mary Blasser, Chapman Tp.
1/30/1851	"	Samuel	"	Catherine Snyder, "
1/24/1850	"	Harrison	"	Hannah Spyer
1/27/1853	"	Fred R.	"	Mary J. Aurand, Chapman Tp.
12/29/1853	"	Henry	"	Martha Fisher, "
2/2/1854	"	"	"	Susan Shaffer "
3/17/1872	"	Wollington	"	Catherine Trutt "
1/28/1869	Heskell, Noble			Emma Holtzapple, Freeburg, Pa.
8/20/1840	Hessrich, Jacob			Caroline Himes
6/28/1846	Hettrick, Jacob			Lydia Lovig
5/4/1847	"	Adam		Catherine Wendt
6/10/1852	"	Daniel	Penn Tp.	Mary Ann Jarrett, Penn Tp.
7/2/1854	Higgins, Frank		Selinsgrove, Pa.	Julia Ann Bertch, Freeburg, Pa.
3/10/1869	Hilbish, Jonathan		Elkhart, Ind.	Jane E. Walter, Penn Tp.
9/29/1842	Hoch, Jacob			Rebecca Schoch, Middlecreek Tp.
1/18/1844	Hoefflich, Joseph F.		Center Tp.	Leah Gift, Perry Tp.
10/10/1852	Hoff, John			Elizabeth Heimbach, Freeburg, Pa.
10/14/1850	"	Samuel		Catherine Charles, "
4/21/1863	"	Geo. W.	Washington Tp.	Elizabeth Hovis, Washington Tp.
12/22/1840	Hoffman, John			Barbara Charles
7/16/1848	"	David	Penn Tp.	Susan Keiser, Penn Tp.
7/1/1855	"	Tillman		Mary Ann Heiges
9/31/1851	Hoke, Joseph			Mary Lenig
5/23/1852	Hollenbach, Henry			Margaret Hoffman, Selinsgrove, Pa.
2/11/1840	Holmes, Leroy			" Keiser
12/15/1868	Holtzapple, George		Freeburg, Pa.	Catherine Bittinger, Washington Tp.
12/18/1870	"	Fred		Mrs. Eliza Winkleman
9/8/1872	"	Henry	Washington Tp.	Catherine Duck (Dock)
10/16/1859	"	John		Mary Ann Haines, Washington Tp.

Date	Name	Place	Spouse
7/8/1849	Hopp, John		Maria Lauver
5/4/1851	Hopp, Peter		Dorothy Roth, Perry Tp.
6/15/1848	Houseworth, Jacob	Chapman Tp.	Polly Fisher, Chapman Tp.
7/31/1864	House, John		Elizabeth Limbert, Juniata Co.
11/29/1863	Hovis, Issac	Washington Tp.	Esther Grissinger, Penn Tp.
10/3/1872	" Jacob	Perry Tp.	Lucinda Mengle, Washington Tp.
8/27/1865	Hosterman, Henry	Penn Tp.	Lucy Ann Hoot, Penn Tp.
11/1/1868	" James	"	Mary Duck, Penn Tp.
6/5/1856	" Franklin		Catherine Haines, Freeburg, Pa.
3/5/1846	Huber (Hoover?) And.	Chapman Tp.	Elizabeth Hummel, Chapman Tp.
11/22/1866	Howell, Aaron	Franklin Tp.	Mary Hoffer, Chapman Tp.
3/3/1867	Hughes, John K.	Penn Tp.	Clara Seebold, Penn Tp.
1/25/1857	" Samuel W.	"	Barbara S. Boyer, Penn Tp.
4/8/1852	" Charles	Washington Tp.	Sarah Snyder
12/25/1845	Hummel, William		Elizabeth Herrold
1/8/1846	" Peter	Chapman Tp.	Anna Kerstetter, Chapman Tp.
12/16/1858	" John	Freeburg, Pa.	Emma Snyder, Penn Tp.
8/8/1869	" Frank		Maggie Duck (Dock), MiddlecreekTp
6/18/1871	" Paul		Catherine Bickel, Washington Tp.
11/11/1860	" John		Lovina Erdly, Penn Tp.
4/4/1861	" Robert		Sarah Bolig, Middlecreek Tp.
4/4/1861	" George		Eliza Boon "
9/25/1859	Hughes, William	Penn Tp.	Mary Kantz, Penn Tp.
11/1/1863	Jacoby, Ezra R.	Williamsport, Pa.	Mrs. Clara Steiver, SelinsgrovePa
1/25/1846	Jarrett, Isaac	Penn Tp.	Anna Keller Penn Tp.
11/12/1848	" Jacob	"	Elizabeth Shannon, Penn Tp.
4/11/1855	" "		Mrs. Harriet Conley, Monroe Tp.
6/28/1868	" Amos		Mary Ann Fretig, Jackson Tp.
3/16/1848	Jarrett, Henry	Penn Tp.	Maria Hain, Penn Tp.
3/9/1875	Jeffries, J. K.	Sunbury, Pa.	Louisa Seasholts, Selinsgrove, Pa.
2/2/1862	Johns, John	White Deer Tp.	Hettie Lauver
5/28/1840	Johnson, Samuel		Mary Charles, Liverpool, Pa.
4/15/1851	Kain, William		Sarah Hummel
11/18/1855	Kantz, Conrad	Penn Tp.	Malinda Apple, Washington Tp.
8/10/1856	" Henry		Mary Strawser, Washington Tp.
4/26/1846	" John	Washington Tp.	Hannah Walborn, "
2/16/1847	" Jacob	Penn Tp.	Elsie Aumiller, Penn Tp.
2/25/1850	" Peter	"	Eliza Beachel, "
11/9/1852	" George W.		Sarah A. Bower
11/6/1859	" Simon		Mrs. Matilda Grush, Penn Tp.
12/8/1859	" Hiram	Penn Tp.	Cassandra Walter, "
12/22/1863	" Luther	Washington Tp.	Caroline Boyer, Washington Tp.
1/22/1865	" Thomas	Penn Tp.	Catherine Romig, Penn Tp.
2/6/1866	" B. Frank	"	Lucinda Erdly, Penn Tp.
12/26/1871	" Simon	Washington Tp.	Sarah Heintzelman, Chapman Tp.
5/23/1850	Kaufman, Samuel M.	Juniata Co.	Elizabeth Gingrich, Washington Tp.
6/8/1852	" Samuel	Union Tp.	Harriet Loudenslager, Penn Tp.
6/8/1847	Keck, Elias	Penn Tp.	Anna Bickel, Penn Tp.
5/16/1875	" Albert B.		Josephine Wolf, Perry Tp.
12/19/1875	Keeler, J. O.	Middlecreek Tp.	Sallie Dietrich, Middlecreek Tp.
3/28/1850	Kehler, George	Juniata Co.	Emoline Snyder, Perry Tp.
10/1/1848	Keller, Joel	Chapman Tp.	Sibilla Heim, Chapman Tp.
3/19/1850	" Jacob		Elizabeth Straub, Chapman Tp.
6/28/1857	" John		Catherine Oldt, Monroe Tp.
10/22/1870	" Jacob C.		Lydia Miller, Selinsgrove, Pa.

11/18/1873	Kemble, Martin	Harriet Weller, Washington Tp.
9/12/1875	Kepler, Riley	Perry Tp.	Mary Yerger, Perry Tp.
5/27/1855	" John	Elizabeth Bender, Perry Tp.
11/18/1847	Kepner, Samuel	Barbara Motz
1/6/1853	" William	Juniata Co.	" Ickes, Juniata Co.
12/26/1854	Kern, Robert	Susan Moyer, Penn Tp.
3/30/1854	" Simon P.	Sandusky, Ohio	Maria Gemberling, Penn Tp.
12/25/1856	Kerstetter, Michael	Susan Minnig, Penn Tp.
12/14/1854	Kerstetter, Benjamin	Barbara Marks, Chapman Tp.
9/19/1842	" Levi	Chapman Tp.	Mary Ann Gangler, "
3/23/1848	" Joseph	"	Catherine Herrold, "
3/7/1852	" Andrew	Perry Tp.	Sophia Marks, Juniata Co.
3/18/1858	" David	Catherine A. Gorman, Perry Tp.
6/26/1859	" Isaac	Betsey Strawser, Chapman Tp.
3/3/1872	Kaltrider, William A.	Polly Reichenbach, Perry Tp.
9/8/1870	Kessler, Henry	Mrs.BarbaraBoyerHughes,Wash.Tp.
8/10/1843	Kerchner, Benj.	Catherine Clemens
12/31/1840	Kine, George	Mary Shadow
10/25/1856	Kinney, Henry	Elizabeth Sauer, Middlecreek Tp.
2/7/1847	Klatfelder, Isaac	Chapman Tp.	Susan Moyer, Chapman Tp.
5/7/1848	" Peter	"	Charlotte Arnold, "
11/1/1854	Kline, Samuel	Union Tp., UN. Co.	Mrs. Amelia Noyer, Chapman Tp.
8/25/1850	" Levi	Troxelville, Pa.	Barbara Kline, Troxelville, Pa.
10/28/1850	" Peter	Leah Noyer, Beaver Tp.
2/7/1854	" Lenhart	Mary Sechrist, Perry Co.
12/23/1859	" Solomon	Barbara "
8/18/1859	Klingler, John	Sarah Crouse, Middlecreek Tp.
9/12/1861	" Joel	Margaret Brouse, Jackson Tp.
12/17/1871	" I. Peter	Jackson Tp.	" Seville Ulrich, Jackson Tp.
6/19/1870	Klose, George	Bellevue, Ohio	Mrs. Sophia Hummel, Freeburg, Pa.
5/18/1841	Kohl, Levi	Mary Miller
2/5/1855	Kohler, Andrew	Richfield, Pa.	Sarah Fisher, Richfield, Pa.
3/21/1854	" Simon	Perry Tp.	Elizabeth Schnee, Perry Tp.
10/28/1869	Koster, B. K.	Juniata Co.	Clara Winey, Perry Tp.
12/18/1845	Knights (Neitz?), Eman.	Chapman Tp.	Elizabeth Houser
9/15/1861	Knights (Neitz?), Philip	Mary Hughes, Penn Tp.
1/24/1850	Kramer, Fred	Mary Ann Heim
1/12/1843	" Perry	Nancy Gilfillin
1/14/1858	Kratzer, Levi	Mrs. Eliza Boyer
11/26/1863	" Michael	Mary Garman, Monroe Tp.
5/21/1865	" Jeremiah	Mrs. Susan Kratzer, Penn Tp.
10/14/1866	" Peter	Susan Worts, Washington Tp.
5/7/1857	Krebs, Alexander	Elizabeth Thursby, Chapman Tp.
3/20/1856	" Joseph	Julia Ann Reigle
12/23/1856	Kremer, John	Louise Kopler, Perry Tp.
3/1/1854	" William	Clearfield Co.	Polly Mengle, Perry Tp.
4/16/1854	" John F.	Catherine Kreigbaum, Perry Tp.
1/2/1845	Kreider, Jacob	Perry Tp.	Elizabeth Houtz
10/3/1850	" Isaac	Penn Tp.	Catherine Bateman, Penn Tp.
3/28/1854	" Henry	Matilda Jarrett, Penn Tp.
2/15/1844	Kreischer, Chas. E.	Buffalo Tp.	Martha Keeler, Buffalo Tp.
11/18/1856	Kreigbaum, Jonathan	Elizabeth Smith, Perry
11/7/1841	Kriner, John	Sarah Reed
12/26/1869	Krissinger, Jeremiah	Catherine Sechrist, Union Tp.
2/17/1848	Krouse, Andrew	Washington Tp.	Lucy Keiper, Washington Tp.
9/12/1861	" Lewis	Catherine Brouse, Jackson Tp.
2/21/1867	" Henry	Mary Ann Gemberling, SelinsgrovePa
11/28/1867	" Samuel	Sarah Kratzer, Penn Tp.

12/24/1854	Kuhn, George W.		Barbara Kantz
2/26/1860	Kuhn, Jacob		Amelia Morr
12/30/1875	Kuhn, William S.	Washington Tp.	Emma J. Gilbert, Washington Tp.
11/21/1854	Kuster, Simon		Catherine Bolig, Center Tp.
3/17/1859	" Henry		Polly Dunkelberger, Penn Tp.
4/13/1870	Landis, Tobias	Washington Tp.	Utica Row, Washington Tp.
2/5/1852	" Benjamin	Juniata Co.	Susan Stock, Perry Tp.
8/10/1858	Laporte, Peter		Mrs. Susan Moyer, Chapman Tp.
3/28/1847	Lark, Simon		Sarah Boyer, Freeburg, Pa.
1/16/1851	Landenslager, Valentine		Mrs. Rachael Brouse, Penn Tp.
9/11/1856	" Andrew		Rosanna Bellman
2/23/1869	" Henry		Susan Knouse, Penn Tp.
1/24/1849	Lauver, Emanuel	Richfield, Pa.	Sophia Winey, Richfield, Pa.
5/31/1849	" Peter	Perry Co.	Susan Keagle, Perry Co.
9/18/1850	" Balthaser		Mary Graybill, Richfield, Pa.
12/4/1851	" Peter	Perry Tp.	Margaret Maurer, Perry Tp.
9/15/1853	" Joseph		Mary Moyer, Richfield, Pa.
11/13/1855	" Michael		Anna Wayne, Perry Tp.
11/22/1855	" Reuben		Elizabeth Graybill, Perry Tp.
5/4/1847	Lawrence, ———		Margaret Grubb, Liverpool, Pa.
3/5/1857	Leach, William		Barbara Arnold, Chapman Tp.
2/27/1873	Lease, John S.		Jane Yerger, Perry Tp.
10/1/1840	" Daniel	Perry Tp.	Salome Schnee, Perry Tp.
11/1/1849	Leiter, John	Selinsgrove, Pa.	Susan Hoffman, Selinsgrove, Pa.
9/9/1856	" George W.	Chapman Tp.	Susan Snyder, Chapman Tp.
10/10/1875	Leitzel, John P.		Margaret Meiser
12/15/1859	" Henry E.		Eve Benfer, Jackson Tp.
1/7/1849	Lenig, George	Chapman Tp.	Hannah Bickhart, Chapman Tp.
2/16/1862	" John		Caroline Troup, Washington Tp.
4/14/1867	" G. Wash.		Catherine Gable, Chapman Tp.
9/1/1867	" Jackson		Anna Dirk, Chapman Tp.
8/25/1870	" Joseph	Perry Tp.	Sarah Kepler, Perry Tp.
3/9/1873	Lesher, George		Jane Stahl, Richfield, Pa.
6/16/1841	Liddick, John	Perry Co.	Elizabeth Parks, Perry Co.
1/26/1843	" "	New Buffalo, Pa.	Catherine Freed, New Buffalo, Pa.
12/3/1840	Light, Philip		Lydia Ulsh
4/29/1856	" Isaac		Catherine Neimond, Chapman Tp.
4/15/1875	Lintner, Henry	Schuylkill Co.	Minerva Heintzelman, Chapman Tp.
9/25/1856	Lloyd, I. E.		Susan Straub, Penn Tp.
1/7/1841	Livingston, Ben		Esther Albright, Perry Co.
1/8/1850	Long, Daniel		Mary Diehl, Perry Co.
12/9/1850	" Solomon	Penn Tp.	Harriet Row, Penn Tp.
1/7/1851	" Jonathan		Judith Diehl
6/10/1852	" Jacob	Penn Tp.	Elizabeth Jarrett, Penn Tp.
2/2/1854	" George	Mifflinburg, Pa.	Susan Boyer, Freeburg, Pa.
2/12/1857	" Samuel		" Oldt, Monroe Tp.
8/4/1861	" "		Harriet Bolig, Middlecreek Tp.
10/10/1875	" Abraham	Selinsgrove, Pa.	Jennie Thomas, Selinsgrove, Pa.
6/8/1854	Look, Frank	Chapman Tp.	Molly Kerstotter, Chapman Tp.
1/9/1845	Lose, Jacob		Susan Nerhood
8/26/1841	Louden, Henry		Rebecca Yeager
12/24/1846	Luck, Jacob		Mary Ann Kerns, Penn Tp.
1/15/1860	" Levi		Mary C. Baker, Selinsgrove, Pa.
10/28/1862	" Joel		Maria Row, Penn Tp.
10/30/1863	" Samuel		Malinda Row, Penn Tp.
9/20/1868	" Charles		Elizabeth Snyder, Penn Tp.
12/24/1868	" William		Rachael Ewing, Penn Tp.
3/23/1842	Lupfer, Jacob		Mary Motter

Date	Name	Place	Spouse
5/15/1843	Maier, John		Susan Shaffer
5/18/1875	" "	Wilkes-Barre, Pa.	Polly Ann Naugle, Washington Tp.
7/22/1858	Malick, Solomon	Selinsgrove, Pa.	Mary Roush, Freeburg, Pa.
5/19/1872	Markle, Peter		Emma Hendricks, Juniata Co.
11/8/1855	Martin, Jacob		Catherine Martin, Perry Tp.
10/10/1861	" "	West Perry Tp.	Mary Yeager, Juniata Co.
10/13/1867	" Samuel		Sarah Graybill, W. Perry Tp.
3/9/1875	" Jacob	Freeburg, Pa.	Mary Ann Forry, Penn Tp.
2/20/1845	Matthias, Jeremiah	Penn Tp.	Judea Morr, Penn Tp.
3/25/1845	" Henry		Matilda Grush, Penn Tp.
12/28/1854	Mauck, Jacob	New Berlin, Pa.	Mrs. Amelia Herrold Bender
12/20/1860	Maurer, Samuel		Elizabeth Luck, Penn Tp.
1/5/1843	MacKenzie, David	Liverpool, Pa.	Margaret Karr, Liverpool, Pa.
3/21/1842	McMorris, Dr. Wm. N.	New Buffalo, Pa.	Catherine Wright
4/1/1844	Meiser, Jonas		Maria Herrold, Washington Tp.
8/12/1845	" Harrison	Perry Tp.	Susan Fisher, Chapman Tp.
10/8/1846	" John	"	" Zeller, Perry Tp.
6/10/1851	" Joseph		Hannah Shadle, Perry Tp.
2/12/1851	" Thomas		Sarah Garman, "
10/20/1862	" Henry		Elizabeth Garman, Perry Tp.
11/13/1862	" Joel		Rebecca Marks, Juniata Co.
2/14/1863	" Frederick		Catherine Lawver, West Perry Tp.
10/17/1865	" "		Sarah Lower, Juniata Co.
6/10/1866	" Perry		Mary Ebright, Perry Tp.
2/4/1869	" Benjamin	Washington Tp.	Catherine Grimm, Washington Tp.
11/7/1869	" John	Middlecreek Tp.	Mary Luck, Middlecreek Tp.
9/10/1871	" Benjamin		Catherine Mengle, Washington Tp.
6/20/1872	" "	Perry Tp.	Anna Phillips, Perry Tp.
3/29/1874	" Jonathan	"	Sarah Snyder "
5/19/1872	Meister, William	"	Alice Landis "
1/19/1845	Menges, Washington	Freeburg, Pa.	Susan Roush, Washington Tp.
4/4/1847	" George		Susan Dietz
11/15/1863	" Jacob		Elira Ann Moyer, Freeburg, Pa.
9/8/1848	Mengle, John	Washington Tp.	Leah Ickes, Washington Tp.
7/24/1851	" Michael	Perry Tp.	Catherine Arbogast, Perry Tp.
11/22/1855	" Daniel		Anna Wendt, Juniata Co.
8/10/1858	" Henry		Elizabeth Arbogast, Perry Tp.
4/3/1845	Mertz, Peter	Freeburg, Pa.	Susan Hilbish, Freeburg, Pa.
11/17/1846	" George		Amelia Hummel
10/30/1853	" Frederick	Center Tp.	Elizabeth Showers, Center Tp.
6/11/1844	" David		Sarah Kime
3/27/1841	Miller, Henry		Elizabeth Shaffer
3/21/1843	" George		Sophia Duck (Dock), Washington Tp.
9/19/1858	" Amos		Sarah Knouse, Juniata Co.
12/3/1846	" Jacob	Selinsgrove, Pa.	Sarah Bower, Selinsgrove, Pa.
3/1/1849	" John	Washington Tp.	Matilda Moser, Center Tp.
8/22/1850	" James	Penn Tp.	Elizabeth Brunner, Penn Tp.
7/1/1852	" John		Susan Strayer, Freeburg, Pa.
8/17/1852	" William	Lycoming Co.	Catherine Aumiller, Penn Tp.
10/26/1852	" Eli		Sarah Keiper, Washington Tp.
8/24/1854	" John	Berrysburg, Pa.	Elizabeth Schoch, Penn Tp.
2/1/1855	" Edward		Sarah Batdorf, Freeburg, Pa.
6/1/1862	" Hon. Charles	Penn Tp.	Lydia Kantz, Middlecreek Tp.
5/30/1867	" William		Susan Straub
8/14/1870	" George	Union Co.	Mrs. Ann Shadle, Perry Tp.
12/27/1872	" John		Harriet Musser, Franklin Tp.
7/23/1871	" Allison	Limestone Tp.	Sallie Frock, Limestone Tp.
12/18/1859	" Joseph	Lebanon Co.	Sarah Fisher, Monroe Tp.
11/27/1853	Minnich, Jonathan		Leah Gilbert, Washington Tp.
11/19/1854	Minnig, Elias		Sophia Garman
1/18/1856	" Moses		Mary Craig, Chapman Tp.

Date	Name	Place	Spouse
11/4/1855	Minium, Benjamin		Mary Ann Helvig
1/17/1869	" Lewis		Mary Fisher
5/23/1869	" Jacob		Catherine Hertz
8/13/1843	" "		Eliza Rathfon
5/24/1860	Mitchell, Jeremiah		Amelia Boyer, Middlecreek Tp.
9/8/1867	Mitman, John		Mary Saners, "
11/8/1866	Mitterling, George S.	Perry Tp.	Margaret Weiss, Perry Tp.
12/23/1865	" Abraham		Emeline Arbogast, "
8/8/1869	" Philip S.		Leah Arnold, "
10/11/1849	Mohr, Moses	Middlecreek Tp.	Caroline Straub, Middlecreek Tp.
4/25/1850	" Austin		Lucinda Klingler, Union Tp.
3/23/1852	Morr, Isaac	Washington Tp.	Anna M. Reichenbach, Washington Tp
4/13/1862	" Jacob		Susan Roush, Washington Tp.
12/15/1861	" Isaac	Freeburg, Pa.	Mrs. Catherine Weaver, Freeburg,Pa
10/2/1870	" Henry	Washington Tp.	Anna Rohrig, Selinsgrove, Pa.
2/28/1865	Moser, William H.		Lydia Kennedy, Middlecreek Tp.
3/20/1842	Motz, Samuel	Freeburg, Pa.	Sarah Rine, Perry Tp.
9/29/1863	" Henry	"	" Swartz, Freeburg, Pa.
10/24/1848	" Henry	Freeburg, Pa.	Elizabeth Moyer, Freeburg, Pa.
8/3/1845	Moyer, William	Chapman Tp.	Amelia Frayer, Chapman Tp.
5/26/1846	" Benjamin	"	Mary Houseworth, "
12/5/1847	" Ellsworth	"	" Phillips "
12/19/1850	" Aaron	Chapman Tp.	Louise Peffer, Chapman Tp.
1/21/1851	" William	"	Anna Traub "
5/29/1851	" George		Catherine Minium
2/19/1852	" Daniel		Maria Renninger, Center Tp.
10/10/1852	" Nathan		Lydia Yeager
3/27/1860	" Henry		Mary Dagle, Penn Tp.
2/10/1861	" John		Matilda Stahl, Chapman Tp.
12/24/1865	" Joseph	Washington Tp.	Catherine Straub, Washington Tp.
6/30/1867	" Evans	"	Fianna Weller, Washington Tp.
1/2/1870	" Philip J.		Maria J. Erlenberger, Freeburg, Pa
12/29/1870	" Henry	"	Alice Hoch, Washington Tp.
12/17/1871	" John C.		Christiana Metzger
1/—/1873	" John A.	"	Catherine Goodling, Perry Tp.
10/10/1875	" Lewis		" Arbogast, Washington Tp.
4/8/1844	" Aaron		" Strayer, Freeburg, Pa.
12/30/1855	Mull, John		" Renninger, Middlecreek Tp.
6/21/1863	" Henry		Susan Long, "
7/31/1864	Musselman, Samuel		Sarah J. Woodling, Monroe Tp.
3/6/1862	Myers, William S.	York Co.	Mary Scholl
3/25/1848	Nangle, Jacob		Sarah Miller, Union Co.
3/11/1856	Nace, George	Northumberland Co.	Catherine Bender
8/5/1860	" Jacob	"	Susan " Perry Tp.
5/17/1866	Naugle, David		Henrietta Bussler, Penn Tp.
8/5/1866	" John B.		Elizabeth Kepler, Perry Tp.
5/17/1870	" Daniel		Catherine Botteigor
7/23/1849	" Benjamin		Sarah Beigle, Washington Tp.
2/21/1864	" John	Liverpool, Pa.	Mrs. Susan Miller, Freeburg, Pa.
4/9/1858	Neiswender, Benjamin		Margaret Fisher
5/17/1851	Nerhood, Adam	Chapman Tp.	Catherine Herrold, Chapman Tp.
3/18/1865	Newman, Thomas		Elisabeth Weiser, Chapman Tp.
9/13/1866	Nipple, Dr. Henry N.		Viola Schnee
7/28/1861	Noecker, Jarius		Mary Kantz
4/26/1858	Oplinger, Benjamin		Catherine Renninger, Penn Tp.
9/11/1856	Ott, George		Amelia Eisenhower

3/12/1858	Pawling, Charles W.	Penn Tp.	Lydia Long, Selinsgrove, Pa.
5/15/1865	" S. B.	" "	Esther " "
8/20/1850	" William	" "	Caroline Row, Penn Tp.
10/6/1872	Parks, Charles	Selinsgrove, Pa.	Louise Kane, Selinsgrove, Pa.
5/9/1843	" John	Penn Tp.	Lydia Gemberling, Penn Tp.
9/29/1867	Philips, Ezra		Satilla Lenig, Chapman Tp.
10/26/1851	Platt, Jacob		Mary Felmly
8/23/1860	Pontius, George		Susan Bickle, Freeburg, Pa.
1/12/1856	Potter, Jacob		Mrs. Catherine Grubb, Liverpool, Pa
2/11/1858	Puffenberger, Harry		Catherine Herman, Selinsgrove, Pa.
10/18/1846	Ramstein, George		Mary E. Gallicker (Gallagher?)
5/27/1855	Rathfon, Wilson	Perry Tp.	Catherine Meiser, Perry
7/1/1855	" John		Mary A. Eovis
9/20/1857	Rathgerber, John		Mrs. Elizabeth Glass
4/13/1875	Reed, Ammon	Northumberland Co.	Laura Erlenmeyer, Freeburg, Pa.
7/24/1873	Reich, George		Sarah Benfer, Middlecreek Tp.
10/6/1850	Reichenbach, Samuel		Catherine Arbogast, Washington Tp.
11/30/1854	" Dr. Charles		Cathorine Arbogast
2/18/1858	" Benjamin		Amelia Moyer, Washington Tp.
8/11/1846	Reifsnyder, John	Liverpool, Pa.	Nancy Musselman, Liverpool, Pa.
2/34/1844	Reigle, Daniel	Washington Tp.	Hannah Hackenberg, Washington Tp.
4/13/1847	" John		Sarah Repass
9/27/1849	" Peter		Catherine Gundrum
6/23/1850	" Daniel	Chapman Tp.	Elizabeth Herrold, Chapman Tp.
5/25/1851	" Jacob	Conter Tp.	Lovina Gill, Center Tp.
4/5/1862	" Benjamin		Mrs. Lucy A. Krouse, Washington Tp.
8/13/1865	" Henry F.		Emma J. Woodling, Washington Tp.
7/11/1867	" Jacob		Kate Kinney, Penn Tp.
3/14/1869	" Henry	Middlecreek Tp.	Charlotte Spade, Middleburg, Pa.
10/19/1873	Reitz, John	Trevorton, Pa.	Lucinda Charles, Freeburg, Pa.
11/11/1858	" Tobias	Juniata Co.	Molly Garman, Perry Tp.
5/21/1857	Renninger, Aaron		Harriet Barber, Franklin Tp.
9/9/1858	" Simon		Abigail Boney, Washington Tp.
6/6/1863	" Henry	Franklin Tp.	Savilla Hummel, Middlecreek Tp.
1/21/1875	" Levi	Middlecreek Tp.	Mary J. Benfer "
2/23/1854	Rine, John		Matilda Arbogast, Perry Tp.
10/26/1854	" Joseph	Chapman Tp.	Elizabeth Straub, Chapman Tp.
12/24/1857	" Jacob		Catherine Apple, Washington Tp.
10/8/1863	" Henry		Malinda Garman
2/9/1865	" Jacob J.		Sarah Lauver, Juniata Co.
2/13/1868	" John M.	Chapman Tp.	Elizabeth Klinger, Gratz, Pa.
9/4/1862	Ritter, Samuel		Mrs. Elizabeth Fisher, Penn Tp.
12/25/1875	Roads, Samuel	Lebanon Co.	Ellen Donmoyer, Franklin Tp.
2/15/1844	Romig, John	E. Buffalo Tp.	Margaret Stettler, E. Buffalo Tp.
12/6/1855	" Andrew		Mary A. Boyer, Penn Tp.
12/3/1846	Roush, Daniel	Liverpool, Pa.	Sarah Shuman, Liverpool, Pa.
3/26/1848	" Nathan	Penn Tp.	Elizabeth Duck, Penn Tp.
8/3/1848	" Philip	Washington Tp.	Caroline Rine, Washington Tp.
12/10/1848	" Aaron		Susan Rohrer
6/2/1850	" Henry		Margaret Fisher
7/20/1851	" Edward		Catherine Heintzelman, Chapman Tp.
3/15/1853	" Jacob		Selena Mohr, Middlecreek Tp.
10/29/1854	" Charles	Freeburg, Pa.	Matilda Straub, Chapman Tp.
7/4/1855	" George		———— Bertch, Freeburg, Pa.
11/6/1856	" Samuel		Malinda Freyman, Middlecreek Tp.
7/26/1863	" Joseph	Washington Tp.	Mary Kline, "
9/7/1865	" Jarius	" "	Emma Courtney "
3/10/1867	" Ezra	" "	Mary Bollinger "
12/1/1872	" Simon	Chapman Tp.	Hannah Heiges, Chapman Tp.

8/10/1848	Row, James	Penn Tp.	Catherine Laudenslager, Penn Tp.
3/15/1849	" David	"	Maria Hain, Penn Tp.
4/4/1852	" George		Mary Boyer
4/5/1855	" Frederick		Rachale Rummel, Penn Tp.
4/24/1856	" Jonathan		Catherine Boyer "
12/25/1856	" Daniel		Anna Ritter "
3/12/1857	" Isaac		Mary Luck, "
5/5/1857	" Frank		Salome Erdly "
7/16/1857	" Jacob	Penn Tp.	Harriet " "
11/10/1867	" Benjamin		Catherine Row "
6/2/1859	" Samuel		Susan Laudenslager'"
8/18/1859	" Isaac	Liverpool, Pa.	Louise Meiser, Perry Tp.
10/16/1860	" Jacob		Hannah Musselman, Penn Tp.
2/5/1861	" Edward		Lovina Duck, "
2/12/1861	" Reuben		Amelia Musser "
12/24/1865	" William H.		Mary A. Herman
10/31/1867	" John		Lydia Luck "
1/5/1868	" Isaac	Penn Tp.	Diana Jarrett "
12/24/1868	" George W.	Jackson Tp.	Lydia Hane, Monroe Tp.
5/22/1852	Ruhl, John		Mrs. Anna Smith
6/21/1874	Saners, Isaac	Middlecreek Tp.	Susan Derk, Middlecreek Tp.
11/7/1872	Sassaman, Jonas, Jr.	Monroe Tp.	Clara Conley, Monroe Tp.
12/31/1865	Saners, Henry		Lydia Dunkelberger, Middlecreek Tp.
4/9/1860	" Adam		Susan Yerger "
10/14/1845	Schlabbig, Nathan	Washington Tp.	" Kants, Washington Tp.
11/29/1840	Schnee, Michael		Anna Deckard, Liverpool, Pa.
2/14/1841	" Philip		Anna Arbogast
6/11/1865	" William	Perry Tp.	Caroline Maurer, Perry Tp.
2/23/1871	" Mathias		Mrs. Eliza Weaver, Center Tp.
8/24/1873	" Philip S.		Ellen Morr, Washington Tp.
10/14/1866	Scholl, Henry		Lizzie Lenig, Chapman Tp.
6/23/1872	" "	Union Tp.	Mrs. Mollie Sechrist, Union Tp.
3/3/1850	Schroyer, William	Selinsgrove, Pa.	Elizabeth Morr, Washington Tp.
11/1/1849	Sears, Jacob		Lydia Mitterling, Perry Tp.
7/9/1871	" George W.		Sophia Mengle, Perry Tp.
12/10/1871	Sechrist, Tobias	Union Co.	Emma J. Mitchell, Center Tp.
9/26/1842	Seebold, Joseph	"	Nancy Springer, Union Co.
3/15/1857	" Henry	"	Anna E. Wetzel, Snyder Co.
12/13/1868	Seiler, John H.	Northumberland Co.	Araminta Meiser, Perry Tp.
10/30/1856	Shadle, John		Margaret Meiser, Perry Tp.
8/15/1841	Shaffer, John		Sophia Garman
12/21/1843	" William	Chapman Tp.	Rebecca Herrold, Chapman Tp.
1/16/1844	" "	"	Barbara Garman "
2/18/1847	" Amos		Caroline Goodling "
2/18/1855	" Daniel		Susan Lenig, Washington Tp.
2/10/1857	" William		Mrs. Lucetta Glatfelder
2/16/1858	" Thomas		Hannah Dressler, Perry Tp.
6/10/1860	" Benjamin W.		Sarah Kantz, Washington Tp.
12/26/1860	" Solomon M.		" D. Kramer
2/21/1864	" George	Perry Tp.	Elizabeth Haas, Perry Tp.
8/9/1870	" Henry C.	Washington Tp.	Araminta Kreider, Penn Tp.
8/20/1871	" David		Caroline Woodling, Freeburg, Pa.
10/18/1874	" Wilson	Perry Tp.	Catherine Hupp, Juniata Co.
9/12/1875	" John	Washington Tp.	Matilda Reichenbach, WashingtonTp
10/9/1845	Shambach, Charles		Elizabeth Bilger
1/29/1857	Shamory, Peter		Mary Gaugler
7/11/1845	Shannon, Joseph	Mifflinburg, Pa.	Mary Stettler, Center Tp.

12/23/1858	Sellers, Joseph	Juniata Co.	Eve Kepler, Perry Tp.
12/10/1874	Seebold, Charles	Middleburg, Pa.	Emma Stahlnecker, Middleburg, Pa.
2/13/1862	Shellenberger, Enoch	Perry Co.	Margaret Berry, Freeburg, Pa.
10/5/1854	" Amos		Mary Berge, Juniata Co.
11/20/1856	" Michael		Barbara Reitz, Richfield, Pa.
11/27/1856	" Jacob		Caroline Brown, Juniata Co.
12/19/1863	Shelly, Abraham	Richfield, Pa.	Catherine Barge, Juniata Co.
1/19/1865	" "	"	" " "
2/10/1857	" Daniel		Polly Bender
3/4/1862	Shetterly, Frederick		Sarah Troup, Perry Tp.
2/24/1867	" John		Mary E. "
10/26/1848	Shidow, Samuel	Perry Tp.	Elizabeth Kauber, Perry Tp.
1/30/1844	Shipton, Robert		Catherine Nerhood
9/9/1869	Shirk, Jacob	Freeburg, Pa.	Jane Keeler, Freeburg, Pa.
7/24/1851	Sholly, Jacob	Chapman Tp.	Susan Snyder, Chapman Tp.
12/21/1854	Shotsberger, John		Sarah Holtzapple
12/20/1857	" Elias	Freeburg, Pa.	Amelia Naugle, Washington Tp.
10/26/1873	" Jonathan		Barbara Steffen, Chapman Tp.
10/4/1870	Showers, Adam		Mary Stauffer, Selinsgrove, Pa.
6/10/1866	Shumory, J. H.	Chapman Tp.	Mrs. Elizabeth Rice, Chapman Tp.
11/4/1858	Shrader, Daniel		Elizabeth Wayne, Franklin Tp.
11/4/1858	Shuler, Joseph	Liverpool, Pa.	Susan Roush, Freeburg, Pa.
1/10/1841	Shuman, Henry		Elizabeth Stalcy
4/1/1847	" Michael	Liverpool, Pa.	" Chesnay, Liverpool, Pa.
1/28/1864	Shurrick, Abel	Juniata Co.	Catherine Aucker, Perry Tp.
12/18/1856	Sieber, Joseph		Mrs. Sarah Motz, Washington Tp.
10/10/1869	Smeigh, John B.	Sunbury, Pa.	Emeline Houtz
10/19/1843	Smith, Philip		Esther Witmer
8/10/1851	" Jonas	Penn Tp.	Mary Ann Row, Penn Tp.
3/28/1852	" Hiram P.	"	Caroline Landenslager, Penn Tp.
11/20/1860	" Jonathan	Fulton Co., Ind.	Mrs. Mary A. Snyder, Chapman Tp.
8/23/1863	" Jacob		Margaret Row, Penn Tp.
8/14/1856	" Henry		Lydia " "
12/24/1857	" George		Susan Apple, Washington Tp.
5/31/1860	" Michael		Elizabeth Kreider
11/21/1869	" Benjamin	Penn Tp.	Sarah Knouse, Penn Tp.
4/16/1871	" George S.		Louisa Hovis, Perry Tp.
4/18/1875	" Philip H.		Mary McLensie, Selinsgrove, Pa.
11/24/1846	Snyder, Benjamin	Perry Tp.	Anna Graybill, Perry Tp.
2/19/1850	" Christian	Huntingdon Co.	Mary Gingrich, Washington Tp.
4/24/1862	" Jeremiah	Penn Tp.	Harriet Smith, Middleburg, Pa.
11/2/1862	" Jacob		Sarah Rine, Chapman Tp.
12/25/1864	" "	Penn Tp.	Clara Amig, Selinsgrove, Pa.
8/12/1866	" Samuel	"	Sallie Brouse, Penn Tp.
11/4/1852	" Edward	Perry Tp.	Elmira Rathfon, Perry Tp.
5/11/1854	" Jonathan		Hannah Golnet, "
9/14/1856	" Henry		Mary Meiser, Perry Tp.
8/9/1857	" Lewis		Louise Mease, Penn Tp.
12/1/1857	" G. Washington		Caroline Hartman, Shamokin Dam, Pa.
9/11/1870	" David	Jackson Tp.	Mary Reigle, Washington Tp.
12/4/1870	" Daniel S.		Emma Mengle, Perry Tp.
2/25/1874	" George S.		Kate Bowersox, Middleburg, Pa.
2/6/1844	Somers, Samuel		Lucinda Maurer, Washington Tp.
2/9/1841	Souloff, Benjamin		Susan Hallman, Perry Tp.
10/11/1846	Spade, George		Phoebe Hendricks
4/6/1854	" Henry		Barbara Stauber, Perry Tp.
8/16/1860	" John		Polly Gerhart "
1/8/1857	Specht, John		Catherine Bender, Franklin Tp.
9/4/1855	Spriggle, John F.		Susan Strawser
3/15/1860	Springman, Augustus		Josephine Burd, Juniata Co.
11/18/1847	Sponeberger, Wm.	Liverpool, Pa.	Catherine Charles, Liverpool, Pa.
8/15/1875	Spotts, Isaac		" A. Heiges, Perry Tp.

9/11/1870	Stahl, William S.	Union Tp.	Lydia Row, Penn Tp.
7/7/1863	Stahlnecker, Elias		Mrs. Maria Smith, Penn Tp.
1/19/1840	Staley, Frederick	Liverpool, Pa.	Abbie Speece, Liverpool, Pa.
2/7/1840	Stark, "		Mary Gontz
1/7/1872	Stauffer, Manoah		Lydia Sechrist, Union Tp.
2/28/1864	Spade, John W.		Sarah Eyster, Franklin Tp.
11/12/1840	Steel, David	Perry Co.	Rebecca Steffen, Perry Co.
10/3/1852	Steffen, John	Washington Tp.	Elizabeth Reigle, Washington Tp.
4/15/1856	" Joseph		Sarah Shotsberger, Chapman Tp.
9/24/1871	" Isaac		Emma Noecker, Chapman Tp.
11/23/1856	Steininger, Christian		Susan Yeager, Franklin Tp.
12/13/1845	" George	Center Tp.	" Steininger, Center Tp.
12/8/1840	Stephen, Daniel (Steffen?)		Ann Hunter, Perry Co.
4/8/1851	Stepp, John	Northumberland Co.	Catherine Keller, Chapman Tp.
2/5/1852	Stettler, John	"	Polly Millhoff, Washington Tp.
9/3/1857	" Benjamin		Elizabeth Row, Penn Tp.
10/—/1874	" "	Penn Tp.	Mrs. Susan Wittenmeyer, Middleburg, Pa
2/23/1875	" George F.	Middleburg, Pa.	Jane Houser, Middleburg, Pa.
4/30/1840	Stevens, Samuel		Mary Johns
5/11/1854	Stiver, John		Salome Steffen, Perry Tp.
3/30/1845	Stock, Lewis	Penn Tp.	Susan Schroyer, Penn Tp.
3/8/1846	Stock, Joseph	"	Esther Hain "
4/29/1850	" John	Perry Tp.	Susan Arbogast, Perry Tp.
9/20/1860	" Benjamin		Catherine " Perry Tp.
8/20/1871	" (Stuck), Waldo		Salome Moyer, Franklin Tp.
2/9/1841	Stohler, George		Mary Arnold
6/17/1845	Straub, John	Perry Tp.	Maria Houser, Perry Tp.
10/12/1845	" Daniel	Chapman Tp.	Lydia Heimbach, Chapman Tp.
4/1/1850	" George B.		Catherine A. Roush
2/9/1871	" E. M.	Penn Tp.	Anna Boyer, Penn Tp.
9/8/1872	" Amos		Sarah Diemer
8/23/1874	" Ben	Washington Tp.	Mary Hepner, Washington Tp.
10/8/1857	" Philip		Maria Erdly, Penn Tp.
6/27/1858	" Jonas		Barbara Steffen, Chapman Tp.
6/17/1860	" Elias		Emma J. Mull, Penn Tp.
12/8/1860	" Samuel	Washington Tp.	Sarah Weyland
6/9/1864	" John S.	"	Catherine Pontius, Washington Tp.
5/4/1843	Strayer, Francis		Anna Bird
7/10/1853	" William	Freeburg, Pa.	Margaret Duck, Freeburg, Pa.
11/24/1853	" John		Elizabeth Arbogast, Perry Tp.
8/20/1850	Strawser, Elias	Perry Tp.	Susan Zimmerman, Perry Tp.
4/25/1849	Summers, Henry		Catherine Morr, Washington Tp.
2/19/1846	Swartz, Daniel		Eve Arbogast
6/10/1855	" David	Chapman Tp.	Caroline Hovis, Chapman Tp.
2/9/1856	Swartzlander, William		Catherine Leitzel, Middlecreek Tp.
12/8/1840	Swineford, Albright	Juniata Co.	Sarah Diehl, Juniata Co.
3/14/1843	" John		Mary Hilbish
9/24/1846	" Henry		Sarah Hassenplug
9/1/1850	Tayer, Ira	Port Trevorton, Pa.	Mrs. Elizabeth Witmer, Chapman Tp.
9/23/1866	Teats, Robert		Elisabeth Womer, Perry Tp.
7/6/1855	Thamer, John		" Kratzer, Penn Tp.
3/1/1855	Thomas, George		Mary M. Benninger
12/22/1864	" John		Amanda Musser, Franklin Tp.
1/29/1857	Thursby, Jacob		Polly Steffen
11/22/1858	" William		Caroline Kelly, Chapman Tp.

3/21/1841	Tobson, Samuel		Isabel Hamilton
7/30/1840	Traub, -----		Elizabeth Roth
4/23/1843	" Samuel		Rebecca Reichenbach, Washington Tp.
12/27/1846	" Frederick		Polly Reichenbach
11/21/1848	" David	Chapman Tp.	Anna Rumfelt, Chapman Tp.
3/18/1852	Trego, Benjamin	Northumberland Co.	Catherine Kratzer, Chapman Tp.
12/9/1852	Treon, Peter		Sarah A. Glass
11/10/1870	Tressler, Benjamin		Mrs. Barbara Kerstetter, JuniataCo.
3/12/1871	Troup, William		Elizabeth Hoffman, Perry Tp.
1/30/1848	Troutman, Isaac		Susan Grubb, Liverpool, Pa.
3/25/1845	Ulrich, John George	Selinsgrove, Pa.(?)	Sarah Row, Juniata Co.
2/13/1851	" Perry	"	Mary Morr, Washington Tp.
11/25/1856	" Benjamin		Angeline Pawling, Penn Tp.
3/7/1854	Ulsh, Josias		Sarah Arbogast, Perry Tp.
6/19/1870	Uplinger, Henry		Mrs. Margaret Diemer
10/4/1840	Van Ormer, George		Maria Comfort
12/10/1848	Vogel, Bernhart	Juniata Co.	Barbara Kohler, Juniata Co.
12/20/1846	Wagner, Jacob	Liverpool, Pa.	Amelia Hains, Liverpool, Pa.
1/16/1851	" Abraham	Beaver Tp.	Mary E. Moyer, Beaver Tp.
6/7/1853	" William		Mary A. Mathias
11/8/1853	" Henry	Penn Tp.	Susan Hain, Penn Tp.
3/13/1856	" "		Amelia Moyer, Beaver Tp.
11/24/1859	" Eli J.		Hannah Gilbert, Jackson Tp.
3/20/1860	" Levi		Catherine Kreider, Penn Tp.
7/9/1854	Walborn, William		Elizabeth Fisher, Penn Tp.
12/27/1866	" Henry		Sarah Mitman, Penn Tp.
11/2/1843	Walter, Edward	Penn Tp.	Mary Laudenslager, Penn Tp.
10/27/1846	" Solomon		Catherine Mark
11/22/1846	" Henry		Matilda Bowersox
12/31/1850	" Samuel	Chapman Tp.	Elizabeth Luck, Penn Tp.
6/30/1853	" Michael	Selinsgrove, Pa.	Elizabeth Fryer, Chapman Tp.
1/30/1872	" Frederick		Susan Hughes, Penn Tp.
8/11/1872	" Dr. Eyer	Mifflinburg, Pa.	Mary Sanders, Center Tp.
5/23/1875	" Frank P.		Margaret Hare, Franklin Tp.
8/14/1845	Waters, Jonathan	Selinsgrove, Pa.	Rebecca Albert, Selinsgrove, Pa.
10/17/1847	Watney, John	Bradford Co.	Adalia Stroh, Selinsgrove, Pa.
12/1/1857	Watts, John G.		Margaret Showers, Richfield, Pa.
4/11/1858	" Samuel W.		Abbie Duck, Freeburg, Pa.
1/16/1848	Wayne, Samuel	Perry Tp.	Sarah Wayne, Perry Tp.
7/28/1846	" Abraham	Juniata Co.	Phoebe Shelly, Juniata Co.
4/8/1849	Weaver, Adam	Center Co.	Catherine Botdorf, Freeburg, Pa.
10/5/1851	" Charles	Lewisburg, Pa.	Sarah Van Ormer, Perry Tp.
7/4/1869	Weirick, Elias		Rebecca Renninger, Washington Tp.
8/14/1869	" Franklin	Selinsgrove, Pa.	Clara Rohback, Selinsgrove, Pa.
3/14/1848	Weiser, Jacob	Chapman Tp.	Rebecca Neimond, Chapman Tp.
12/8/1848	" Isaac		Catherine Houseworth, Chapman Tp.
3/8/1849	" Josiah	"	Mary Fryer, Chapman Tp.
7/8/1856	Weist, John	Philadelphia, Pa.	Emma Boyer, Freeburg, Pa.
1/21/1844	Weller, William	Perry Tp.	Mary A. Lauver, Perry Tp.
7/5/1849	" "	Washington Tp.	Lucy Ann Roush, Washington Tp.
3/29/1866	" Levi		Mary A. Rathfon, Perry Tp.
10/18/1853	Wentzel, Adam		Catherine Rine, Chapman Tp.
11/25/1841	Werner, Moses	Perry Co.	Rebecca Zeiders, Perry Co.
10/7/1858	" Philip	Chapman Tp.	Catherine Reichenbach

4/8/1852	Wetzel, Samuel	Union Co.	Susan Hummel, Union Co.
12/26/1858	" William		Sarah Aurand, Penn Tp.
2/10/1870	" Miles		Emma J. Roush, Freeburg, Pa.
5/10/1874	" Cornelius	Washington Tp.	Matilda Holtzapple, Washington Tp.
11/7/1875	" Solomon J.		Jane Kratzer, Jackson Tp.
3/3/1859	Wayne (Winey?), Amos		Rachael Rinninger, Franklin Tp.
9/22/1857	Willis, Henry	Middleburg, Pa.	Susan Schoch, Middlecreek Tp.
4/15/1852	Wilt, Washington		Sarah Houseworth
10/15/1857	" Lewis		Polly Keely, Juniata Co.
3/28/1860	Winey, William G.		Sarah Scholl, Richfield, Pa.
12/5/1867	" Christian I.	Juniata Co.	Amanda Landis, Richfield, Pa.
6/6/1875	" Foster	Richfield, Pa.	Hannah Garman, Richfield, Pa.
10/29/1840	Wirt, John		Catherine A. Dirk
12/21/1854	Witmer, David		Sarah Miller, Penn Tp.
10/14/1865	" Daniel		Mary Schnee, Perry Tp.
6/15/1845	Wittenmeyer, Amos	Center Tp.	Elizabeth Hassinger, Center Tp.
6/13/1867	Wolf, Daniel	Washington Tp.	Louise Adams, Washington Tp.
9/9/1866	Womer, Jonathan	Perry Tp.	Mary Kepler, Perry Tp.
8/24/1842	Woodling, Samuel		Julia Stricker, Washington Tp.
1/17/1847	" William	Penn Tp.	Mary Musselman, Penn Tp.
8/29/1852	" "		" Smith "
7/1/1852	" Isaac	Washington Tp.	Catherine Gilbert, Washington Tp.
1/15/1850	" Levi	"	Caroline Glass "
8/6/1854	" Henry		Susan Snyder, Penn Tp.
1/11/1856	" Eli	Penn Tp.	Mary Pontius, "
2/2/1860	" Samuel		Elizabeth Fisher, Penn Tp.
11/24/1870	" Henry		Mary J. Kratzer, Penn Tp.
11/14/1847	Worley, Samuel	Center Tp.	Hannah Woirick, Center Tp.
1/28/1841	Wright, Charles		Eliza Hunter
4/15/1841	" John	Greenwood Tp.	Jane Bonsall, Greenwood Twp.
11/26/1840	Yeager, John		Barbara Sechrist
12/6/1868	" William		Sarah Rine, Washington Tp.
6/4/1865	Yorger, Henry B.		Catherine Kramer, Middlecreek Tp.
7/12/1868	" William		Elizabeth Bingaman, Perry Tp.
8/4/1870	" Henry		Mrs. Nancy Smith, Middlecreek Tp.
10/30/1870	" Jacob J.	Perry Tp.	Caroline Rine, Perry Tp.
5/19/1859	Yoder, Jacob	Lewisburg, Pa.	Mrs. Margaret Kohler
12/29/1870	" Jonas		Emma Arnold, Juniata Co.
11/16/1848	Young, John	Union Co.	Sarah Warion, Union Co.
11/5/1871	Zechman, Henry	Center Tp.	Mary Walter, Center Tp.
8/20/1841	Zeiders, Jacob		Rebecca Finchel
2/11/1840	Ziegler, Daniel		Mary Keiser
3/22/1846	" Harrison	Chapman Tp.	Cathrine Snyder, Chapman Tp.
5/14/1864	" John		" Lenig, Washington Tp.
11/5/1840	Zimmerman, Jacob		Catherine Shaffer
2/22/1853	" Henry	Perry Tp.	Mary Landis, Perry Tp.

PART VII

MARRIAGES OF SOME PENNSYLVANIA SOLDIERS AND PATRIOTS OF THE REVOLUTIONARY PERIOD.

DATE	NAME	COUNTY	WIFE
?	Acker, Jacob	Northampton	Eberhartine Heisler
	" "	Lancaster	Anna Graybill (John)
2/13/1776	Adam, Simon	Berks	Catherine Eck
	Adams, Albert	Cumberland	Agnes Blain
	" David	York	Mary ———————
	" George	Snyder	Catherine ———
4/26/1756	" Capt. James	Cumberland	Isabel Weldon
	Albion, Ens. William	Westmoreland	Jane ———————
	Aldridge, John	"	Elizabeth Vees
	Alexander, Alexander	Philadelphia	Catherine ———————
10/——/1778	" Hugh	Bedford	Margaret Elder (Robert)
2/17/1789	" "	"	Mary Bell (Joseph)
1789	" James	Mifflin	Rosa Reed, Franklin Co.
	" John	Mifflin	Mary Clark
1789	" William	Cumberland	Margaret Call
11/11/1770	" Capt. William	Bedford	Isabella Alexander (Cousin?)
	Allen, Adam	?	Nancy ———————
	" David	Juniata	Mary Nelson (Robert)
1798	" Josiah	Westmoreland	Susan Dickerson
	" William	Washington	Susan Ruckman
	Allison, Andrew	Cumberland	Sally Barr
5/7/1789	" Archibald, Jr.	Union	Eleanor McCormick
	" John	Washington	Mary Herron
9/13/1771	Alter, John	Lancaster	Helenor Sheetz
	Anderson, Capt. James	"	Jane Tate (Rev. Joseph)
	" " "	"	Margaret Chambers
	" William	"	Jane Bell
11/10/1766	Angst Daniel	Berks	Magdalene Fisher (G.Ulrich)
4/17/1774	Apgar, William	(New Jersey)	Catherine Pickle (Bickle)(Conrad)
	App, Mathias	Snyder	Elizabeth Buch (Book, or Buck)
	Applegate, Benjamin	Northampton	Phoebe Grimes
	Archibale, Thomas	Westmoreland	Mary Kent
	Armstrong, Lt. John		Tabitha Goforth
	Arnold, Lawrence	Northumberland	Mary ———————
1761	Atcheson, Matthew		Jane Reed
1793	Aughe, Harmon	Philadelphia	Mary Hunger
	Aurand, Lt. Daniel	Union	Mary Appolinia ———————
	" Henry	Snyder	Rebecca Dreisbach (Martin)
	" John	Union	Anna Christina ———————
	" "	Union	Mary Elizabeth Pontius
	Avit, Richard	Philadelphia	Jane ———————
7/26/1759	Awl, Jacob	Lancaster	Sarah Sturgeon (Jeremiah)
1781	Ayers, John	Dauphin	Mary Montgomery (Gen. William)
1786	" "	"	Jane Lytle (Joseph)
	" William	"	Mary Kean (Charles)
	Bailey, George	Northumberland	Barbara Lehman (Tobias)
1777	Baird, Thomas	Cumberland	Esther Kilgore
	Baldwin, John	Washington	Jane House
	Baldy, Christopher	Union	Susanna ———————
	" "	"	Mrs. Eva. Metzger, widow of Daniel
8/3/1777	Balsbough, Valentine	Dauphin	Elizabeth Miller (George)
1779	Barber, Phineas	Northumberland	Ann Kennedy
4/29/1784	Barnet, John	Dauphin	Mary McEwen
	Bernhart, Mathias	Union	Margaret ———————
	Bartges, Christopher	Snyder	Barbara ———————
2/16/1782	Bartholomew, Capt. Benjamin	Chester	Rachael Dewees
	Bashore, John Michael	Union	Elizabeth Swartz (Peter, Sr.)
	Baxter, James	Cumberland	Rachael Riddle

	Baxter, Co. William		Elizabeth ————
	Bayley, Thomas	Lancaster	Elizabeth Kelly (William)
1759	Beale, Capt. Thomas	Cumberland	Sarah Todhunter
	Beatty, Alexander, Sr.	Union	Agnes ————
1768	" James	Dauphin	Alice Ann Irwin
ca.1784	" John	Union	Jane Banks (William)
	Bell, Ens. Walter	Lancaster	Catherine ————
1787	Benefield, George	Cumberland	Mary Buchanan
	Benfer, J. George	Snyder	Mary Magdalene Miller (J. Fred.)
11/2/1784	Best, John	North'd.	Mary Haas
	" "	Northampton	Susanna ————
	Betz (Beats), Urban	Cumb.	Dorothy Baker (or Barker)
	Bickel, Henry	Union	Esther Regina Sharp
	Bickel, Lt. Jacob	Snyder	Mary Magdalene Ulrich(J.George,Sr.)
	Bickel, John	"	Catherine ————
	Bickel, Simon	"	Cath. Elizabeth Buchtel (John)
	Bickel, Tobias, Jr.	"	Catherine Anmiller (John)
	Bieber, Adam	Lycoming	Magdalene Reber
1778	Biggs, Robert		Jane ————
	Bickel, Thomas	Snyder	Barbara Weaver (Capt. Michael)
	Bilger (Bilgear),Fred.	Lancaster	Elizabeth ————
4/6/1779	Bingaman, Frederick	Snyder	Christina Huffnagle (Christopher,Sr.)
9/—-/1808	Bisbiny, George	Philadelphia	Elizabeth ————
	Bitting, Capt. Adam		Deborah ————
ca.1770	Black, James	Westmoreland	Jane McDonough
	" "		Ruth ————
	Blaine, Co. Ephraim	Cumb.	Rebecca Galbraith
	Blair, Thomas	8th Pa.	Mary Ann Jones
	Blunt, Andrew	West'd.	Mary Calhoun
1785	Boas, Henry	Lancaster	Dorothea Baumgartner
	Boevard, Capt. James	Union	Hannah Beatty (Alexander, Sr.)
	Boggs, Alexander	Lancaster	Anna Alricks, (Hermanus)
	" Capt. Andrew,Jr.	"	Mary ————
	Bohner, Nicholas	North'd.	Margaret Stahr
	Bolich, Andrew, Jr.	Berks	Margaret ————
	Bonine, Daniel	Lancaster	Elizabeth ———— 1st wife
			Sarah Miller 2nd wife
			Mary Copeland 3rd wife
	Boob (Boop, Bub)George	Snyder	Maria Margaret ————
	Book (Buch), Jacob		Mary ————
	Boone, Capt. Hawkins	Union	Jane ————
	Born, Peter	"	Barbara ————
2/14/1782	Bower, Jacob	Lancaster	Anna Rohrer
	Bowman, John	Bedford	Mary Magdalene ————
	Bowman, Philip Casper	Lancaster	Katherine Foust
1793	Bowyer, Peter	2nd Pa. Art.	Catherine Shellman (2nd wife)
1784	Boyd, Adam	Dauphin	Jeannette MacFarlane
5/13/1794	Boyd, Capt. John	North'd.	Mary Rebecca Bull (Gen. John)
	Boyd, William Y.	Northamp.	————Davidson
	Boyer, Charles B.	Berks	Mary Magdalene Reitnour
	" "	"	———— ————
6/24/1755	Boyer, J. Valentine	Phila.	Maria Christina Winck (Christian)
	" Leonard	"	Margaret ————
	" Philip	Lancaster	Elizabeth Nungesser, 1st wife
11/26/1801	" "	Snyder	Catherine Keely 2nd wife
	" "	Mont.	Catherine ————
7/29/1777	" Samuel	Berks	Catherine Enser
	Brandon, William	Dauphin	Agnes Wiggins (John)
1783	Bratton, James, Jr.	Mifflin	Bathsheba Ripley
	" Capt. Wm.	"	Hester Hamilton
	Brannon, John		Elizabeth, Harborn

	Brenneman, Christian	York	Mary Cressner
	Brent, Lt. George	Lancaster	Elizabeth Edmunds
	Brenton, William		Fannie ————
	Bretz, Benjamin	Dauphin	Margaret Paul
ca. 1781	Brewer, Benjamin	Westmoreland	Katie Mellinger
1785	Bridgewater, Levi	"	Patience Stillwell
11/11/1745	Brinkerhoff, Joris	Adams	Laeltic Isabella Demarest
12/25/1790	Britton, Joseph	Snyder	Hannah Frank, Montgomery Co.
	" Samuel	Phila.	Mary ————
10/26/1780	Brobst, John	Union	Catherine ————
5/14/1804	Brotherton, Robert	Erie	Dorthea Reichard (Henry), 2nd wife
5/3/1807	Brown, Nathan	"	Tamar Samons
	Brosius, J. George	North'd.	Mary Catherine ————
		"	Maria ————
	Brown, Johnston	Mifflin	Keziah ————
	Brown, Matthew	Union	Eleanor Lytle
5/11/1767	" Roger	Perry	Tabitha Morrison
	Brownlee, James	Washington	Jean Rankin
	Bryson, Lt. Samuel	Juniata	Ann Harris (John)
	Buchanan, Robert	Mifflin	Dorcas ————
ca. 1774	Buck, Capt. Aholiab	Luzerne	Lucretia York (Amos)
	Burdge, Samuel	Cumb.	Nancy McCartney (McCartney) 1st wife
			Agnes Ann Johnson, 2nd wife
2/25/1790	Burrows, Hubbard B.	Erie	Mary Wilkins
	" John	Lycoming	Jane Torbert, 1st wife
1807	" "	"	Mary McCormick, widow of William
	Bussinger, Conrad	Northamp.	Barbara Yuncer
	Butler, Benjamin	Chester	Hannah ————
	Byers, Ens. William	Washington	Mary Munn, wid. of Sol Froman, Sr.
			Hannah Bunnell, 2nd wife
	Byrn, Lawrence	3rd Pa. Reg.	Elizabeth ————, Philadelphia, Pa.
10/1/1771	Caldwell, Andrew	Dauphin	Martha Cochran
7/26/1783	Campbell, Christopher	Union	Martha Everitt, Lebanon, N. J.
	" Daniel	"	Catherine Klinesmith (Baltzer)
	" John	Washington	Rosanna ————
	" John	North'd.	Elizabeth Stauts
	" John	Lancaster	Martha ————
	" McDonald	Union	Margaret Tingeley, 1st wife
			————Valentine, widow, 2nd wife
	" Michael	North'd.	Sarah ————
2/6/1755	" Patrick	Dauphin	Eleanor Hayes (Patrick)
	" Capt. Robert	Phila.	Mary ————
8/3/1782	" Robert	North'd	Mary Reynolds, N. J.
1791	" William	Phila.	Rachael Robinson
	" William	Cumb.	Margaret Riddle
	Carbaugh, Peter	Lancaster	Mary ————
3/26/1784	Carner, Anthony	Snyder	Catherine Strombeck, Philadelphia P.
	Carr, Capt. Thomas	Westmore	Hannah Coombs
	Carson, Capt. Walter		Mary ————
	Cartwright, John	Northamp.	Margaret ————
	Catt, Philip	8th Pa. Reg.	Sarah ————
1781	Caughey, Andrew	Erie	Elizabeth Caughey, a cousin
1758	Chamberlin, Col. William	Union	Elizabeth Ten Broeck, 1st wife
3/3/1771	" " "	"	Ann Park, 2nd wife
1782	" " "	"	Margaret Park, 3rd wife
8/16/1794	" " "	"	Mary Kemble, 4th wife
	Chambers, Ens. Robert, Sr.		Cath. Klinesmith, Wid. of Dan Campbell
1781	Chandler, Josiah	Warren	Eunice Dana, Pomfret, Conn.
12/—/1778	Cheeseman, Benjamin	Erie	Sarah Howe, Roxbury, Mass.
	Cherry, Aaron	Westmore	Mary Phillips
	Christ, Sgt. Adam	Union	Elizabeth Follmer

	Clark, Brice, Sr.	Lancaster	Mary Crawford, 1st wife
			Marg. Clark, wid of Robt.Anderson
	Clark, John	Washington	Julia Ann Hooker
	Clark, Col. John	Union	Florence Watson
	" Robert, Sr.	"	Jane ————
	" "	Perry	Mary Alexander (Pugh, Sr.)
4/10/1797	" Samuel	Warren	Catherine Reese
	" Lt. Co. William	Cumberland	Nancy Brown (George)
	" Capt. William	Union	Elizabeth Boan (Rev. John)
	Clemens Michael	Snyder	Eve ————
1805	Clement, Joseph	North'd.	Hannah Hazen (Ezra), New Jersey
	Clingan, Thomas	Lancaster	Mrs. James McFarland
6/11/1778	Clingan, Lt. Wm. Jr.	Union	Jane Roan (Rev. John)
1790	Cochran, John	North'd	Sarah Lattimore
12/4/1760	" Dr. John	Dauphin	Gertrude Schuyler (Sister of Gen Phil)
ca.1779	" John	"	Caroline ————
11/22/1770	" James	"	Mary Montgomery
	" Samuel	"	Margaret
12/11/1777	" Samuel, Jr	"	Mary Shorer
9/17/1761	Coe, Lt. Ebenezer	Westmorel'd	Eunice Jaggar, Morristown, N. J.
12/29/1774	Cohoon, Nathaniel	Erie	Abia Stuart, Kent, Conn.
9/—/1777	Cole, Barbabas	"	Sarah Alworth, Dutchess Co., N.Y.
1750	Cole, Col Philip	Union	Elizabeth Edie
1788	Colglazier, Lt. David	Westmorel'd	Cynthiana May
	Colpetzer, Adam	Union	———— Boto (George)
1780	Commons, Robert	Chester	Ruth Hayes
	Cook, David	Lancaster	Martha ————
9/20/1764	" Elihu	Erie	Carinda Cook (Ebenezer)
1796	" Isaac	Phila	Ann (Stephens) Masterson
	" Samuel	Lancaster	Ann Allison (John)
	Cooke, Col. William	North'd	Sarah Simpson (Samuel)
	Cool, Capt. Simon	"	Mary ————
	Cooper, Adam	Dauphin	———— Shott (Ludwig)
ca.1783	Cook, William	Erie	Margery Watts (David), Carlisle,Pa.
11/7/1825	Cooper, John	Dearborn Co.,Ind.	Anna Barbara Trout
ca.1784	" Michael	Berks	Mary Griffin
1790	Coryell, George	Union	———— Van Buskirk
ca.1779	Cotton, Capt. John	Washington	Lucy ————
	Courtright, Cornelius	Erie	Catherine ————
3/20/1777	Cowden, Capt. James	Dauphin	Mary Crouch (James)
	Craig, Col.Thomas (Daniel)	Northampton	Jean Jamison
	" Gen. Thomas	"	Dorothy Breinig
ca.1797	Crane, Abiathar	Erie	Ruth McClelland (James)
ca.1790	" Elihu	"	Ruth Park (Christopher)
	Crawford, Maj. James	North'd.	Rosanna Allison (John) 1st wife
			Agnes McDonald, 2nd wife
	Crawford, Richard	Montour	Elizabeth ————
	" Col William	Westmorel'd	Hannah ————
	Cribbs, John	"	Catherine Harrold (Christopher)
	Cromer, John	Lancaster	Sophia ————
9/22/1757	Crouch, James	Dauphin	Hannah Brown
1788	Cummins, Lt. John	Mifflin	Amelia Foreman
1/25/1780	Currier, Samuel	Erie	Anna Collins, New Hampshire
	Curtis, Capt.Marmaduke W.	Erie	Mary ————
1772	Daggett, John	Erie	Sarah Hawkins, Sharzee, Vt. 1st wife
			Polly Smith, Greenfield,Pa 2nd "
			Nancy Smith, Fairview, Pa. 3rd "
	Dale, Capt. Samuel	Union	Elizabeth Futhey(Samuel) 2nd wife
	Dalrymple, Davie	Warren	Mary Corning, 1st wife

ca.1787	Dauberman, Peter	Snyder	Catherine Eliz. Bartges(Christopher)
	Davis, David	Cumberland	Anne ————
1781	Davis, Elijah	Warren	Desire Lytle, Elizabeth, N. J.
	Dawson, Edward(d. in Ind)	(7th Pa.)	Hannah ————
5/21/1789	" Nicholas	Westmorel'd	Violet Littleton (John)
1801	Deal, Daniel	Lancaster	Catherine Shake
	Dean, William	Cumberland	Martha ————, Franklin Co.
	Decker, John, Sr.	York	Diana Kuykendall
	Decker, Joseph	York	Florinda ————
	" Luke	Chester	Sarah Kuykendall, 1st wife
			Trenny Claypool, 2nd wife
	De Long, John	Northampton	Mary ————
	Denny, Capt. Walter	Cumberland	Mary ————·
	Derr, George	Union	Fanny Yentzer
	Derr,(Durr), Leonard	Lancaster	Elizabeth ————
	Derr, Ludwig	Union	Catherine ————
	Dersham, Ludwig	"	Barbara ————
10/16/1785	Dewaltz, Peter	Erie	Hannah Davey, Kindon, N. Y.
12/4/1804	DeWitt, William	Bedford	Elizabeth White Connor
1789	Dickerman, John	(New York)	Thankful Smith (Col. Seth)
1779	Dickson, Capt. James	Erie	Mary Morris (Daniel), N. H. Conn.
5/3/1753	Dieffenderfer, Godfrey	Northampton	Anna Margaret Mattorn
	Diehl, Philip	(Ohio)	Elizabeth ————
	Diehlman, Michael	Snyder	Christina ————
3/—/1782	Ditto, Francis	"	Elinor Gift (J. Adam)
	Dilley, Caleb	Washington	Rebecca Martin
8/1/1777	Dillman, Andrew, Jr.	Snyder	Barbara Roush (Casper)
1791	Dixon, John	(Indiana)	Elizabeth Garrison
	" Joseph	Cumberland	Elizabeth Hurst
	Dixon, Lt. Sankey	Union	Ann ————
ca.1789	Donnell, Thomas	Cumberland	Nancy Barr
	Dorman, Ludwig	Union	Mary ————
	Dorough, Ephraim	"	Deborah Peak (James)
1777	Dougherty, William	Chester	Lydia Cox
	Douglass, Ens. David	York	Jean Buchanan, 1st wife, no issue
			Elizabeth Reay, 2nd wife
1788	Dowers, Conrad	Phila	Mary Shields
	Dreese, John	Snyder	Maria ————
	Druckenmiller,Frederick	"	Christina ————
	"	"	Anna Mary ————
	Drummond, James, Jr.	Cumberland	Nancy Griffiths
	Drown, John	Erie	Sally Ayres
ca.1795	Drum, Maj. Charles	Snyder	Catherine Snyder,wid.of Anthony Selin
4/29/1782	Duck, John	"	Elizabeth Aumiller (John)
	Dugan, Henry	Blair	Polly ————
9/20/1744	Dull, Capt. Casper	Mifflin	Hannah Matthews
1789	Duke, John	(Indiana)	Sally McNeal
1768	Dunlap, Alexander	Chester	Agnes Guy
ante 1776	" John	Lancaster	Voney Robins ————
10/3/1760	Dunn, Lt. Justice	Erie	Experience Stolle
	Dunn, Isaac		Jerusha Blackwell
1789	Dunn, Samuel	Chester	Anna Stagg
	Dusing, Nicholas	Snyder	Dorothy
4/6/1797	Dyal, John	Washington	Christina Davis, Mason Co., Ky.
	Dye, John	(11th Pa.)	Ruth Applegate
	Eakers, Dr. Joseph	Union	Elizabeth Blythe (Lt. William)
	Eckhart, Jacob	Snyder	Mrs Christina Druckenmiller(wid.of Fred)
1790	Edwards, John	Lancaster	Mary Jackson
	Ebersole, Christian	Erie	Frances Zuck

	Egle, Casper	Dauphin	Elizabeth Mentges (Francis, Sr.)
1796	" Valentine	"	" Thomas
	Elder, Col. Robert	"	Mary Jane Thompson
7/8/1784	Ellis, David	Erie	Sarah Washburn
	Emrick, David	Union	Catherine
4/11/1765	" Valentine	Berks	Cath. Fredrica Shott (Jacob)
5/13/1764	Enders, Philip C.		Anna Degen (Conrad)
	Engle, J. George	Snyder	Elizabeth ————
12/2/1783	Enslow, George	Bedford	Elizabeth Martin
	Ent, Peter	(New Jersey)	Sarah Kent
ante 1780	Etzweiler, J. George Jr	Snyder	Mary ————
	Evans, Edward	(11th Pa.)	Jemima Applegate
ca. 1753	" Col. Evan	Chester	Margaret Niven (William)
4/16/1793	" Maj. Samuel		Frances Lowery (Alexander)
	Everett, John	Northampton	Sarah ————
	Ewig, Christian	Snyder	Magdalene ————
1795	Ewing, Alexander	Cumberland	Charlotte Griffiths
5/——/1776	Eyer (Eyerly) Abraham	Union	Catherine ————
6/——/1792	Fagley, Christian	Northumberland	Magdalene Lehman
10/9/1770	Fahnestock, Benjamin	Adams	Catherine Garber
ca. 1760	" Casper	Lancaster	Maria Cath. Gleim (Gottlieb)
	" Charles	"	Susan Smith
1773	" Daniel	"	Ellen Lust, 1st wife
	" "	"	Catherine Rider, 2nd wife
1766	" John	"	Rebecca Groff, 1st wife
ca. 1774	" "	"	Catherine Studebaker, 2nd wife
	" Samuel	"	Hannah Studebaker
ca. 1771	Farley, Lt. Caleb	Union	Charity Pickel (Bickel) N. Jersey
3/29/1824	" "	"	Rebecca Wolf (Michael), 2nd wife
	Farnesworth, Moses	Warren	Annie Wilson, 1st wife
	" "	"	Zheuhana Beckwith Crocker, 2nd
12/1/1797	Featherly, Henry	Erie	Polly Dodge (Moses),Herkimer Co.,N.Y.
6/16/1791	Fee, John	Huntingdon	June ————
	Fasnacht, John	Lancaster	Susanna B. ————
	Faust, J. Henry	Northampton	Catherine ————
	Feehrer, Joseph	Snyder	Maria Barbara Ott, 1st wife
	" "	"	Sarah Rupp
	Fertig, Adam	Lancaster	Elizabeth ————
	Fink, J. George	Northampton	Catherine Barbara ————
	Finley, Maj.Joseph L	(8th Pa.)	———— Blair (Rev. Samuel)
	Finney,Ens. Lazarus	Union	Elizabeth Fulton, 1st wife
	" "	"	" Cchiltree, 2nd wife
4/26/1768	Fisher, J. Adam	Snyder	Margaret Eliz. Ried (Frederick)
12/3/1743	" J. Jacob	Berks	Mary Elizabeth Frederick (John)
ca. 1752	" J. Michael	"	Maria Aker
10/10/1773	" John	(New York)	Elizabeth Enders, Schoharie Co. N.Y.
6/5/1764	" Joseph	Northumberland	Catherine Minegar, New Jersey
	" Paul	Union	Katherine Kishter
	" Peter	Snyder	Anna Maria Faer
	" Lt. William	Northumberland	Mary Murray (Alex) Cumberland Co.
ca. 1784	Fleck, Adam	Cumberland	Elizabeth Stuff
	" George	Blair	Catherine ————
2/6/1783	Fleming, Robert	Dauphin	Margaret Wright (John)
	" Archibale "Hans"	Clinton	Annie ————
1775	Focht, Ens. Michael	Union	Elizabeth Shively
10/5/1786	Forster, Thomas	Erie	Sarah Montgomery (Rev. John)
	" Capt. John	Union	Jane ————
ca. 1780	" Robert	"	Esther ———— 1st wife
			Elizabeth ———— 2nd wife
9/12/1790	Fox, Aaron	Erie	Lydia Kellogg, Castleton, Vt.

	Fox, John	Dauphin	Anna Mary Rupert
	Frazee, Jonathan	(2nd Pa)	Mary Bradford
	Frederick, Peter	Union	Elizabeth —————
	Fruit, Robert, Sr.	"	Catherine McClure, Dauphin Co.
	" " Jr.	"	Elinor Clark (Robert Sr.)
4/6/1774	Fuller, Ichabod	Erie	Martha Cummins, Coventry, R. I.
1779	Fullerton, Thomas	"	Hannah Kennedy
	Fulton, Samuel	Northumberland	Mary Huston
4/2/1781	Fulkerson, John	"	Catherine Slaght
	Gablo, Frederick	Northampton	Elizabeth —————
1/17/1760	Galpin, Caleb	(Conn.)	Eunice Lee, Farmington, Conn.
1/1/1786	Gardiner, Nathaniel B.	Erie	Hannah Briggs
	Garman, Henry	Snyder	Elizabeth —————
	" Jacob, the elder	"	Anna —————
	" John	"	Margaret —————
	Gast, Christian, Jr.	Blair	Margaret Boyer (or Borer)
	Gast, J. Nicholas	Center	Catherine Knipe (or Kipe)
	Gaugler, Nicholas	Snyder	Mary —————
	Geddes, William	Cumberland	Sarah McCallen
	Geer, Asa	Warren	Olive Harris, 1st wife
	" "	"	Mary Stead, 2nd wife
1779	Geiger, Barnhart, Sr.	Dauphin	Mary Smith
	Galbraith, Col. Bertram	Lancaster	Ann Scott (Josiah)
	" Lt. Col. James	Cumberland	Elizabeth Bertram (Rev. William)
	Galloway, Joseph	"	Agnes Cross, 2nd wife
	Gardner, Dr. Joseph	Chester	Isabella Cochran (Robert)
ca. 1751	Garst, Dewalt	Lancaster	Maria Statthalter
ca. 1779	Gaylord, Justus, Jr.	Luzerne	Elizabeth Garner
	" " Sr.	"	Elizabeth —————
	Goiger, Peter	Berks	Mary —————
ca. 1767	Gemberling, J. Jacob	Snyder	Catherine Wolfersberger
	Gerhart, Capt. Jacob	Northumberland	Katherine Kline, New Jersey
	Gerred, John	Erie	Sarah —————
	Gifford, William	"	Elizabeth ————— ,
	Gillam, Jonathan	Washington	Mary ————— , 2nd wife
ca. 1762	Gift, J. Adam	Snyder	Anna Catherine —————
ca. 1792	Gilbert, Adam	"	Barbara Arney, 2nd wife
	" Henry	"	Elizabeth —————
1769	Gilson, John	Warren	Patience Graves, Suderland, Mass.
6/11/1767	Glass, J. George	Snyder	Eva Albright
6/—/1737	Graves, Jedediah	(Conn.)	Elizabeth Allen
1/19/1786	" Amos	Erie	Hannah Kennedy
	" Nathaniel	"	Sarah —————
	Gray, Matthew	"	Elizabeth Boggs
9/12/1782	" William	"	Mary Allison, 1st wife
	" "	"	Jane ————— , 2nd wife
	Gillespie, John	"	Jane —————
	Goy, J. Frederick	Snyder	Anna Catherine Zeller
	Gobin, William	(8th Pa.)	Rebecca Braudy, 1st wife
	" "	"	Unity Durham, 2nd wife
	Goodlander, Jacob	Berks	Catherine Stump
	Graham, Capt. James	Cumberland	Elizabeth Black
	" John	Dauphin	Ann Barnett
	Gray, David	Bucks	Nancy Blackburn
	Gray, Lt. Col. Nigel	Union	Mary —————
	" Capt. William	"	Agnes Rutherford
ca. 1750	Graydon, Alexander	Dauphin	Rachael Marks
1760	Green, Timothy	"	Effie Finney, Wid. Jas.Robinson
	" Capt. Joseph	Union	Margaret Abbott, 1st wife
1784	" "	"	Mary Irwin, 2nd wife
	Graybill, John, Sr.	Juniata	Barbara —————

	Groninger, Leonard Sr.	Union	Elizabeth ————
	Grove, Peter	"	Sarah Witmore (Witmer?)
	Grove, Wendall	"	May ————, 1st wife
		"	Jane Coon, 2nd wife
ca. 1778	Gross, John	Dauphin	Rachael Sahler (Abraham), N.Y.
	Grubb, Jacob	Snyder	Elizabeth ————
	Guffy, Lt. James	Washington	Jane ————, and Sally————.
177-	" Alexander	Northumberland	Margaret Scott (James)
	Gullion, John O.	Westmoreland	Mrs. Catherine Riffle Tanner
	" Robert	Washington	Barbara ————
ca. 1790	Gustin, Amos	(Ohio)	Susanna Jones
1770	Guthrie, Lt. George	Blair	Margaret Campbell
3/13/1771	Guthrie, Capt. John	Washington	Lydia Baldwin
	" William	Westmoreland	Margaret ————
	Gwynn, Hugh	Union	Margaret ————
8/13/1776	Haas, Peter	Northampton	Maria C. Trexler (Peter)
	Hafer, Andrew	Snyder	Mary E. Druckomiller (Peter)
1801	Hahn, Michael, Jr.		Nancy ————
	Hackney, Joseph	Warren	Margaret McGrady, maybe 2nd wife
	Hafflich, Jacob	Snyder	Margaret ————
	Hager, John		Elizabeth ————
	Hagerty, William	Erie	Anna ————
	Haggerty, William	(1st Pa.)	Nancy Hastings Burford
	Haines, John	Snyder	Regina Schuster
	" John George		Margaret ————
1781	Hall, William	(8th Pa.)	Sarah ————
12/——/1772	Hamilton, John	Dauphin	Margaret Alexander (Hugh)
	" William	Erie	Tabitha ————
ca. 1782	Hammersly, John	Snyder	Regina Garman (Jacob)
	Harding, John	Westmoreland	Magdalene Kier
1784	" Thomas		Sarah Payne
	Hare (Hair) Michael	Erie	Elizabeth ————
	Harman, John	Lancaster	Margaret ————
	Harper, Ebenezer	Philadelphia	Elizabeth ————
6/2/1768	Harris, James	Dauphin	Mary Laird (William)
1749	" John	"	Elizabeth McClure,
1749	" John	Juniata	Jane Poer McClure, 1st wife
	" John	"	Jane Harris, 2nd wife
11/1/1764	" John	Dauphin	Mary Read (Adam)
10/4/1752	" William A.	"	Mary Simpson (Samuel)
1758	" Capt. Samuel		Elizabeth Bonner, Philadelphia, Pa.
1755	Hartlein, George	Berks	Mary Catherine Boehm (Conrad)
	Hayes, Capt. Patrick	Lycoming	Susan McNutt
3/25/1762	" Robert	Dauphin	Margaret Wray
10/6/1767	" William		Jean Taylor of Virginia
	" Andrew		Jean Alcorn of Ireland
	Harrison, Maj. William	Westmoreland	Sarah ————
1786	Harry, Charles	Washington	Barbara ————
1779	Harvey, Henderson	Cumberland	Martha McConnell
	Hay (Hoy), Adam	Northampton	Anna Maria ————
	Hayes, David (Capt.Pat)	Lancaster	Martha Wilson (James)
	Hayes, Capt. Joseph	Chester	Joanna Passmore
	Hayes, John, Sr.	Lancaster	Eleanor Elder (Rev. John), 1st wife
	" "	"	Elizabeth ———— 2nd wife
	" Lt. Solomon	Chester	Mary Craig
10/16/1760	Hays, John, Jr.	Crawford	Barbara King
	Hassinger, J. Jacob,Sr.	Snyder	Elizabeth ————
	Heim, Paul	"	Catherine Shaffer (Christopher,Sr.)
	Heimbach, Peter	"	Mary Barbara ————
	Heisler, Henry	"	Catherine Elizabeth ————

	Herman, John	Snyder	————Miller, 1st wife
	Henry, James	Bedford	Elizabeth ————
	Henderson, Matthew	Cumberland	Margaret H. ————
	Hessler, Ens. John	Snyder	Susanna ————
ca. 1751	Herrold, Capt. J. George	"	Anna Maria Elizabeth Benesch
1775	" John	Westmoreland	Barbara Altman
ca. 1780	" Lt. Simon	Snyder	Elizabeth ————
	Hettrick, Christian	Union	Agnes ————
1785	Hill, Henry	Northumberland	Rachael Swartz (Peter, Sr.)
4/1/1784	Histed, Thaddeus	Erie	Esther Sayles
	Histed, Abraham	Northampton	Magdalene Strickler
	Hillis, Dr. William	Washington	Jane Carruthers
	Hinkle, Nathan	Lancaster	Marie Magdalene Zureker
1784	" Wendell	"	Elizabeth Fox
	Hobaugh, Philip	(8th Pa.)	Catherine Huver (Huber, Hoover)
	Hoffman, Christian	Dauphin	Susan Deibler (Albright)
	" John	"	————Kauffman
4/22/1772	" J. Nicholas	"	Margaret Harman, Berks County
11/14/1776	Holliday, Adam	Bedford	Sarah Campbell
	" Capt. John	Blair	Dorcas ————
	" William, Sr.	"	Mary McClellan
ca. 1797	" Samuel	Erie	Jeannette Campbell
	Hoffman, Henry	(Indiana)	Margaret Boo 1st wife
12/25/1788	" "	"	Mary Ann Drum, 2nd wife
	Hogeland, Capt. John	Washington	Jane ————
	Holeman, Eli	Union	Agnes McGrady (Alexander)
	Holmes, William	Cumberland	Elizabeth Love
	Hood, William	Northumberland	————Lee (maybe daughter of Maj.John)
	Horton, Daniel	Chester	Martha Terry
1/6/1803	Hoskinson, Basil	Erie	Eleanor Downs
	Hosterman, Jacob, Jr.	Center	Christina ————
	Hosterman, Col. Peter	Snyder	Elizabeth ————
	Houser, Jacob	"	Susanna ————
	" Martin, Sr.	Cumberland	Elizabeth Hess
	" " Jr.	"	Mary Snavely
5/6/1773	Houston, Dr. John	Lancaster	Susan Wright
6/28/1773	Hubbell, John, Jr.	Erie	Sarah Curtis
	Huber, Henry	Montour	Margaret Kern
4/11/1763	Huck (Hucki), Paul	Berks	Juliana Zweier
	Huff, Benjamin	Warren	Mary ————
	Huckleberry, George	Westmoreland	Rosanna Wise
	Huffman, John	Lancaster	Margaret,Upp, 1st wife
1786	" "	"	Nancy Sprenkle, 2nd wife
	Hulbert, John	Erie	Lucy ————
ca. 1788	Hueings, Thomas	Perry	Elizabeth Watts (Gen. Fred)
1787	Hume, John	Lancaster	————Crawford
	Hummel, Geo. Adam	Snyder	Magdalene ————
3/3/1789	" J. George	Northumberland	Christiana ————
	" Frederick, Sr.	Dauphin	Rosina ———— 1st wife
1769	" Frederick, Sr.	"	Barbara Blessing, 2nd wife
	" Frederick, Jr.	"	Rachael Rickert (Jacob)
	" David	"	Mary Toot (David)
	Hunter, James, Sr.	Erie	Elizabeth Hunter, Dauphin Co.
1796	Hunt, Josiah	(8th Pa.)	Bethia Reeve
	Hunter, John	Cumberland	Mary ————
	" Patrick	Washington	Nancy Jack
3/25/1786	Huston, Mathias	Northumberland	Hannah Cox, Philadelphia, Pa.
	" Lt. William		Susanna ————
	Iddings, William	Union	Eve ————
ca. 1782	Irwin, John	Cumberland	Mary Welsh

	Irwin, Capt William	Union	————Armstrong, 1st wife
	" " "	"	Jane Forster (John)
	Isherwood, P. Francis	Erie	Elizabeth ————————
1/3/1782	Jackson, Lyman	"	Dodamia Durban, Pownal, Vt.
	Jacquot, Lt. Joseph	(1st Pa.)	Susan ————————
1781	Jarrett, Lt. Jacob	Snyder	Catherine Ott (J. George)
	John, Jehu	Chester	Elizabeth David
	Johnston, Lt. Michael	Lancaster	Ruth ————————
1793	" Thomas	?	Sarah Foster
4/17/1775	Jones, Benjamin	Union	Rachael ————————
	" Isaiah	Warren	Mary Randolph, 1st wife
	" "	"	Mary Lindsey, (David), 2nd wife
	Jordan, John	Chester	Sarah Scott
9/7/1786	Judd, Freeman, Sr.	Erie	Deborah Boughton, Norwalk, Conn.
1787	Justice, James	Cumberland	Nancy Campbell
	Kantz, Christian	Snyder	Anna Margaret Menges (J. Adam)
	Kauffman, Philip	Northumberland	Magdalene Seaman
1786	Koan, John	Dauphin	Mary Whitehill (Robert)
1788	Keesling, John	Berks	Eva Miller
	Kelker, Anthony	Dauphin	Mary Magdalene Meister (George)
	Keller, John	Blair	Dorothea ————————
1765	" John Christian	Dauphin	Catherine Dolp (J. Nicholas)
1780	Kelly, John	Erie	Mary Robinson
	Kelly, Maj. John	Union	Sarah Pock (James)
	Kemplin, Capt. Thomas	"	Mary ————————
	Kennedy, Dr. Samuel	Chester	Sarah ————————
	Kepler, John	Northampton	Helen De. Avarle
	" Matthias	?	Elizabeth Shaffer
	Kern, J. Yost	Snyder	Eva Maria Weiss of Germany
1785	Kerstetter, George	"	Elizabeth Snyder
	" Leonard, Jr.	"	Catherine Richter (Christian)
	" Martin	"	Elizabeth ————————
	Kesler, Jacob	York	Catherine ————————
	Kessler, George	Snyder	Barbara Broucher
	Kostler (Kneedler)Fred	Northumberland	Catherine ————————
	Kidd, Robert	(New York)	Jane ————————
1781 or 1782	Kilburn, Benjamin	Cumberland	Diana Danning, Carlisle, Pa.
	Kindig, Jacob	Snyder	Mrs. John Snyder
	King, Adonijah	Erie	Diadema ———— 1st wife
6/1/1786	King, "	"	Rachael Bliss(Tim),Royalston,Mass
	" Capt. Robert	"	Mary McCullough
	Kimney, Jacob	Snyder	Catherine ————————
ca. 1776	Kinsloe, Patrick	Mifflin	Dorothy West
ca. 1772	Kinter, Philip	Erie	Mary ————————
	Kirk, William	Cumberland	Jane ————————
1784	Kimmer (Keimer),Nicholas	(4th Pa.)	Sarah Taylor
1778	Kleckner, John	Union	Anna B. Koch of Northampton Co.
	Kline, Barnhart	Snyder	Margaret ————————
	Klinesmith, Baltzer	Union	Mary ————————
	Klase, Valentine	Northumberland	Mary Eva Smith
	Klose, Ernest	Northampton	Margaret ————————
	Knouse, Christian	"	Elizabeth Hoffman
1780	" Abraham	"	Elizabeth Boeckel (Bickel)
ca. 1767	" Daniel	Lehigh	Elizabeth Ritter
ca. 1755	" "	Northampton	Salome ————————
	" David	"	Christina ————————
3/17/1771	" Geo. Frederick	"	————Rhoads (Francis William) 1st
	" "	"	Mary M. Saeger (J. Christian)
	" Gottfried, Jr.	"	Anna Maria Griesemer (John)

-79-

Date	Name	County	Spouse
	Knouse, Henry	Berks	———— Brant, 1st wife
5/4/1781	" "	"	Elizabeth Von Rith
4/22/1766	" Henry	Northampton	Anna Maria Ehrenhardt
4/10/1787	" Jacob	"	Anna Rosina Kreiter
4/21/1789	" John	"	Elizabeth Hay (Adam)
4/27/1779	" J. Daniel	Northampton	Susannah Meirer
11/25/1783	" J. Ludwig	"	Mary Magdalene Klein
	" Jonathan	"	Anna Maria Knappenberger
3/31/1772	" John	"	Catherine Romig (Frederick)
12/15/1769	" Leonard	"	Joanna Salome Miller
	" Ludwig	"	Elizabeth ————
ca. 1874	" "	"	Elizabeth Shumaker
6/12/1780	" Michael	"	Ann Elizabeth Romig (J. Frederick)
	" Capt. Paul	"	AnnaCatherineGriessmer(John)1st
	" " "	"	Magdalena ————, 2nd wife
	" Philip		Mary Magdalene Fatzinger
	Koch, Daniel	Snyder	Anna Maria ————
	Koenig (King,) Jacob	Northampton	Catherine Illick
	Kohl, George	"	Maria ————
	Kratzer, Benjamin	Snyder	Elizabeth ————
	Kreider, Christian	Lancaster	Susanna Ellenberger
	Krick, Jacob	Snyder	Catherine ————
1/3/1769	" Lt. Philip	"	MargaretHahn(George),BerksCounty
	Kuhns, Phineas	(2nd Pa.)	Elizabeth ————
5/4/1779	Kunkle, Christian	Dauphin	Catherine Hoyer
	Kyle, Joshua	Bedford	Mary Stewart (Alexander)
	Larue, George	Dauphin	Anna Maria Forehner
8/30/1781	Latsha, Henry	Northumberland	Mrs. Catherine (Shott) Emerick
5/—/1775	Laudenslager,ValentineSnyder		Magdalene Kochendorfer (George)
	" J. George "		Catherine ————
	Leap, John	Bucks	Barbara Dirth
	Loe, Capt. Daniel	Erie	Patience Callender
5/8/1777	", Isaac	Blair	Mary Boone (William)
	Leebrick, J.F.Nicholas	Dauphin	Catherine Franks
	Loer, Jacob	(10th Pa.)	Frances Stutsman
	Leitch, John	Westmoreland	Jean ————
	Le Gore, John	(4th Pa.)	Margaret Funk, 1st wife
	" "		Esther ———— 2nd "
	Lemon(Lemon),Matthias	Northumberland	MaryRunnel(orRummel),2ndwife
	" " Thomas	"	Margaret Haugh (Matthias)
	Leploy, Jacob	Snyder	Catherine ————
	" Michael		Mary Ann ————
	Lepper, John	Erie	Mary Brame (or Prime), N. Y.
	Lesher, Abraham	Berks	Elizabeth Rumden
1/3/1756	Levers, Robert	Northampton	Mary Church
	Lewis, Elijah	Erie	Lucy Odell
	Lewis, Lt. Samuel	Northumberland	Rebecca ————
	" Paschal	Union	Elizabeth Boude (Maj. Thomas)
	Lincoln, Michael		Rachael Thompson
	Lindsay, William	Chester	Elizabeth Mace, 1st wife
	" "		Clarissa Prior, 2nd wife
4/15/1787	Lindsey, David	Warren	Sarah ———— of Mifflin County
	Lingle, Thomas	Dauphin	Anna Mary ————
	Lilly, John	Erie	Roxanna ————
4/8/1804	Linn, John	Union	Jane ————————2nd wife
1780	" "	"	Ann Fleming (John), 1st wife
	List, Andrew	Snyder	Elizabeth ————
	Little, Joseph (Zph.)	Lancaster	Nancy ————
	" Nathaniel	"	Christina ————
	Livingood, George	Snyder	Anna Maria Werner (Henry)
	Littel, Absalom	(Indiana)	Mary Norris
	Lochry, Col. Archibald	Westmoreland	Mary ————

1780	Logan, Patrick	Westmoreland	Sarah Nancy Harper
8/---/1792	Long, George	Warren	Isabelle McCormick, Lycoming Co.
	" Jacob	Snyder	Elizabeth ---------
4/---/1789	" Joseph	Union	Christina Bernett
	Loomis, John	Erie	Salome Scott, 1st wife
	" "	"	Elizabeth Standish, 2nd wife
6/17/1757	" Seth	"	LuranaKnapp,Westfield,Mass.1stwife
9/21/1801	" "	"	Mindwell Potter, 2nd wife
4/---/1778	Louder, John	Bucks	Martha Vastine (Jeremiah)
	Lower, Adam	Berks	Nancy ---------
5/21/1779	Luther, Dr. John	Dauphin	Barbara Weaver, Philadelphia, Pa.
8/15/1804	" " "	"	Eva Hisser
5/---/1783	Lybarger, Nicholas, Jr.	Erie	Christiana ----------, Bedford Co.
	" " Sr.	Bedford	Mary Ann ----------------
	Lyons, Lt. Thomas	Erie	Jean Bennett
3/27/1760	Lowden, Capt. John	Union	Sarah ---------
1775	" " "	"	Ann ---------
	Lowray, Col. Alexander	Lancaster	Mary Watters
	" " "	"	Ann West, widow of Hermanus Alricks
	" Robert	Cumberland	Mary Johnson
11/10/1773	Maclay, Col. Samuel	Union	Elizabeth Plunkett (William)
4/11/1769	" Hon. William	Dauphin	Mary McClure Harris
5/---/1780	Magee, James	Warren	Margaret McCracken of Mifflin Co.
1783	Mallery, Truman	Erie	Olive Hubbell (Silas)
3/16/1798	Mallory, Nathaniel	"	Sarah Boyd
	Mann, John	(7th Pa.)	Ann Dean
9/10/1782	Marsh, Simeon	Warren	Jane Cole
	" Capt. William	Chester	--------- Cornwallis
1753	Martin, Dr. Christian F.	Northampton	Rosina Shertlin (Rev. Jacob)
1/10/1768	" " "	"	Mary Wilhelmina Miller (Andrew)
	" Jacob	Lancaster	Catherine Wilson
	" Peter	Philadelphia	Sarah ---------
	Mathers, William	Cumberland	Esther Thorn
	Matteson, David	Erie	Anna ---------
	Mead, Darius	Warren	Ann Hoffman
12/---/1782	" John	"	Katherine Foster
	" Michael	(Ohio)	Patricia ---------
3/20/1783	Means, Hugh	Huntingdon	Rosanna ---------
4/1/1783	Mease, Baltzer	Somerset	Anna Baker
	Meredith, Gen. Samuel	Philadelphia	Margaret Cadwalader
	Morrill, Jesse	Warren	Rhoda ---------
1797	Miller, Abraham	Lancaster	Elsie Thomas
	" George	Union	Catherine Markle
	" Jacob	Berks	Eva Fix
	" James, Sr.	Lancaster	Jean Boyd (?)
	" Capt. John	Philadelphia	Margaret ---------
	" John	(8th Pa.)	Margaret Bowler
1785	" John	Berks	Catherine Reber
	" Capt. Samuel	(8th Pa.)	Jane ---------
1745	" Steven	?	--------- Philpot
1/4/1781	" Stephen	Erie	Jemima Winston
	Miles, David	"	Mary Watts, Carlisle, Pa.
	" Robert	Warren	Catherine Watts
	" Solomon, Jr.	"	Betsy Crane of Connecticut
3/23/1786	Milligan, David	Mifflin	Mary Beatty
6/---/1795	Mitchell, Andrew		Margaret,w/o Capt. John Hamilton
	Maurer, Michael, Jr.	Snyder	Elizabeth Krick (Jacob)
	" Peter	"	Catherine ---------
	Meiser, Henry	"	Anna Maria ---------
	Menges, J. Adam	"	Anna Margaret ---------------
	Merts, Lt. Philip	"	Anna Maria Rossman (Jacob)

-81-

9/—/1776	Miller, John		Lancaster	Rosanna Ulrich
10/23/1812	Mitchell, John		?	Susan Osborn
	"	Gen. David	Cumberland	Mary West (Francis)
	"	John	Washington	Esther Gibson, 1st wife
	"	"	"	Mary McPheeters, 2nd wife
	"	"	Westmoreland	Jane ——————
	"	"	Dauphin	Judith Hollinger
1775	"	Robert, Sr.	Cumberland	Ann Espy
	Montgomery, James		(8th Pa.)	Martha ————, Westmoreland Co.
1765	"	Rev. John	?	Elizabeth Reed (Andrew), 1st wife
2/11/1770	"	" "	"	Mrs. Rachael Russ Boyce, 2nd wife
1784	"	Hugh	Dauphin	Eve Hartman
1793	Moore, Andrew			Elizabeth Shepard (John)
1780	"	"	Juniata	Margaret Banks (James)
	"	John	Westmoreland	Esther ——————
	"	Zachariah, Jr.	Lancaster	Mary Boggs (Andrew, Sr.)
3/3?/1769	Moorhead, Capt. James		Erie	Catherine Byers
1/10/1778	Morey, Charles		"	Phoebe Blanchard (James)
8/5/1783	Morrison, James, Jr.		"	Hannah Gunn
	"	" Sr.	Warren	Margaret Rice, 1st wife
	"	" "	"	Martha Griffin, 2nd wife
	Morrow, John			Elizabeth Pollock, 1st wife
				Abigail Miller, 2nd wife
ca. 1771	Motz, Capt. Michael		Snyder	Barbara Meyer (J. Jacob, Sr.)
3/25/1784	Mowland, Richard		Chester	Rachael Williams
8/1/1784	Moyer, Jacob		Huntingdon	Elizabeth Hold
1783	"	Nicholas	Union	Rosanna Reasoner
	"	Philip	Snyder	Margaret Morr (Andrew)
	"	J. Jacob, Jr.	"	Julia " "
	"	J. George	"	Elizabeth Buchtel (John), 1st wife
	"	" "	"	Mary Brosius, 2nd wife
	Mounts, William		Westmoreland	Nancy Crawford
11/6/1777	Muhlenberg, Gen. J. Peter G.		(Pa. & Va.)	Anna Barbara Meyer
	Murray, James		Dauphin	Rebecca McLean
12/29/1762	"	Jonathan	"	Margaret Hayes (Andrew)
9/2/1786	"	Patrick	"	Mary B. Beatty
1767	Musgrave, Samuel		Cumberland	Elizabeth ——————
	Musser, Peter		Lancaster	Margaret ——————
	McCalay, Zachariah		Westmoreland	Clarana ——————
1781	McCasland, William		Cumberland	Eleanor ——————
	McClanahan, James		Union	Sarah ——————
	McClellan, John		Juniata	Elizabeth Martin
ca. 1776	McClelland, Capt. Daniel		Cumberland	—————— ——————, 1st wife
11/12/1787	"	" "	"	Margaret Holmes, 2nd wife
	"	James	Washington	—————— Hughes
	"	Col. John	Fayette	Martha ——————
	McClintock, Lt. Alex.		Montgomery	Mary ——————
	"	"	Philadelphia	Sarah ——————
	McClure, Daniel		Cumberland	Martha Baird
	"	George	"	Jane Gilmore
1786	"	John	"	Jane McGuire
1787	"	Capt. William	"	Margaret Mossman
ca. 1762	"	William	Dauphin	" Wright (Robert)
11/10/1768	"	Jonathan	"	Sarah Hayes
	McCombs, William		Washington	Elizabeth ——————
11/26/1764	McCord, Mark		Dauphin	Catherine ——————
1785	McCoy, John		Erie	Mrs. Elizabeth Fraser Arbuckle (Jos.)
1775	"	William	Washington	Elizabeth Rice (or Royce)
3/15/1774	McCormick, James		Union	Isabella Dixon
ca. 1811	McCrabb, Dana			Sarah Lynch
	McCracken, Henry		Union	Mary ——————
12/16/1765	McCreary, Joseph		Dauphin	Agnes Ann Grubb
1824	McCune, Joseph		Lancaster	Maria Redenbaugh

-82-

1/1/1794	McDaniel, John	Warren	Bathsheba Cramplin
	McDonald, William	Cumberland	Hester ————
	McDowell, James	Westmoreland	Mary ————
8/14/1788	" Thomas		Mary Conner
	McEntire, William	(8th Pa.)	Mary ————
1788	McGahay, William	Cumberland	Prepare Clark
6/15/1798	McGill, Arthur	Warren	Elizabeth Arters
	McGuire, Hugh	"	Patience ————
	McHenry, John, Sr.	Columbia	Susan McNeal
	McHenry, Dr. Matthew	Northampton	Margaret Gregg (Robert)
	McKee, Andrew	Armstrong	Mary Blandford
	" (McKay), Neal	Erie	Nancy Montgomery
	" William	Mifflin	Sarah Jane Taylor
	McKinsey, Samuel	Cumberland	Mary ————
1821	McMillan, William	Mercer	Nancy Anderson
	McKnight, John	Chester	———— Hazelitt
	McMullen, Hugh		Susannah ————
	McNiell, Laughlin	Philadelphia	Ann ————
	McTeer, Capt. Robert	Snyder	Elizabeth Martin, 3rd wife
	McWhinney, Thomas	Cumberland	Eleanor Fryar
	McWilliams, Robert	Northumberland	Elizabeth ————
	" William		Sarah Johnston
11/12/1777	" " (TOOK OATH OF ALLEGIANCE IN NORTHUMBERLAND COUNTY, PA.)		
	McVey, John Sr.	Mifflin	Sarah Wakefield (Mathias)
ca. 1800	Nagle, Richard		Catherine Baum
1781	Neely, Joseph	Lancaster	Martha Johnston
	Neese, Peter	Center	Christina Hess
	Neil, John	Cumberland	Susannah ————
	Nerhood, Henry	Snyder	Mary Krick (Jacob)
ca. 1779	Northrup, Gideon	Warren	Esther Munson
	Oberholtzer, Abraham	Philadelphia	Magdalene Detweiler
	" Henry	"	Catherine Shoemaker (Jacob)
	O'Crosson, James		Rosanna White
	Ohl, Lt. Henry	Northampton	Abbie Lark
1782	Oliver, John	Mifflin	Mary Lyon (James)
	" Stephen	Erie	Elizabeth Cochran (Charles)
7/3/1822	" "	"	Polly Gracey, 2nd wife
	Olney, Capt. Stephen	Warren	Martha Aldrich
	Orr, William	Westmoreland	Mary ————
8/10/1778	Orwig, George	Union	Mary Magdalene Gilbert
	Osborne, Nicholas		Margaret Conrad
	Ott, J. George	Snyder	Mary Catherine ————
1776	Otto, Dr. J. Augustus	Berks	Catherine Hilner (George)
1787	Overlin, William	Cumberland	Letitia McKinney
1753	Overmire, Capt. J. George	Union	Eva Rosenbaum, 1st wife
1760	" "	"	Barbara Focht (Jonas)
ca. 1790	" J. George, Jr.	"	Maria Rearick
1783	" J. Peter	"	Maria Eva Haney (Christopher)
	Overturf, Martin	Washington	Catherine Deitch
8/—/1787	Owen, John	Warren	Lydia Gilson (John), 3rd wife
	Page, Thomas	Warren	Margaret ————
3/10/1790	Parker, Nathaniel	Erie	Eunice Doubleday (Joseph), Conn.
	Parry, Lt. Col. Caleb	Phila.	Elizabeth ————
	Parsons, Lt. Thomas	"	Bathsheba ————
	Pattern, John	?	Elizabeth White
	Patterson, James	Lancaster	Elizabeth Witherow
1765	" Lt. Samuel	"	Martha Agnew
ca. 1820	Patton, James	?	Catherine Neiman

1794	Paul, John	Westmoreland	Sarah Thornberry
1781	" Thomas	?	Catherine DeCamp, Philadelphia,Pa.
	Pedan, Capt. Hugh	Lancaster	Mary Boggs (Andrew), 1st wife
" " "			Sarah " (Widow Margaret),2ndwife
	Petterson, James	Cumberland	Letitia Gardner (Robert)
1784	Phelps, Jonathan	Warren	Charity Beckwith, E. Haddam, Conn.
	Phillips, Amasiah	Erie	Sarah ————
"	David	Chester	Mary Thomas
1779	" Esquire	Warren	Ann Gates
"	Josiah	Chester	Sarah Thomas
"	Thomas	"	Jane Blair
8/27/1765	" Thomas	Lancaster	Elizabeth Carson
	P P iercy, Jacob	(2nd Pa.)	Abby McDowell (or McDonnell)
1792	Piety, Thomas	?	Mary Duncan
	Piper, Lt. Col. James	Cumberland	Lucinda ————
1786	Pollock, David	Erie	Ann Rowland
175-	" James	Northumberland	Mary Heron
ca. 1770	Pontius, Lt. Henry	Union	Catherine Wolf
2/—/1778	" Nicholas	Union	Maria Appolonia Wilhelm
3/28/1790	Pomeroy, Medad	Erie	ElisabethMorrell(Hugh),Boston,Mass.
	Porter, William	"	Mary ————
5/9/1784	Portman, John	Warren	Catherine Godling
	Potter, Gen. James	Union	Elizabeth Cathcart, 1st wife
" " "	"		Mary Petterson (wid. Thos.Chambers)
	Powell, Nathan	Chester	Sarah Nickels
	Powers, Lewis	?	Martha ————
	Prigg, William	Lancaster	Susan Wells
	Protzman, John	Northampton	Nancy Barbara Reckner
ca. 1780	Putnam, Jesse	Warren	Mrs. Rachael Putnam Carleton
1776	Ragin, Thomas	?	Hannah ————
12/24/1757	Randall, David	Erie	Anna Maxon (Joshua)
"	Stephen	"	Cynthia Wells
	Rank, George	Lancaster	Martha ————
11/—/1787	Raymond, Zaccheus	Warren	Sarah Sears
	Rea, Samuel	Erie	Mary Eaton
4/6/1774	Redcay, Elias	Berks	Elizabeth Hunter
	Reed, Capt. Casper	Snyder	Anna ————
5/17/1772	" Frederick (Casper)	"	Barbara Wertz (John)
ca. 1769	" Lt. Col. Seth	Erie	Hannah Harwood
	Reddick, William	?	Margaret Trump
	Reed, David	Westmoreland	Rachael ————
1782	" Isaac	Northumberland	Margaret Baker
"	Timothy	Northampton	Judith ————
"	William	Washington	Mary ————
	Rees, Thomas	Erie	Ann ————
	Roger, Adam	Snyder	Charlotte ————
	Reichenbach,Jacob(John,Sr)	"	Elizabeth Steffen (J. Adam)
"	John, Sr.	"	Catherine ————
"	" Jr.	"	Mary ————
1770	Reigle, Andrew	Dauphin	Catherine Hoffman
3/9/1775	Reid, Adam	Erie	Martha Shields (Joseph)
1788	Reid, James	Chester	Jean Black
	Reiley, John	Cumberland	Mary McIlvane
5/20/1773	Reily, John	Dauphin	Elizabeth Myer (Isaac)
	Reish, Peter	Berks	Susannah ————
10/28/1799	Reishner, Daniel	Franklin	Christiana Croft, widow
	Reynolds, John	Phila.	Catherine ————
	Riblet, John	Erie	Catherine Keiper (Michael)
	Richter, Lt. Christian	Snyder	Julia Ann ————
	Riddle, Samuel	Westmoreland	Martha Johnson

-84-

	Righter (Richter), Sam'l.	Chester	Christiana ————
	Rine, Henry	Snyder	Christina ————
	Ritz (Reitz), Michael	Northumberland	———— Schnope
	Roads (Rhoads), Francis	W. Snyder	Hannah ————
ca. 1766	Roberts, Joseph	Bedford	Agnes ————
1/8/1756	" Gideon, Sr.	Erie	Mary Lawrence
3/8/1780	" " Jr.	"	Jerusha Pitcher (James)
7/11/1771	Rockwood, Simeon	"	Demaris Olds, Brookfield, Mass.
	Rogers, Thomas	Chester	Elizabeth ————
	Roller, Baltzer	Bedford	Alse ———— 2nd wife
	Rolls, James	?	Margaret Heter
	Roseborough, Isaac	Huntingdon	Rachael ————
	" Rev. John	Northampton	Jane Ralston (James)
1779	Ross, Ens. John	Lancaster	Charlotte Natcher (Nacher)
	" Jonathan	Cumberland	Elizabeth ————
	Rothrock, Philip	Mifflin	Martha Labaugh (Abram)
ca. 1741	Roush, Casper	Snyder	Anna Maria ————
ca. 1779	" J. George	"	Christina Morr (Andrew), 1st wife
ca. 1792	" " "	"	Barbara Potter, 2nd wife
ca. 1774	" J. Jacob	"	Barbara Wittenmeyer
	Row, George, Sr.	"	Mary Magdalene ————
ante 1778	" " "	"	Margaret ————
ca. 1795	Royer, Sebastian	"	Mary Elizabeth Weaver
1786	Rudd, John, Sr.	Erie	Clara Hill
	Rudisill, John	York	Katherine ————
	Rue, Capt. Benjamin	?	Mary Taylor
1/27/1750	Rupp, J. George	(Alsace)	Ursilla von Petersholtz
	Rush, John	Washington	Amy Laycock (Abner)
	Russell, John	Warren	Mary ————
	" James, Sr.	Westmoreland	Sarah ————, maybe 2nd wife
2/4/1762	Rutherford, Capt. John	Dauphin	Margaret Parke
9/12/1769	Robinson, James	Dauphin	Martha Cochran
ca. 1778	" John	Bucks	Jane Rowland
	Saltzman, Sgt. Anthony	Northumberland	Rosanna ———— (Mrs. Robt. Ritchie)
	Sample, John, Sr.	Union	Mary ————
	Sargeant, John	?	Julia Comegys
	Sassaman, Henry	Snyder	Catherine ————
10/1/1761	Sawyer, William	Dauphin	Jean Wilson
12/16/1794	Saylor, George N.	Franklin	Anna Wilk
	Schaeffer, Peter	Lancaster	Catherine ————
1763	Schertz, Jacob	?	Elizabeth Roush (Casper), Lebanon Co.
	Schip, Michael	?	Catherine Smith
	" Thomas	?	Mary Smith
	Schoch, John	Snyder	Catherine ————
	" Matthias	"	Mary Margaret ———— 1st wife
	" "	"	Catherine Sipe Gruver, wid. 2nd wife
	" George	Union	Mrs. Esther Regine Sharp Bickel
	" John	Snyder	Margaret ————
	Schweitzer	Northampton	Elizabeth Kolp
1790	Scott, John	Cumberland	Hannah ————
10/31/1765	Scott, William	Dauphin	Jean Hayes (Patrick)
	Seal, Joseph		Mary Montgomery
	Sechrist, Lt. Christian	Snyder	Nancy ————
1788	Seebold, Christopher	Union	Anna Eva Hochlander, Lancaster Co.
	Seitz, George	Union	Catherine Burkhart
ca. 1790	Selin, Maj. Anthony	Snyder	Mary C. Snyder
	Shadle, Henry	Snyder	Maria Ohlinger
	Shaffer, Andrew		Cath. Elizabeth ————
	" Christopher	"	Maria Eva Rosina ————
	" George	"	Catherine ————

	Shaffer, Jacob	Berks	Katherine ―――
	" John Peter, Sr.	Snyder	Eve ―――――
	" Michael	"	Salome ―――――
	" John	"	Anna Maria Reichenbach
1785	Shannon, George	Washington	Ann Reid
	" Capt. Samuel	Westmoreland	Elizabeth ―――
5/25/1770	Shattuck, John	Erie	Abigail Fairbanks (Jabez)
	Sheely, Michael	Westmoreland	Sarah ―――――
	Sheehy, Daniel		Jane McLean (Robert)
	Shenefeld, John	Cumberland	Rose Ann Galt
2/6/1759	Sherer, Capt. Joseph	Dauphin	Mary McClure, later Mary McCracken
	Shetterly, Andrew	Snyder	Anna Maria ―――――
	Shipton, Thomas	"	Nancy ―――――――, 2nd wife
	Shively, Christian, 3rd	Union	Catherine Van Groote Smith
	Shirk, Andrew	Berks	Martha Hamilton
	Shirley, John	Warren	Hannah Stevens, Chester, N. H.
	" Richard	Bedford	Rachael ―――――, later Mrs. Gartral
	Shively, Henry	Lancaster	Mary Banta
	Shoemaker, Abraham		Mary ―――――
	" Peter	Snyder	Catherine ―――――
	Sierer, John	Union	Mary ―――――――― 1st wife
ca. 1810	" "	"	Louisa McMillen, 2nd wife
11/8/1762	Sigfreid, Andrew	Berks	Mary Agatha Zweier
5/5/1791	Silliman, James	Erie	Mary Hunter
	Silverthorn, William		Jane ―――――
	Simeral, Lt. Alexander	Westmoreland	Martha McGrew
	Simon, Jacob	Washington	Elizabeth Degen (Martin)
	Simonton, John	Dauphin	Mary Wiggins (John)
11/17/1777	" Dr. William	"	Jean Wiggins (Dr. John)
	Simpson, Ens. Andrew	Westmoreland	Sarah ―――――
	" Lt. Murray	Dauphin	Margaret Murray (Capt. James)
ca. 1776	" Thomas	"	Mary Huling (Marcus)
1759	Sloan, Archibald	"	Margaret Sloan, 1st wife
1766	" "	"	Mary Craig, 2nd wife
	" Lt. David		Mary ―――――, later Mrs. Robt. Orr.
	Smith, David	Union	Barbara Shively (Christian, Sr.)
10/17/1792	" Conrad	York	Anne Black, widow
	" Lt. Col. Matthew	Northumberland	Agnes Wilson (Lt. Col. William)
	" Oliver	Erie	Betsey ―――――
	" Robert	Cumberland	Keziah Stewart
8/13/1802	" Thomas	Huntingdon	Betsey Boyles
ca. 1768	Snyder, Lt. Casper	Northumberland	Elizabeth Furster
	" John	Lancaster	Juliana ―――――
	" Harman, Jr.	Snyder	Magdalena Grabill (John)
	" John, Sr.	"	Susanna ―――――
	" Leonard B.	Lancaster	Juliana ―――――
	" Gov. Simon	Snyder	Elizabeth Michael, 1st wife
	" " "	"	Catherine Antes(Col.Fred.),2ndwife
10/16/1814	" " "	"	Mrs. Mary Slough Scott, 3rd wife
	" William	Lancaster	Susanna Barkman
1781	Solesby, Daniel		Rachael Bircham
	Sommerville, James	Blair	Charlotte Bicknell
	Southworth, William	Erie	Sally ―――――――, 2nd wife
	Spangle, Zacharias	Snyder	Mary ―――――
	Spangler,Geo.Christian,Sr	Union	Anna Maria ―――――
	" " " Jr	"	Catherine ―――――
	Sparrow, Stephen	Erie	Susan Robertson, 1st wife
12/3/1813	" "	"	Lydia Harris, 2nd wife
	Spatz, John	Northumberland	Anna Maria Keiser
5/9/1786	Specht, Christian		Barbara Sensendorf (Martin)
12/4/1789	Spencer, Orange	Erie	Sarah Bostwick

5/—/1775	Spong, Jacob	Cumberland	Elizabeth Miller
	Spotz, Matthias	Snyder	Barbara —————
	Stafford, David	Erie	Sally —————, 2nd wife
	Stembach, Philip	Cumberland	Anna Maria —————
2/25/1792	Stancliff, Lemuel	Erie	Mehitable Goff
11/12/1783	" Samuel	"	Olive Balcom
	Staub, Adam	Snyder	Eva —————
	Steel, James	Westmoreland	Elizabeth McMasters
	Steese, Jacob	Union	Margaret —————
	Steese, J. Jacob	Snyder	Margaret Eckbert
	" John	Union	Barbara Frantz
12/20/1757	Steffen, J. Adam	Snyder	Agnes Pfrang, Lebanon County
	Stephenson, Capt. Steph.	Lancaster	Ruth Bayley (James)
	Sterrett, Ens. James, Jr.	"	Mary Allison, 1st wife
			Margaret McClure, 2nd wife
	" James	Erie	Ann McKnight
ca. 1755	" " Sr.	Lancaster	Sarah Montgomery
	" Robert	Erie	Margaret McComb
	" William	Lancaster	Sarah Woods (Thomas)
ca. 1770	Stevens, Giles	Blair	Nancy Tipton
	Stevenson, James	Chester	Hannah Bull, 1st wife
	" "	"	Catherine Moore, 2nd wife
ca. 1770	Stewart, James, Jr.	Westmoreland	Rebecca Marchant
1/18/1780	" William	Dauphin	Mrs. Mary Hulings Simpson, 1st wife
ca. 1800	" "	"	Nancy Templeton (Robert)
	Stillwagon, Jacob	Lancaster	Elizabeth —————
1784	Stillwell, Capt. Richard	Bucks	Sarah Enlow
	Stock, Melchoir, Sr.	Snyder	Anna Mary —————
	Stockman, James		Nancy Lewis
	Stonebraker, Sebastian	Lancaster	Susan Yeakle
	Stonesifer, Henry	York	Elizabeth Hoffhainze
	Stork, John	Chester	Nellie —————
10/12/1796	Stoops, Andrew	Bucks	Sarah Shaw
	Stough, Nicholas	Erie	Eve —————
	Stout, Job	Northampton	Rhoda Howell
	Strain, Lt. William	Cumberland	Jane Lemon
5/1/1787	Straub, Andrew	Northumberland	Mary Eve Walter
	" Charles, Sr.	Snyder	Catherine —————
1780	Strevay, Paul	Northampton	Mary —————
	Struthers, John	Washington	Mary Foster
	Stuckey, J. Frederick	Lancaster	Barbara Seemp
	Stump, George		Elizabeth —————
1804	Summers, George	York	Prudence Gross
	Sutton, Benjamin	Westmoreland	Sarah Tingely
	Swan, Capt. Richard	Erie	Catherine Boggs
4/10/1783	Swenk, Jacob N.		Elizabeth Reimer (John)
ca. 1752	Swineford, Albright, Sr.	Snyder	Margaret —————
	" George Michael	"	Susan —————, 2nd wife
	" John	"	Barbara —————
	Swengle, Michael	"	Elizabeth —————
	Tallmadge, Elisha	Erie	Maria Brasee
	Tate, Adam	Lancaster	Jean Hayes (Robert)
	Tate, Edward, Sr.	Union	Barbara Gast (J. Nicholas)
1780	Taylor, Maj. James	Lancaster	Mary Ann Cully
10/6/1761	Teal, John	Erie	Elizabeth Frizer
	Temple, Jacob	Northumberland	Hannah —————
	Telker, George	Philadelphia	Anges —————
ca. 1779	Thom, Joseph	Washington	Elizabeth Craig
1780 or 1781	Thomas, Henry	Northumberland	Mary —————
	" Jacob	Erie	Dorcas Hurd
1767	" Martin	"	Ursilla Miller (John)

		Thompson, Andrew	Erie	Martha ————
ca.	1778	" Isaac	Juniata	Martha Larimore, 1st wife
ca.	1783	" "	"	Jane Evans Well, 2nd wife
		" Robert	Cumberland	Mary Gordon
11/24/1785		" Rufus	Erie	Sarah Burley (Josiah)
		" William	Northumberland	Jane ————
		Thornton, John	Snyder	Magdalene Witmer (Peter, Sr)
		Tietsworth, William	Northumberland	Mary Campbell
		Toey, Simon	Lancaster	Catherine ————
		Tollen, Cornelius	"	Rosanna ————, 1st wife
		" "		Katherine Duffy, 2nd wife
		Torrence, John		Jane Jolly
		Townsley, John		Hester Martin
		Trask, Rufus	Erie	Hannah Stacy, Salem, Mass.
		Treaster, Martin, Jr.	Snyder	Elizabeth ————
10/24/1771		" Michael, Jr.	"	Rosina Bickel (Tobias, Sr)
		Treon, Jacob	"	Barbara ————
		Treese, John	Huntingdon	Barbara ————
		Troutman, Philip	Berks,	Magdalene Troutman
		" John	"	Maria E. Hoffman
		Truesdale, John	Cumberland	Hannah Robinson
		Tull, Handy Thomas		Eleanor ————
		Turnor, Robert	Chester	Ann Carlisle
5/13/1787		Uffer, Francis	Berks	Maria Zweiler
12/19/1775		Ulrich, J. George, Jr.	Snyder	Catherine Laudenslager (George)
		Utter, Abraham	Cumberland	Martha Lycan
ca.	1769	Umholtz, Henry		———— Rouch
		Van Camp, Moses	Erie	Anna Riggs, 2nd wife
		Van Campen, Maj. Moses	Northumberland	———— McClure (James)
10/4/1781		Van Deventer, Peter	Erie	Mary ————
		Van Dyke, Henry	Union	Elizabeth Campbell
1777		" " John	"	Martha Moore
		" " Lambert	"	Margaret McMichael
6/16/1771		Van Worken, Martin	Erie	Mary Winne
		Vincent, Cornelius	Northumberland	Phoebe Ward
		Wadsworth, Henry	Erie	Mary Noble
		Wales, John	Union	Anna Mary ————
		Walker, David		Anna Banks (James)
		" John, Sr.	Northampton	Mary Ann Blackburn
3/—/1779		" "	Cumberland	Mary Rowan
10/28/1787		" Joseph	Erie	Celia Cooley
		" Josiah	Westmoreland	Nancy Poke (Polk)
ca.	1791	" Nathaniel		Sarah Franklin
		Wallace, Nathaniel	Washington	Mary Wallace
		" Thomas	Chester	Jane ————
		Walls, John	York	Mary Elizabeth Patterson
		Walter, Christopher		Mary Stotts (?)
3/16/1787		" David	Snyder	Susan Barbara Eberhart (Bernard?)
7/24/1757		" J. Jacob	"	Maria Kauffman
		Watson, Col. David	Lancaster	Jean Hamilton
		" David	Union	Jane Clark (Capt. John)
7/25/1784		" Dr. John	Lancaster	Margaret Clemson (James)
ca.	1749	Watts, Gen. Frederick	Cumberland	Jane Murray
		Watt, James, Sr.	Northumberland	Anna ————
		Weaver, David	Center	Eva Wolf
		" John	"	Anna Mary ————
ca.	1754	" Capt. Michael	"	Anna Barbara Moyer (J. Jacob, Sr.)
10/27/1785		Webster, William	Erie	Anna Hodge (Benjamin)

	Weiser, Capt. J. Conrad	Snyder	Barbara Boyer
	" Conrad	Berks	Elizabeth Klinger (Philip)
1751	" Frederick	"	Anna Amelia Zoller
2/2/1772	Weise, Adam	"	Margaret Wingard, 1st wife
8/23/1818	" "	"	Mrs. Mary Bitterman Keeley
12/10/1820	" "	"	Mrs. Catherine Neimond Patton
11/16/1784	Weirick, Michael	York (?)	Elizabeth Rimby
1797	Welch, Samuel	Cumberland	Jane Cunningham
12/11/1775	Wells, Ezekiel	Erie	Alice Collins
	Wheeler, John	Columbia	Mary Revel (?)
	White, Charles		Gretchen Margaret Busch
5/13/1788	" John	Westmoreland	Eleanor Williams
	Whitley, Capt. Michael	Lancaster	Martha ————
	Whitehill, John, Jr.	"	Mary Middleton
11/1/1774	" Robert		Mary Cochran (Andrew)
ca. 1780	White, Giles	Warren	Sarah Dodd (Ebenezer)
8/17/1756	Wiley, Thomas		Mary Cochran (Andrew)
	Wilkins, Capt. John	Cumberland	Catherine ————
12/17/1790	Willard, Ephraim B.	Erie	Mindwell Loomis
	Williamson, Joseph	Cumberland	Margaret Fox (Fuchs)
5/18/1784	Wilson, Alexander	Erie	Catherine Davison
	" Ephraim		Catherine ————
	" Lt. Col. George	Philadelphia	Sabina ————
2/17/1790	" Hugh	Union	Catherine Irwin (Capt. William)
	" James		Martha Willock
2/26/1787	" John	Union	Nancy Agnes Forster (Capt. John)
1782	" John	Mifflin	Margaret Fleming (John)
	" John	Cumberland	Jennet ————
	" Lt. Joseph	Bucks	Mary Britton
	" Nathaniel	Cumberland	Susan Riddle (Yost?)
1774	" "		Eleanor McAllister
1770	" Peter	Union	Jane Galbreath
	" Capt. William	Northumberland	Mary Scott (Abraham)
1793	" William	"	Sarah Riddle (Yost?)
	Wilt, Thomas	Bedford	Barbara ————
1778	Winters, John	Lancaster	Martha Jones
	" Thomas	Westmoreland	Mary Jane ————
	Wirt, Lt. George	Philadelphia	Mary ————
	Wise, Frederick	Union	Barbara Kurtz (?) (Michael)
	Witmer, Abraham	Snyder	Mary ————
	" Christopher	Northumberland	Hannah Reed (Capt. Casper)
ca. 1757	" Peter, Sr.	Snyder	Maria Salome ————
12/19/1787	" " Jr.	"	Magdalene Overmire (Capt.J.Gcorge)
	Wittenmeyer, Andrew	"	Susan ————
1766	Wolf, George Wendel	Union	Ann Elizabeth Ried
1807	Wood, Abraham		Nancy Bolin
ca. 1785	Woodling, J. George	Snyder	Hannah Herb
1802	Woodworth, Richard		Sarah Ann Robinson
	Work, Samuel		Jean McEwen (or McCune)
1799	Wright, Robert		Agnes Holmes, 2nd wife
1748	Yoder, John	Berks	Catherine Leister
10/15/1752	York, Amos	Bradford	Lucretia Miner
	" Jeremiah		———— Brown
1765	Yost, Maj. Casper	Union	Catherine Cole (Col. Philip)
1747	" John	"	Mary Foster
	Zearing, Henry	Lebanon	Elizabeth Rupp
	Zehring, Christian	Lancaster	Maria Bouch, 2nd wife
4/2/1771	Zerbe, John	Berks	Maria Margaret Angst
1789	Ziegler, Maj. David		Lucy Ann Sheffield
	Zeller, Peter	Union	Catherine Wilhelm

	Zimmerman, Abraham	Berks	Bernice Werley
	" John	Lancaster	Christina ——
1/16/1844	Zinn, John	Berks	Nancy Mullikan
6/6/1777	Zweier, Anthony	"	Maria Dreese
4/11/1779	" Joseph	"	Catherine Scharg (Sherk)
4/23/1770	" John	"	Eva Becker
6/13/1763	" Stephen	"	Anna Mary Stahl